THOUGHTS
A studybook for moral education

THOUGHTS
Education for Peace and One World

A studybook for moral education

compiled and introduced
by
Irene Taafaki

with drawings by
Susan Reed

GEORGE RONALD
OXFORD

GEORGE RONALD, Publisher
46 High Street, Kidlington, Oxford OX5 2DN

First Reprint 1986
Second Reprint 1989
Third Reprint 1992

British Library Cataloguing in Publication Data

Thoughts, education for peace and one
world : a studybook for moral education.
1. Moral education
I. Taafaki, Irene
370.11'4   LC268

ISBN 0-85398-221-X
ISBN 0-85398-222-8 Pbk

Phototypeset by Sunrise Setting, Torquay
Printed in the United States of America

Contents

How to use this Book

The 'thoughts' or spiritual and moral concepts included in this book have been arranged in alphabetical order. The treatment given to each 'thought' is not intended to be complete but rather provides a beginning for more detailed study of each idea.

The structure of each chapter follows the same format. Section 1 provides short quotations from the scriptures of the world or other writings. Many of these are suitable for children to memorise, or they may be used as captions for pictures children might draw illustrating each thought. Section 2 provides longer quotations from religious texts. Each 'thought' includes stories or poems which illustrate the theme, and these are grouped under Section 3. Many of the 'thoughts' are quite difficult for children, especially young children, to grasp, and Section 4 includes questions which will stimulate the children into thinking about the concepts and how they relate to their own lives.

The sources of the quotations have been kept deliberately short within the text, but detailed lists of references and sources are included at the end of the book. Authors of stories and poems are cited at the end of their works. All quotations in Sections 1 and 2 are within quotation marks. In Sections 3 and 4, text for which there is no reference, or which is not in quotation marks, is by the compiler.

The source books and religious teachers most often cited in the text refer to the following religions:

Upanishads, Vedas, Bhagavad Gita – Hinduism
Yaçna – Zoroastrianism
Dhammapada – Buddhism
Old Testament – Judaism
New Testament – Christianity
Muhammad – Islám
The Báb – Bábí Religion
Bahá'u'lláh, 'Abdu'l-Bahá – Bahá'í Faith

Foreword

Thoughts was originally compiled and written to be used as a teaching aid in various situations in an international residential school, the New Era High School in Panchgani, Western India. It was intended to be a means of directing the attention of the staff and students towards acceptable standards of behaviour.

The research and compilation of the material was done over a period of two years while Irene Taafaki was serving as the co-ordinator of the moral education programme and as one of the moral education teachers in the primary and secondary section of the school.

She accepted the challenge of trying to provide a means of inculcating the concept of world-mindedness and the ideal of the oneness of God in the minds of students who came from tremendously varied national, religious and socio-economic backgrounds. *Thoughts* is one of the teaching materials which resulted in response to that challenge. As with most good ideas, the idea for *Thoughts* is basically very simple: to elicit a desire to attain those personal virtues which reflect the attributes of God. Such virtues as trustworthiness, honesty, purity, trust, and faith make up a universal, spiritual thread which runs through all the great world religions; so it was natural to reveal that single thread coming from many sources. The material also deals with the problem of teaching moral values, which are born out of religious experience, without promoting any particular religion or dogma.

The brief and pointed quotations from the Scriptures of different religions and from the writings of great thinkers in the East and West can be easily understood and explained, even to primary school children. The questions section can help parents, teachers and group leaders to launch a group discussion and to initiate a variety of other learning activities. The stories which illustrate and support the ideas have been enjoyed by both younger and older students and often lend themselves to dramatisation and to role-playing activities. Creative parents and teachers will use private and public libraries to find other stories related to the themes that may be more suited to the needs of the children they know well.

Thoughts was, and still is being, used in a variety of ways and settings. In the international school in which it was developed, a 'thought' is used as the lesson subject in the structured moral education classes where it is dealt with in depth. In a large gathering, such as the daily school assembly, one quotation from the week's 'thought' is read. One quotation is written on a prominent chalkboard in the main school corridor to serve as a reminder to all who pass by and read it. The 'thought' for the week is the moral theme emphasised in the dormitories and used as a standard for the granting of rewards for improved, or consistently good, behaviour of students in the residential setting.

This collection of 'thoughts', now published in book form and distributed more widely, can be very helpful as a resource book for parents, teachers and youth leaders in meeting their responsibilities for the character-building of the children in their charge. *Thoughts* uses the creative power of the word of God as the prime means to effect positive change in attitude. Parents may wish to use *Thoughts* as a fitting part of their morning family devotional before the disturbing influence of a hectic world begins to distract and influence young minds.

Using the 'thoughts' as the stimulus, the classroom teacher may choose to begin the school day with a brief reading and discussion. They may be used as the basis for learning activities which help the students to recognise, evaluate and come to terms with their own ideas and provide them with the standard on which to base their own efforts to improve their behaviour and to raise their level of moral reasoning.

It is indeed rare to find teaching material which students and teachers from all backgrounds can find acceptable. Those of us who have been in the field of education for some time, who have searched for and found so little material, will welcome *Thoughts* as a valuable educational tool. This is one approach which demonstrates the unity in all of God's religions.

Let us hope that this form of teaching universal virtues will assist in the spiritualisation of our children who are destined to be the future leaders and citizens of one world family.

Dr Ray Johnson

Acknowledgements

I would like to acknowledge the assistance of the following people: Mrs Gloria Faizi who inspired the idea of *Thoughts* and gave initial guidance and encouragement; Dr Ray Johnson, Principal of the New Era High School from 1971 to 1983, for his constant support and enthusiasm; Tahirih Mihrshahi and Farzaneh Jehani for their typing of the original manuscript; and especially to Dr Wendi Momen for her careful editing.

Irene Taafaki

To Munirih, Jane, my husband Falai-Riva
and the children of the New Era High School

Animals

1

'[The true seeker] should show kindness to animals.'[1]   *Bahá'u'lláh*

'To the blessed animals . . . the utmost kindness should be exercised; the more the better it will be.'[2]   *'Abdu'l-Bahá*

'All cattle, that which lives under the water, under the heaven, the birds, the wide-stepping, the beasts with claws, praise we.'[3]

Yaçna

'May I regard all beings with the eye of a friend.'[4]   *Yajur Veda*

'Him I call indeed a Brahmana who without hurting any creatures, whether feeble or strong, does not kill nor cause slaughter.'[5]

Dhammapada

2

'If an animal is sick they [the children] should endeavour to cure it; if it is hungry, they should feed it, if it is thirsty, they should satisfy its thirst, if it is tired, they should give it rest.'[6]   *'Abdu'l-Bahá*

3

Muḥammad and the Animals

A man once came to him [Muḥammad] with a bundle, and said, 'O Prophet, I passed through a wood and heard the voice of the young birds, and I took them and put them in my carpet, and their mother came fluttering round my head.' And the Prophet said: 'Put them down'; and when he had put them down the mother joined the young. And the Prophet said: 'Do you wonder at the affection of the mother towards her young? I swear by Him who has sent me, Verily, God is more loving to His servants than the mother to these young birds. Return them to the place from which ye took them,

and let their mother be with them.' 'Fear God with regard to animals
. . . ride them when they are fit to be ridden, and get off when they
are tired. Verily, there are rewards for our doing good to animals,
and giving them water to drink.'[7]

The Locusts in the Garden of Riḍván

We returned to the garden [Riḍván], where Abul-Qásim
[Bahá'u'lláh's gardener] made tea for us, and there he told us the
story of the locusts. How that during one hot summer there had
been a pest of locusts and they had consumed most of the foliage in
the surrounding country. One day Abul-Qásim saw a thick cloud
coming swiftly towards the garden, and in a moment thousands of
locusts were covering the tall trees beneath which Bahá'u'lláh so
often sat. Abul-Qásim hastened to the house at the end of the garden
and coming before his Lord besought Him, saying: 'My Lord, the
locusts have come, and are eating away the shade from above Thy
blessed head. I beg of Thee to cause them to depart.' The Manifestation smiled, and said: '*The locusts must be fed; let them be.*' Much
chagrined, Abul-Qásim returned to the garden and for some time
watched the destructive work in silence; but presently, unable to
bear it, he ventured to return again to Bahá'u'lláh and humbly
entreat Him to send away the locusts. The Blessed Perfection arose
and went into the garden and stood beneath the trees covered with
insects. Then He said: '*Abul-Qásim does not want you; God protect you.*'
And lifting up the hem of His robe He shook it, and immediately all
the locusts arose in a body and flew away.

    When Abul-Qásim concluded this story he exclaimed with
strong emotion as he touched his eyes: 'Oh, blessed are these eyes to
have seen such things; oh, blessed are these ears to have heard such
things.'[8]   *May Maxwell*

4

A. Mrs Froth died last night. She left all her money to build a home
    for stray dogs and cats in the city. What do you think about her
    action?

Bahá'u'lláh says: 'He [the seeker] should show kindness to animals,
how much more unto his fellow-man, to him who is endowed with
the power of utterance.'[9]

B. Is our attitude towards animals only a one-way affair? Can you think of the many ways animals assist man?

C. Why do the Holy Books teach us not to be cruel to animals?

D. How can our understanding of the Kingdoms of God help us in our attitude towards animals?

Backbiting

1

'. . . backbiting quencheth the light of the heart, and extinguisheth the life of the soul.'[1] *Bahá'u'lláh*

'. . . good is restraint in speech . . . [he] who is controlled in tongue, who speaks wisely . . . sweet, indeed, is his speech.'[2]

Dhammapada

'. . . find not fault with one another, neither revile one another by nicknames . . . O ye believers, eschew much suspicion, for some suspicion is a sin. And do not spy, neither backbite one another. . .'[3]

Muḥammad

'O Son of Man! Breathe not the sins of others so long as thou art thyself a sinner. Shouldst thou transgress this command, accursed wouldst thou be, and to this I bear witness.'[4] *Bahá'u'lláh*

2

'Lord, who shall abide in Thy Tabernacle? Who shall dwell in Thy holy hill? . . . He that backbiteth not with his tongue nor doeth evil to his neighbour . . . shall never be moved.'[5] *Old Testament*

'O Emigrants! The tongue I have designed for the mention of Me, defile it not with detraction. If the fire of self overcome you, remember your own faults and not the faults of My creatures, inasmuch as every one of you knoweth his own self better than he knoweth others.'[6] *Bahá'u'lláh*

'. . . the tongue is a smouldering fire, and excess of speech a deadly poison. Material fire consumeth the body, whereas the fire of the tongue devoureth both heart and soul. The force of the former lasteth but for a time, whilst the effects of the latter endureth a century.'[7] *Bahá'u'lláh*

In the Bible, the Epistle of St James 3:3 has much to say on this subject. You may like to read it.

3

Children are full of curiosity – it's a sort of mental hunger. Try to encourage their thinking and reasoning to be about objects and events rather than about individuals.

Control your Tongue

One day a rich lady went to a saintly man to ask his advice. She said that she wished to be a saintly woman, but there was one fault which she found difficult to overcome. The saint told her that there was no fault one could not overcome if one wanted to overcome it.

Then the lady told the saint how she was in the habit of gossiping about others and how she had failed to overcome that fault although she had tried very hard.

'Can you help me?' she asked the holy man. 'I will do anything you ask me to do.'

'Very well,' answered the holy man, 'go to the market and buy a fowl. On your way back home, pluck the fine feathers of the fowl and throw them on the street as you walk along. Come and see me after you have done this.'

The rich lady was surprised to hear this, but she respected the holy man. So she did as she was told and faithfully obeyed his orders.

The next day she went and told the holy man that she had obeyed his commands.

'Very good,' answered the saint. 'You have done the first part of your task very well. Now comes the second part. Go to the market and walk along the street again and try to pick up the feathers which you threw on the road yesterday.'

'That's impossible!' said the rich lady. 'The wind has already blown them in all directions. How can I collect the feathers again?'

'That is so,' answered the holy man. 'The same happens when you gossip about others. Your words are passed from mouth to mouth and it is impossible to stop the evil spreading, once it has started. The best thing to do is not to start it.'

The lady was so impressed by this object lesson that she went home determined never to speak evil of anybody again.

4

For younger children

A. Have you heard of a tattle-tale? What does it mean?
B. What are other ways of telling a bad thing?
C. What should we do instead of those bad things?

For older students

D. Read the words of Muḥammad again. Why is suspicion a sin?
E. How do you feel when you have discussed another person?

Cleanliness

1

'Be the essence of cleanliness among mankind . . .'[1] *Bahá'u'lláh*

'. . . purity and holiness, cleanliness and refinement, exalt the human condition, and further the development of man's inner reality.'[2] *'Abdu'l-Bahá*

'Blessed are the pure in heart: for they shall see God.'[3]
New Testament

'Truly, God loves those who repent, and He loves those who cleanse themselves.'[4] *Muḥammad*

'Naught . . . in the sight of God is more loved than purity and immaculate cleanliness.'[5] *The Báb*

'Well awakened ever the disciples of Gotama arise: they who by day and by night always contemplate the body.'[6] *Dhammapada*

2

'Be the essence of cleanliness among mankind . . . under all circumstances conform yourselves to refined manners . . . let no trace of uncleanliness appear on your clothes . . . Immerse yourselves in pure water; a water which hath been used is not allowable . . . Verily We have desired to see in you the manifestations of Paradise on earth, so that there may be diffused from you that whereat the hearts of the favoured ones shall rejoice.'[7]
Bahá'u'lláh

'God loveth those who are pure. Naught in the Bayán and in the sight of God is more loved than purity and immaculate cleanliness . . .

'God desireth not to see, in the Dispensation of the Bayán, any soul deprived of joy and radiance. He indeed desireth that under all conditions, all may be adorned with such purity, both inwardly and

outwardly, that no repugnance may be caused even to themselves,
how much less unto others.'[8]   *The Báb*

3

Ṭúbá Khánum, daughter of 'Abdu'l-Bahá, leaves us this childhood
impression of her Grandfather, Bahá'u'lláh:

We children looked upon Bahá'u'lláh as another loving Father; to
Him we carried all our little difficulties and troubles. He took an
interest in everything which concerned us . . .
    He was always punctual, and loved daintiness and order.
    He was very particular and refined in his personal arrangements,
and liked to see everybody well groomed, and as neatly dressed as
possible. Above all things, cleanliness was desirable to Him.
    'Why not put on your prettiest frocks?' He would say to us.[9]

Ṭúbá Khánum

In February 1849 the Bábí defenders of Fort Ṭabarsí had been
besieged for four months. Nabíl leaves us this account of the
behaviour of Mullá Ḥusayn on the day before his martyrdom:

The scarcity of water had, in the meantime, compelled those who
were besieged to dig a well within the enclosure of the fort. On the
day the work was to be completed . . . Mullá Ḥusayn, who was
watching his companions perform this task, remarked: 'To-day we
shall have all the water we require for our bath. Cleansed of all
earthly defilements, we shall seek the court of the Almighty, and
shall hasten to our eternal abode. Whoso is willing to partake of the
cup of martyrdom, let him prepare himself and wait for the hour
when he can seal with his life-blood his faith in his Cause.'[10]   *Nabíl*

4

A. What is cleanliness? What is delicacy? What is sanctity? Use a
    dictionary to help you define these words.
B. How clean should we try to be?
C. How can cleanliness have an influence upon spirituality?
D. How important is cleanliness? Is not dirt natural? Why must it be
    avoided?

E. Is cleanliness only a physical thing or is it also a mental attitude? Explain.

F. Why should we wish our school to be clean and free of litter and other rubbish?

G. What can we do to keep ourselves, the school, our country clean?

Compassion

1

'Well awakened ever the disciples of Gotama arise; they who by day and by night delight in harmlessness.'[1] *Dhammapada*

'Be a home for the stranger, a balm to the suffering, a tower of strength for the fugitive.'[2] *Bahá'u'lláh*

' . . . let thy aim be the good of all and then carry on thy task in life.'[3] *Gita*

'Happiness is a great healer to those who are ill.'[4] *'Abdu'l-Bahá*

2

'We should all visit the sick. When they are in sorrow and suffering, it is a real help and benefit to have a friend come. Happiness is a great healer to those who are ill. In the East it is the custom to call upon the patient often and meet him individually. The people in the East show the utmost kindness and compassion to the sick and suffering. This has greater effect than the remedy itself. You must always have this thought of love and affection when you visit the ailing and afflicted.'[5] *'Abdu'l-Bahá*

3

. . . Mrs Getsinger was in 'Akká having made the pilgrimage to the prison city to see the Master. She was with Him one day when he said to her that He was too busy to call upon a friend of His who was very ill and poor and He wished her to go in His place. Take him food and care for him as I have been doing, He concluded. He told her where this man was to be found and she went gladly, proud that 'Abdu'l-Bahá should trust her with this mission.

She returned quickly. 'Master,' she exclaimed, 'surely you cannot realise to what a terrible place you sent me. I almost fainted from the awful stench, the filthy rooms, the degrading condition of that man and his house. I fled lest I contract some terrible disease.'

Sadly and sternly 'Abdu'l-Bahá regarded her. 'Dost thou desire to serve God,' He said, 'serve thy fellow man for in him dost thou see the image and likeness of God.' He told her to go back to this man's house. If it is filthy she should clean it; if this brother of yours is dirty, bathe him; if he is hungry, feed him. Do not return until this is done. Many times had He done this for him and cannot she serve him once?[6]   *Howard Colby Ives*

Albert Schweitzer

In 1952 the Nobel Peace Prize was awarded to Albert Schweitzer. He has often been called the 'greatest man in the world' and on this occasion the leaders of many nations of the world wrote to congratulate him.

Even in his youth Albert Schweitzer thought of the many unfortunate people of the earth living in faraway places, suffering and dying needlessly for want of proper medical attention. He remembered the words of the Bible, 'all ye are brethren', and so in 1914 he left his home in France and went to the place he was needed most – the jungles of French Equatorial Africa. He learnt medicine so that he could treat people who were unwell. He spent his life teaching the people who lived there. He built hospitals, planted trees and made gardens, living his religion in his everyday life. After his daily work was over he would devote his leisure time to his music, and in the heat of the tropical night, the sweetest melodies of Bach, his favourite composer, could be heard.

His love and compassion for his fellow, but less fortunate, human beings caused him to live deep in the jungle in a very simple house. He brought Western medicine and surgery to people who otherwise would have lived in pain, or who would have been ostracised by their village for being lepers. There were some tribes which looked on twins as bad luck and which turned the mother and babies out into the jungle at the mercy of the wild beasts. Albert Schweitzer made his hospital a refuge for people such as these. Even those who had been cured of their sickness remained near the hospital under the eye of the man who understood that all life is sacred, who saved their lives and freed them from pain.   *Adapted by Irene Taafaki*

The story of Florence Nightingale is a classic for any discussion of compassion:

Florence Nightingale

When Florence Nightingale was small she loved dolls like many other small girls. But her dolls were different. They were always sick or breaking bones in some way which gave her the chance to nurse them back to health.

Florence was born in 1820 into a very wealthy English family whose daughters were supposed to spend their time doing needlework, playing the piano or reading. They could help the poor with a bowl of soup or a basket of fruit occasionally but that was all. In those days it was thought unladylike for women to go out into the world and work.

However, Florence was different. She greatly admired Elizabeth Fry who had long worked to improve prison conditions in England. Florence wished to become a nurse.

In France the Catholic Sisters of Mercy were trained to care for the sick, but there was no place in England where nurses could be trained. In fact, hospitals were terrible places where patients died through lack of care. In Germany a man called Pastor Fledner had seen what Elizabeth Fry had done almost single-handed and made up his mind to do the same for the sick in his own country. It was at his small hospital that Florence wished to be trained. After much family opposition, she was allowed to go there to study.

On her return to England Florence volunteered to go east to Turkey to help the soldiers who had been wounded in the Crimean War.

Today it seems natural that trained nurses should be sent to a scene of war, but in 1854 the idea was shocking and Florence was mocked.

However, together with a few other compassionate and courageous ladies, Florence left England for the Crimea.

When they arrived they found the wounded men living in very poor conditions indeed. There were no towels, no soap to wash the patients, no bowls, no dishes and not even any medicine. The food was inedible and the bedsheets on the few beds that there were were so rough that the men asked for them to be taken away.

However, through the persistent effort of Florence Nightingale, this hospital became a well-equipped institution in a few months. Before the nurses arrived, sixty per cent of all patients had died; afterwards only one per cent did so.

At the end of the war the name of Florence Nightingale was known by everyone in England. Returning soldiers told how she was awake twenty hours every day to save their lives and cheer their spirits. Everyone spoke of her courtesy, her sweet and unfailing kindness and patience, of the letters she wrote home for men too sick to write themselves, the hours she spent comforting the dying.

She returned to England as quietly as she had left. Florence thought so little of her own importance that she did not even let her family know when she was arriving. She was content to have saved the lives of thousands of British soldiers and to have made people respect the women in the nursing profession.

Adapted by Irene Taafaki

4

A. How can you show compassion to a friend who is ill in hospital?
B. Is compassion just feeling sorry for someone?
C. Does compassion involve action?
D. Are we to be compassionate only to those who are ill?

Concern

1

'Be a home for the stranger, a balm to the suffering, a tower of strength for the fugitive.'[1] *Bahá'u'lláh*

'. . . let your manner be sympathetic. Let it be seen that you are filled with universal love.'[2] *'Abdu'l-Bahá*

2

'What profit is there in agreeing that universal friendship is good, and talking of the solidarity of the human race as a grand ideal? Unless these thoughts are translated into the world of action, they are useless.

'The wrong in the world continues to exist just because people talk only of their ideals, and do not strive to put them into practice. If actions took the place of words, the world's misery would very soon be changed into comfort.

'A man who does great good, and talks not of it, is on the way to perfection.

'The man who has accomplished a small good and magnifies it in his speech is worth very little.

'If I love you, I need not continually speak of my love – you will know without any words. On the other hand if I love you not, that also will you know – and you would not believe me, were I to tell you in a thousand words, that I loved you.'[3] *'Abdu'l-Bahá*

3

Ned the Lonely Donkey

Ned, the little grey donkey, had lived all alone on his hill for as long as he could remember. He had lived there, among the furze bushes and near the little hurrying stream in summer and in winter, in sunshine and in rain.

One sunny afternoon after he had run races with his shadow and jumped the stream over and over again, he felt tired and thirsty. He took a long drink of cool water, and lay down on the short springy grass.

He got up and went to look for a sheep. There were very few of them on the hill, and they were generally too busy eating to have any time for talking. At last he found one.

'Are you lonely?' he asked.

'Lonely?' said the sheep, lifting her head from the grass. 'I never have time to think about it. Are you?'

'Yes, I think I am,' said Ned. I'd like someone to talk to and play with.'

'I've no time for things like that,' said the sheep. 'Eating grass takes all my time.' And she went on eating.

Ned walked slowly away. 'I don't want to eat all the time,' he thought. 'I like doing other things. Eating isn't everything.' Just then he met a hurrying rabbit.

'Wait a minute,' he called. The rabbit stopped and turned around.

'Yes,' she said, 'what is it? I've no time to spare.'

'Are you lonely?' asked Ned.

'Lonely?' cried the rabbit. 'Me, lonely? I've a husband and eight children, and you can't be lonely with a family that size! I must go. Everyone will want their tea!' And she dashed away.

Ned wandered back to his stream absent-mindedly. Suddenly he stopped, for he had almost stepped on a peewit sitting on her nest.

'Look where you're going!' said the peewit.

'I'm sorry,' said Ned. 'I'm afraid I was thinking and not watching where I was going.'

'What were you thinking about?' asked the bird.

'I've decided that I'm lonely,' the little donkey said, 'and I'm wondering what I can do about it.'

The peewit looked at him with her bright eyes. 'Go and ask the wise owl in the dark wood,' she suggested.

That evening Ned trotted by the light of the moon to look for the wise owl. There were queer noises in the wood and frightening shadows, but he went on until he was in the thickest part of it. Then he stopped and listened.

'Whoo-hoo-hoo-oo,' he heard. He looked carefully through the trees and at last saw the wise owl sitting on the branch of an oak tree. He looked very wise indeed.

The owl looked down at Ned and asked what he wanted.

'I've come to ask for your help,' said Ned. 'I live on the hill by myself. Sometimes I see a sheep or a rabbit, but they have no time to spare. I play by myself, I eat by myself, and I sleep by myself. I am lonely. What can I do about it?'

The owl stared at him a moment and then said, 'The best thing to do is to find someone else who is lonely. If you put two lonely people together, usually neither of them is lonely any more.'

Ned thought about this, then nodded. 'I see,' he said. 'Thank you very much.' And he trotted away.

Next morning the grey donkey galloped down the hill to the farm in the valley. He looked in all the fields for a little donkey like himself, but there wasn't one to be seen. He talked to some black and white cows.

'I thought there might be a lonely donkey here like me,' he said.

'I don't think you will find anyone lonely here,' answered one of the cows. 'We aren't, there are so many of us,' and they all moved away to a very green stretch of grass.

Ned spoke to some pigs in the sty, but they only opened their sleepy eyes for a moment before shutting them again.

There were two big brown horses harnessed to a plough in one of the fields. Ned asked them whether he would be able to stay at the farm, but they thought not.

'You see,' they told him, 'everyone here has something to do, and that may be why they never have time to think of being lonely. But a donkey, well, what can a donkey do?'

'Nothing special, I suppose,' Ned said sadly. 'No, I can't think of anything I could really do well. I can quite understand that I would still be lonely here.' And he trotted away down the high road.

Soon he came to the seaside. He looked down the cliff and, there on the sand, he saw ten little grey donkeys. Each donkey wore a gay coloured hat and each had a child riding on its back.

'At last,' cried Ned, and he trotted down the path to the shore. The donkeys were all walking slowly in a great circle. As Ned approached they looked at him. He wasn't wearing a hat, and he didn't have a child riding on his back.

'Who are you?' they called to him.

'I'm Ned. I live in a field near a stream. May I join you?'

But the other donkeys just laughed at him. He did not know how to be a seaside donkey. He was too fat to carry the children. The donkeys turned away from him and continued their walk around the circle.

Ned sighed. 'I can see I would still be lonely here,' he said to himself. The grey donkey continued his walk. Soon he came to a high fence. He walked along the fence until he came to an iron gate. Ned looked through the gate and saw a lovely big house and beautiful gardens. As he looked, his nose rubbed against the gate and it slowly opened. Ned was curious to see what the rest of the garden looked like, so he pushed the gate harder and walked inside.

He looked across a stretch of green lawn and saw a gardener sweeping a path. He thought the gardener would chase him out of the garden, so he slowly trotted out of the gardener's sight. He turned a corner and there, sitting on a garden chair was a little boy. He was all alone and he sat quite still, staring in front of him. There were a few toys on the grass but he had none in his hands.

'He looks – he looks lonely,' said Ned to himself.

A magpie flew down and landed near Ned. 'That boy is so sad,' said the magpie to Ned. 'His mother and father have been away for some time and he has nobody to play with. He is well looked after, but he is lonely.' And the magpie flew off again.

'Oh,' said Ned. 'I see. Yes, of course, I see.' And the next moment he was trotting towards the little boy.

The little boy jumped up and stared, then he ran forward and put his arms around Ned's neck and hugged him.

'Have you come to play with me?' the little boy asked. 'May I have a ride on your back?'

He climbed on Ned's back and held firmly to his mane. Ned trotted around the lawn all afternoon.

Soon the gardener came hurrying to the little boy and Ned.

'Where did that donkey come from?' he asked.

'He's mine,' cried the little boy. 'I'm going to make a stable for him.'

'But he isn't really yours, you know,' said the gardener. 'Someone will claim him.' He didn't know that Ned belonged to no one at all.

'I'll keep him until someone does,' said the little boy. The gardener rubbed his chin, but finally agreed the donkey could stay.

The donkey was taken to a comfortable shed at the other end of the garden. The little boy and the gardener worked very hard, putting hay and water ready for Ned, and making him a bed of straw. Ned could hardly believe what was happening to him.

'The wise old owl was right,' he said to himself. 'I will not be lonely here, and the little boy will not be lonely any more either. And the horses were right, too, about doing things. The little boy is busy helping me, he is concerned for my welfare and happiness, so he doesn't have time to be sad and lonely. I must try to make him happy too.'

But what Ned did not know was that by playing with the little boy, Ned was making him happy.   *Adapted from a story by Noel Barr*

4

A. How can we learn to understand the needs of others without intruding?

B. How can we sympathise without prying into other people's business?

C. How can we learn when to act and when to help another by keeping silent?

D. If we are concerned with the well-being and happiness of others, will we be the cause of sorrow? 'Be not the cause of grief, much less of discord and strife.'[5] *Bahá'u'lláh*

Will we sadden anyone? 'Ye know full well how hard it is for this Youth to allow, though it be for one night, the heart of any one of the beloved of God to be saddened . . .'[6] *Bahá'u'lláh*

Will we talk about anyone? '. . . observe silence and refrain from idle talk. For the tongue is a smouldering fire, and excess of speech a deadly poison.'[7] *Bahá'u'lláh*

Will we wish the humiliation of another? ' . . . and wish not the abasement of anyone, that thine own abasement be not exposed.'[8] *Bahá'u'lláh*

E. How can we keep track of our progress of learning concern for others?

'Bring thyself to account each day . . .'[9] *Bahá'u'lláh*

F. Ask yourself, 'Am I a giver or a taker?'

G. How can we try to make certain that in this life we are going to give – give love, care, time, money or whatever – not only take?

For younger children

'Abdu'l-Bahá says: 'Be kind to the strangers . . . Help to make them feel at home; find out where they are staying, ask if you may render them any service; try to make their lives a little happier.'[10]

H. How can we show new children at school that we really care about them?

I. Sometimes new students will seem to be very naughty, always fighting with others, never keeping still for a moment. Can you think of some reasons why they behave like this? What can you do to help?

J. Towards what other people can we have a caring attitude?

Contentment

1

'O Son of Spirit! Ask not of Me that which We desire not for thee, then be content with what We have ordained for thy sake, for this is that which profiteth thee, if therewith thou dost content thyself.'[1]
Bahá'u'lláh

'. . . contentment is the greatest wealth . . .'[2] *Dhammapada*

'Put away all covetousness and seek contentment; for the covetous hath ever been deprived, and the contented hath ever been loved and praised.'[3] *Bahá'u'lláh*

'Do not covet that whereby God in bounty has preferred one of you above another.'[4] *Muḥammad*

'O Son of Man! Be thou content with Me and seek no other helper. For none but Me can ever suffice thee.'[5] *Bahá'u'lláh*

'May there now come . . . contentment, blessing, guilelessness, and wisdom of the pure.'[6] *Yaçna*

'. . . godliness with contentment is a great gain.'[7] *New Testament*

2

'The virtues and attributes pertaining unto God are all evident and manifest, and have been mentioned and described in all the heavenly Books. Among them are trustworthiness, truthfulness, purity of heart while communing with God, forbearance, resignation to whatever the Almighty hath decreed, contentment with the things His Will hath provided, patience, nay, thankfulness in the midst of tribulation, and complete reliance, in all circumstances, upon Him. These rank, according to the estimate of God, among the highest and most laudable of all acts. All other acts are, and will ever remain, secondary and subordinate unto them . . .'[8] *Bahá'u'lláh*

'In Europe, on one occasion, remembering the desperate days in Ṭihrán when Bahá'u'lláh was incarcerated, their home sacked and their properties confiscated, 'Abdu'l-Bahá could yet say, "Detachment does not imply lack of means; it is marked by the freedom of the heart. In Ṭihrán, we possessed everything at a nightfall, and on the morrow we were shorn of it all, to the extent that we had no food to eat. I was hungry, but there was no bread to be had. My mother poured some flour into the palm of my hand, and I ate that instead of bread. Yet, we were contented."[9] *'Abdu'l-Bahá*

3

The Bitter Melon

A master had a slave who was completely devoted to him. One day he gave the slave a melon which when cut open looked most ripe and delicious. The slave ate one piece, then another and another with great relish (the day being warm) until nearly the whole melon had

disappeared. The master, picking up the last slice, tasted it and found it exceedingly bitter and unpalatable. 'Why, it is bitter! Did you not find it so?' he asked the servant. 'Yes, my master,' the slave replied, 'it was bitter and unpleasant, but I have tasted so much sweetness from thy hand that one bitter melon was not worth mentioning.'[10] *'Abdu'l-Bahá*

The Discontented Village

There was once a village that had every reason to be the happiest in the world. It was situated in a pleasant valley with protecting mountains all around. It had fertile fields, industrious workers, and a prosperous market-place. But instead of being the happiest village in the world, it was the saddest.

It was not happy because there lived in it not one contented person. Each person believed himself weighed down with troubles like an old nag with bones. And what is more, each believed his troubles were heavier than any of his neighbours'. If you saw a little group of people standing together and sidled over to hear what they were talking about, you would find yourself listening not to good talk about the weather, or crops, or the price of cheese, or the arrival of a new baby. No – you would hear nothing but talk about trouble.

'Ah me,' like as not one would be saying, 'was there ever a more unfortunate man than I? Things are so bad with me that trouble has moved right into my house and is now a permanent boarder.'

'What do you know about trouble?' his neighbour would answer. 'Trouble is so familiar with me, he calls me by name.'

'Have you heard?' a third might chime in. 'Trouble is calling me brother.'

It is said where there is smoke, there must be fire. Perhaps there is a good reason for such talk. Let us see.

Here is the miller, a fine man, sole owner of a busy mill, completely free and master of himself. He earns more than one pretty penny and no one to tell him what to do with it. But is he happy? No. Why not? Because he has no wife.

'The baker, now,' sighs the miller, 'the baker is a happy man. When he comes home at the end of the day his place is neat and his supper hot upon the table. What does he know of having to shift for himself? What does he know of trouble?'

And the baker – is he happy? No. And why not? Because he has no child.

'What is the use of putting up with the restrictions of married life,' mumbles the baker, 'if there is no child to look after a man in his old age? It is an unfair world. Here I have none and the carpenter has six.'

And the carpenter, is he happy? No. And why not? Because he has too many children. All day long the carpenter complains, 'By my hammer and nails, is there a curse on me? Other men's children grow like weeds and are soon farm hands and wage earners. But mine, now, they stay on all fours forever and the cradle is never empty. Ah me, does any man have such troubles as I?'

And what about the people whose children are grown – are they happy? No. And why not? Listen, and you shall hear.

Here is the tailor with a good steady son, a dreamer and a scholar.

'Of what use are dreamers and scholars?' moans the tailor. 'The world is too busy for dreaming and too much learning leads but to destruction. Now why, if only one child was given me, could it not have been a strong, ambitious lad like the tinker's or a pretty girl like the widow's – a girl who will marry well and keep her mother in comfort?'

But the tinker is unhappy because his strong, ambitious lad is ever off adventuring, and the widow is unhappy because her pretty daughter will have none of the rich farmer's son but is casting soft glances in the direction of the scholar. And so the tinker and the widow complain too.

'Children seldom grow up good and steady and obedient,' they both wail. 'Children are best when they are in the cradle. Yes, the carpenter with his little ones, and the baker and the miller with no children at all, they are happy men.'

And the carpenter and the baker and the miller? We have already heard them.

And so it went. The people who worked envied those who loafed, and those who loafed envied those who worked and made money. And the young longed for the irresponsibilities of old age, and the old wept for their lost youth. And if they didn't have any immediate reason for being unhappy, you can be sure that they looked hard enough until they found one.

So day by day this discontent grew, and the moans and groans and mumbles and grumbles rose like a great thick fog. And one day the fog hid the sun. So busy were the people at first with their troubles that they paid no attention; but when many sunless hours went by, it occurred to them that here was trouble indeed, touching all of them.

'Truly we are an unhappy folk,' they now cried, all together. 'Even the sun won't shine on us.'

Out of the gloom one day came a traveller. It had been murky for so long that no one expected any visitors, and the first the villagers knew of his approach was the sound of a merry voice singing gaily:

Heigh ho,
Life is jolly.

Content is wisdom,
Complaint is folly.

The people gathered in the main street to see who it was that subscribed to such an outlandish theory. And presently there emerged out of the gloom a tall figure. It was a man, not old, not young; not well dressed, not shabby; not loaded with provisions, yet not entirely bereft, for the small bundle slung over his shoulder seemed comfortably full. He stopped in front of the people and put down his bundle.

'Greetings,' he said. 'Forgive me, my friends, for not giving you the good of the morning or the evening, for by my life, how is a man to tell in this gloom if it be day or night here?'

'The sun has deserted the world,' said one of the villagers. 'And,' he added severely, 'small cause for singing, I should say.'

The stranger smiled. 'The sun is shining warm and bright somewhere, I warrant. When this fog lifts, you will see.'

The villager regarded him suspiciously. This cheerful comment was not to his liking. 'Who are you?' he asked bluntly.

'I?' The stranger shrugged his shoulders. 'I am no one and every one. I am a homeless wanderer who owns the earth.'

'Poor man,' said another villager.

'Trouble has addled your brain.'

'Trouble?' said the stranger. 'Now that is a word I do not know.'

The people crowded round him and examined him closely.

'Are you ill?' they asked in amazement. 'How can you say you know not trouble with no hearth or fire or chick or child to call your own? Wandering over the face of the earth, and walking without rest. That does not make for any foolish philosophy of content-ment. That makes for trouble. Trouble in the form of weary legs.'

'Ah well,' said the stranger, 'there is no ill but somewhere a cure exists for it. And as for weary legs, the best cure is to take the weight off them.'

And down he sat, under a tree.

The villagers gathered around him open-mouthed as the stranger calmly sat there. Finally the miller said, 'Well, now, since you are so much-travelled, perhaps in your wanderings you have heard of a cure for fog?'

'Perhaps,' said the stranger. He rose, turned his long nose up, then down, then this way, then that. He sniffed like a dog. Then he stuck out his tongue, tasted the fog, and made a wry face.

'This is no ordinary fog,' he said, 'for, unpleasant as it is, fog is still nothing but vapour, and vapour is nothing but water which neither smells nor tastes bad. Still this looks like fog, and it feels like fog. It must be some special kind, caused by something most disagreeable. If I know the cause, I might know the cure.'

'We do not know the cause,' said the baker. 'The sun suddenly left us. I remember it was some time ago. I was thinking of how unhappy I was when . . . '

'Yes,' interrupted the carpenter. 'I was thinking of how little reason others have for unhappiness, compared to me, when . . . '

The tailor interrupted the carpenter and the tinker interrupted the tailor and soon everyone was shouting.

And as they shouted the fog grew thicker and thicker.

'Stop!' cried the stranger. 'It needs no Solomon to see what is wrong here. Well, well. There is no ill but somewhere a cure exists for it. Yes, even for this ill.'

'And what might the cure be?' asked the widow, eagerly.

'Simple,' said the stranger, 'if you will listen carefully and follow instructions.'

All the people solemnly and silently nodded their heads.

The stranger sat down again.

'Now then,' he said, 'let's see. You must string up a stout line from one end of the market-place to the other. Then you must each go home and put your troubles into a sack . . . '

'No sack in the world is large enough to contain mine,' cried the carpenter.

'Nor mine,' sighed the widow.

'Nor mine,' wailed the tailor.

'Nor mine,' cried everyone.

The stranger frowned. 'Well, then, if you will not listen and will not obey . . . '

He began to rise once more.

And the fog grew thicker and thicker.

'Stay!' cried the people. 'We will manage somehow. Let us hear the cure.'

The stranger sat back once more.

'Then you must each go home and put your troubles into a sack,' he said again, 'and bring the sacks down to the market-place and hang them up on the line. Then you must step back, a good way back, and wait until I give you the signal. At the signal each of you may rush forward and take any sack he wishes off the line. For the fog will not lift until you stop complaining.'

The people were entranced. Their eyes gleamed and thoughts rushed through their heads like scurrying mice. No doubt you have already guessed what these thoughts were. Each person saw himself quickly getting rid of his troubles by grabbing his neighbour's sack. And each hugged the wicked thought close to himself, for fear his neighbour might catch it.

The stranger leaned back against the tree and, peering through the gloom, watched the villagers string up the line. Then they made for their homes. Presently they returned to the market-place in a long line, each person lugging a sack. With much panting they hung the sacks up on the line.

Then they drew back, a good way back, and stood or sat in little groups.

The stranger did not move. Every eye was fastened on him, but he gave no sign.

And so they waited. Still no sign.

And still they waited. And still no sign.

Finally the people took their eyes off the stranger and fixed them upon the line of sacks. Each person heaved a mighty sigh as he looked at his own sack and compared it with his neighbour's, for of course to each one his own sack looked largest and heaviest. They looked again at the stranger. Still no sign. So they turned back to the sacks. And they gazed and they gazed, and as they gazed they began to think, and as they thought, their musing took an unusual turn.

The carpenter's eyes had been darting from the sack of the tailor to the sack of the tinker; from the sack of the tinker to the sack of the widow. Presently he fixed his gaze on the widow's sack. The carpenter sat up with a start. Is it possible? Can that be the widow's sack dragging on the ground, while his, the carpenter's, swings gaily and lightly above? The carpenter recalls it is many weeks since the village has seen ribbon or flounce of the widow's pretty daughter. The girl went off to her aunt vowing she would not return until the scholar was made welcome in the widow's home. Poor widow. Poor lonely woman. Into the carpenter's ears comes the joyous sound of his little children's jolly voices, and into the carpenter's heart comes the proud knowledge that disobedience is unknown in his home. But for how long?

'Ah me,' thinks the carpenter, 'how short a while are children little; how short a time do they obey us; how quickly are they grown up and become wilful and independent; how apt to go off and leave the home empty and the parents lonely and sorrowful.' For the first time in his life, the carpenter remembers gratefully the extreme youth of his own children. He turns in pity to the widow, but the widow's eyes are glued on the carpenter's sack. A terror grips the carpenter.

The tailor's gaze is fixed on the tinker's sack. Suddenly he sits up with a start. Is it possible? Can the tinker's sack be bigger than his? Into the tailor's mind flashes the rumours he has been hearing of war. He sees the tinker's strong, ambitious son march off. His own son, the frail scholar and dreamer, stays behind. Will the tinker ever see his son again? The tailor's heart almost stops beating. Into his mind comes the thought: when the world is weary of hate and destruction and sick over the loss of the young and the strong, it will turn to the comfort which the dreamers will bring and the healing the scholars will send. For dreams are ever made of hope, and from learning comes understanding, and in understanding lies man's salvation. The tailor's eyes grow moist. He looks in compassion at the tinker. But the tinker's gaze is fixed on the tailor's sack.

The miller had been keeping one eye on the stranger and one on the baker's sack. But when he turned both his eyes on the baker's sack, he sat up with a start. Was it possible? Could it be that the baker's sack was larger than his? The miller stares and thinks. It occurs to him that he never sees the baker in the tavern of an evening. 'That wife of his,' the men say, 'she won't let him enjoy a glass of ale with us. Poor man, he cannot call his soul his own.' The miller thinks and stares. 'Everyone knows,' he recalls his cronies saying, 'that the tongue of the baker's wife is tied in the middle and wags

from both ends. Poor man, he knows not one peaceful moment.'
The miller looks with sympathy at the baker. But the baker had
decided that little children mean large troubles, and a wife means
trouble all the time. So he does not meet the miller's sympathetic
look. His eyes are riveted on the miller's sack. A sudden terror grips
the miller.

And so it happened that as each one of the villagers turned greedy
eyes on some one else's sack, it was only to see that the sack he
coveted was always bigger and heavier than his own. And gradually
each pair of eyes came to rest on its own sack and each heart beat
impatiently for the signal. And as the people's hearts filled with
thoughts of pity and compassion and sympathy and gratitude and
content the fog began to lift. The air became sweet and cool and
clear. A full moon sailed the sky, lighting up the whole market-
place. Like a silver ship, the moon followed her starry course and
eventually disappeared in the west. In the east a faint glow appeared
behind the mountains. The glow turned pink and gold and orange,
and when the happy face of the sun just peeped over the mountains,
the stranger rose and stretched himself.

The people were overjoyed to see the sun. And now they noticed
too that the fog had gone. They breathed deeply of the sweet, cool,
clear air. Oh never again would they pollute it with complaints.

But the sign. Would it never be given? They turned anxiously to
the stranger. He picked up his bundle, slung it slowly over his
shoulder, and called out: 'Go!'

Off like a shot went each of the villagers. As straight as an arrow
did each one head for his very own sack.

How light each felt to its owner as he took it off the line. And how
happy was each man to have his own sack once more.

They turned to thank the stranger – but there was no one under
the tree. The soft morning breeze brought them back the echo of
song:

> Heigh ho,
> Life is jolly.
> Content is wisdom,
> Complaint is folly.

4

A. What is true contentment?

'[The seeker] should be content with little and free from all inordinate desire.'[11]   *Bahá'u'lláh*

'Ah, happily do we live without yearning amongst those who yearn; amidst those who yearn we dwell without yearning.

'Ah, happily do we live, we who have no impediments; feeders of joy shall we be even as the gods of the Radiant Realm.'[12]   *Dhammapada*

B. If we are always dissatisfied with what possessions we have, can we be happy?

C. Do you think most people in the world today are contented with what they have? Does this race to have more and more possessions necessarily make people happy?

'O Son of Man! Upon the tree of effulgent glory I have hung for thee the choicest fruits, wherefore hast thou turned away and contented thyself with that which is less good? Return then unto that which is better for thee in the realm on high.'[13]   *Bahá'u'lláh*

D. What do you think the 'choicest fruits' are?

E. What do you consider to be those things that are 'less good'?

Co-operation

1

'Deal ye one with another with the utmost love and harmony, with friendliness and fellowship.'[1] *Bahá'u'lláh*

'. . . association is always conducive to union and harmony, and union and harmony are the cause of the order of the world and the life of nations.'[2] *Bahá'u'lláh*

'. . . attraction, harmony, unity and Love, are the cause of life . . .'[3]
'Abdu'l-Bahá

'And hold you fast to God's bond, together, and do not scatter . . .'[4]
Muḥammad

2

The United Nations building in New York was designed by the best architects from fifteen nations as a symbol of man's striving for peace. These words of the prophet Isaiah are carved in stone outside the building to greet the thousands of visitors who come daily:

'. . . they shall beat their swords into plowshares, and their spears into pruninghooks: nation shall not lift up sword against nation, neither shall they learn war any more.'[5] *Old Testament*

'Liken the world of existence to the temple of man. All the limbs and organs of the human body assist one another; therefore life continues. When, in this wonderful organism, there is a disconnection, life is changed to death and the parts of the body disintegrate. Likewise, among the parts of existence, there is a wonderful connection and interchange of forces, which is the cause of the life of the world and the continuation of these countless phenomena. When one considers the living beings and the growing plants, he realises that the animals and man sustain life by inhaling the emanations from the vegetable world, and this . . . element is called oxygen. The vegetable kingdom also draws life from the living creatures in the substance called carbon. In brief, the beings of sensation draw life from the growing beings and in turn the growing things receive life from the sensitive creatures.'[6]   *'Abdu'l-Bahá*

3

The Only Clock in the Town

Once upon a time there was a nice little town in a corner of the world. The town had a small square and a few narrow lanes. In the middle of the square stood a high pillar with a very big clock which always worked accurately. Once a week the official clockwinder of the town would come and wind up the clock.

This big clock was the only clock in the town. There was no other clock or watch to show the time, and people would arrange their business according to the clock in the square.

Once, at midday, when the sun was really hot and everybody was at home having a meal, a very strange thing happened. As the short hand of the clock was underneath the long one at twelve o'clock, suddenly the long hand said to the short one, 'Hello friend. How are you? Ticking away, are you?'

'Yes,' answered the short hand, 'I am all right. Just doing my job.'

The long hand complained, 'You know, I am really fed up. Out of all the wonderful and interesting things in the world, I've only known the face of this clock. I move round and round myself all the time. The only thing I have done is to show the minutes.'

'It's the same with me,' said the short hand, 'except that I move more slowly than you. My only job is to show the hours. But I am much happier than you because my job is more important.'

'But, my dear friend,' the long hand flushed with anger, 'my job is no less important than yours. If I didn't show the minutes, the people wouldn't know the exact time.'

He continued, 'Let's find out about this. For a while you hide under me and together we will show the minutes only. Then I will stop while you move along and show only the hours. In this way we can find out which one of us is the more important.'

So they did as they had planned. The short hand moved along with his partner and remained hidden by the long hand. At five o'clock, when people were leaving work, only one hand could be seen on the face of the clock. Such a thing had never happened before.

'The long hand has killed the short one,' said one person.

'The long hand has got rid of the short one,' said another.

Just then, the Mayor came along. With him was the only man responsible for winding the clock. The mayor asked all the people to move aside. He told the clockwinder to go up the pillar and investigate the matter.

The clockwinder, who was a bit frightened, climbed up, opened the glass of the clock and looked into it. Then, looking down at the crowd, he shouted happily, 'Ha, ha! Don't worry! Everything is all right. It's just that the short hand was hidden under the long one.'

He tried very hard to release the short hand, but alas, he couldn't. He came down, and as nothing else could be done, everybody went home.

After a few days, the people were getting used to the new situation. But they just couldn't do anything on time. For example, if somebody wanted to invite a friend to his house he would say, 'Come to my house tomorrow at five minutes to seven minutes.' The poor guest, who couldn't make out what it meant, would go at the wrong time, and both he and his host would be embarrassed.

A few weeks passed by. Then one morning people on their way to work noticed that the long hand had stopped at six but that the short hand was showing the right hours.

People rushed to the Mayor and told him to call for the clockwinder to repair the clock. The Mayor said that it was impossible at that time. So the people left and their lives changed again.

For example, when someone was supposed to meet a friend, he might have to wait for one hour because the short hand would remain at one number for an entire hour and only then move on to the next. So no one could be punctual.

Finally they couldn't stand it any more. One afternoon all the people of the town gathered at the Town Hall and told the Mayor that they wanted a brand new clock. He promised to buy one since the old clock obviously was no longer working.

'We should buy a clock whose hands work together in unity,' the Mayor said.

When the hands of the clock heard these words, they whispered between themselves for a while and then started to work together again.

Can you guess what they whispered to one another?

4

A. Why is co-operation important?
B. In how many situations can we co-operate?
C. If we are going to co-operate with others, what things must we try to remember? (e.g. Is everyone the same as we are?)
D. Now think about the family. Why should all members of the family work together?
E. In team games, what is one feature of the winning side?

Courage

1

'O Son of Man! For everything there is a sign. The sign of love is fortitude under My decree and patience under My trials.'[1]

Bahá'u'lláh

'Freedom from fear, purity of heart . . . these are the treasures of the man who is born for heaven.'[2] *Gita*

'Stay steadfast and unwavering.'[3] *Rig Veda*

'Wait on the Lord: be of good courage, and he shall strengthen thine heart . . .'[4] *Old Testament*

'He whose mind is not wetted, he who is not affected, he who has discarded both good and evil – for such a vigilant one there is no fear.'[5] *Dhammapada*

2

'Ismu'lláh had memorised a great number of Islamic traditions and had mastered the teachings of Shaykh Ahmad and Siyyid Kázim. He became a believer in Shíráz, in the early days of the Faith, and was soon widely known as such. And because he began to teach openly and boldly, they hung a halter on him and led him about the streets and bazaars of the city. Even in that condition, composed and smiling, he kept on speaking to the people. He did not yield; he was not silenced. When they freed him he left Shíráz and went to Khurásán, and there, too, began to spread the Faith, following which he travelled on, in the company of Bábu'l-Báb, to Fort Tabarsí. Here he endured intense sufferings as a member of that band of sacrificial victims. They took him prisoner at the Fort and delivered him over to the chiefs of Mázindarán, to lead him about and finally kill him in a certain district of that province. When, bound with chains, Ismu'lláh was brought to the appointed place, God put it into one man's heart to free him from prison in the middle of the night and guide him to a place where he was safe. Throughout all these agonising trials he remained staunch in his faith.

'Think, for example, how the enemy had completely hemmed in the Fort, and were endlessly pouring in cannon balls from their siege guns. The believers, among them Ismu'lláh, went eighteen days without food. They lived on the leather of their shoes. This too was soon consumed, and they had nothing left but water. They drank a mouthful every morning, and lay famished and exhausted in their Fort. When attacked, however, they would instantly spring to their feet, and manifest in the face of the enemy a magnificent courage and astonishing resistance, and drive the army back from their walls. The hunger lasted eighteen days. It was a terrible ordeal. To begin with, they were far from home, surrounded and cut off by the foe; again, they were starving; and then there were the army's sudden onslaughts and the bombshells raining down and bursting in the heart of the Fort. Under such circumstances to maintain an unwavering faith and patience is extremely difficult, and to endure such dire afflictions a rare phenomenon.

'Ismu'lláh did not slacken under fire. Once freed, he taught more widely than ever.'[6]   *'Abdu'l-Bahá*

3

Life in 'Akká and Haifa in the reign of 'Abdu'l-Hamíd was full of tension and danger. Palestine was a tinder box. Tribes fought each other. Crime was rampant. The streets of 'Akká were too narrow for bandits to roam free, but in Haifa they were a constant threat. Shots were heard every night but murderers were never apprehended. Whenever 'Abdu'l-Bahá was in Haifa, the Bahá'ís feared for His life and watched His movements. Frequently He went to visit the poor alone at night, refusing an escort or even a lantern-carrier. However, at a distance a Bahá'í would secretly watch His progress to the very door of His house.

One night it was Yúnis Khán's turn to follow the Master. 'Abdu'l-Bahá was returning home past midnight when in the dark three shots rang out from a side street. Having become inured to the sound of gunfire, Yúnis Khán paid no attention to the first shot. The flash of the second shot sent him running towards the Master. He had reached the intersection when the third shot was fired and saw two men running away. He was now no more than a step behind the Master. 'Abdul-Bahá walked on without changing His pace or turning His head. His tread was firm and dignified. He had paid no attention to what had occurred but quietly murmured prayers as He walked. At the gate of His house He acknowledged Yúnis Khán's presence, turning to him and bidding him goodbye (*'fí amáni'lláh'* – under God's protection).[7] *Kazemzadeh*

During this same period of danger and crisis the Spanish Consul put an Italian freighter at the disposal of 'Abdu'l-Bahá in order that He might escape during the night, but He refused to flee to safety, though the Bahá'ís begged Him to do so. Instead He sent a message to the ship's captain: 'The Báb did not run away . . . ' After three days and nights the freighter departed without the Master.'[8]

Honnold

The White Silk Dress

One night Ṭáhirih called the Kalantar's wife into her room. She was wearing a dress of shining white silk; her hair gleamed, her cheeks were delicately whitened. She had put on perfume and the room was fragrant with it.

'I am preparing to meet my Beloved,' she said. ' . . . the hour when I shall be arrested and condemned to suffer martyrdom is fast approaching.'

After that, she paced in her locked room, and chanted prayers. The Kalantar's wife stood at the door, and listened to the voice rising and falling, and wept. 'Lord, Lord,' she cried, 'turn from her . . . the cup which her lips desire to drink.' We cannot force the locked door and enter. We can only guess what those last hours were. Not a time of distributing property, of saying good-bye to friends, but rather of communion with the Lord of all peoples, the One alone Beloved of all men. And His chosen ones, His saints and His Messengers, They all were there; They are present at such hours; she was already with Them, beyond the flesh.

She was waiting, veiled and ready, when they came to take her. 'Remember me,' she said as she went, 'and rejoice in my gladness.' She mounted a horse they had brought and rode away through the Persian night. The starlight was heavy on the trees, and nightingales rustled. Camel-bells tinkled from somewhere. The horses' hooves thudded in the dust of the road.

And then bursts of laughter from the drunken officers in the garden. Candles shone on their heavy faces, on the disordered banquet-cloth, the wine spilling over. When Ṭáhirih stood near them, their chief hardly raised his head. 'Leave us!' he shouted. 'Strangle her!' And he went back to his wine.

She had brought a silk handkerchief with her; she had saved it for this from long ago. Now she gave it to them. They twisted it round her throat, and wrenched it till the blood spurted. They waited till her body was quiet, then they took it up and laid it in an unfinished well in the garden. They covered it over and went away, their eyes on the earth, afraid to look at each other.

Many seasons have passed over Ṭihrán since that hour. In winter the mountains to the north have blazed with their snows, shaken like a million mirrors in the sun. And springs came on, with pear blossoms crowding the gardens, and blue swallows flashing. Summertimes, the city lay under a dustcloud, and people went up to the moist rocks, the green clefts in the hills. And autumns, when the boughs were stripped, the dizzy space of plains and sky circled the town again. Much time has passed, almost a hundred years since that night.[9]   *Marzieh Gail*

4

One definition of courage is that strength of character which equips us to meet and endure danger and troubles resolutely. Courage is of two kinds: physical and moral.

A.   What is physical courage? Can you think of some examples from your personal experience when someone has shown physical courage?

B. If someone shows a lack of physical courage in any situation are you going to help him by ridiculing this inability?

C. How can we help one another face physical dangers?

D. Is a person truly courageous if he puts others in danger whilst trying to demonstrate his own valour?

E. Is a person who always picks fights with others showing courage?

F. If we have resolve to do and say what we consider to be right, even if it means we become unpopular or have to suffer, are we showing courage?

G. What sort of person do we have to be, and what sort of qualities do we need to have, in order to defend ourselves against other people's opinions?

A very vivid description of courage is found in the *Dhammapada*: 'Realising that this body is (as fragile) as a jar, establishing his mind (as firm) as a (fortified) city, he should attack Mara [evil temptations] with the weapon of wisdom; he should guard his conquest, and be without attachment.'[10]

Bahá'u'lláh teaches us that: 'The source of courage and power is the promotion of the Word of God, and steadfastness in His Love.'[11]

H. Discuss the meaning of these two verses.

I. Does it take courage to be steadfast in God's love?

History is full of people who have shown great physical and moral courage. Encourage the children to think of examples and recount them.

For younger children

Possibilities for discussion include:

J. People who have physical difficulties and yet overcome them to live useful lives.

K. The difference between being courageous and being reckless.

L. Whether a bully is a brave person.

Any of the stories about the early Bábís will help children understand more about physical and moral courage.

Courtesy

1

'[Courtesy] is the prince of virtues.'[1] *Bahá'u'lláh*

'Courtesy is, in truth, a raiment which fitteth all men, whether young or old.'[2] *Bahá'u'lláh*

'Beware lest ye contend with any one . . .'[3] *Bahá'u'lláh*

'Whoever, seeking his own happiness, harms not with rod pleasure-loving beings, gets happiness hereafter.'[4] *Dhammapada*

'And when you are greeted with a greeting, greet with a fairer than it, or return it; surely God keeps a watchful count over everything.'[5]

Muḥammad

2

'O people of God! I admonish you to observe courtesy. For above all else it is the prince of virtues. Well is it with him who is illumined with the light of courtesy and is attired with the vesture of uprightness. Whoso is endued with courtesy hath indeed attained a sublime station. It is hoped that this Wronged One and everyone else may be enabled to acquire it, hold fast unto it, observe it, and fix our gaze upon it. This is a binding command which hath streamed forth from the Pen of the Most Great Name.'[6] *Bahá'u'lláh*

'Beware! Beware! Lest ye offend any heart!
Beware! Beware! Lest ye hurt any soul!
Beware! Beware! Lest ye deal unkindly toward any person!
Beware! Beware! Lest ye be the cause of hopelessness to any creature.'[7] *'Abdu'l-Bahá*

3

While 'Abdu'l-Bahá was in England, He continually received visits from the Bahá'ís there. Lady Blomfield, His hostess, related the following story:

Two ladies had written from Scotland asking if it were possible that 'Abdu'l-Bahá would spare them one evening.

They accepted my invitation to dinner. Having come straight from the train, and being about to return the same night, every moment was precious.

The Master received them with His warm, simple welcome . . .

Everybody was feeling elated at the prospect of a wonderful evening, unmarred by the presence of any but the most intimate and the most comprehending of the friends.

Not more than half an hour had passed, when, to our consternation, a persistent person pushed past the servitors, and strode into our midst. Seating himself, and lighting a cigarette without invitation, he proceeded to say that he intended writing an article for some paper about 'Abdu'l-Bahá . . . He talked without a pause in a far from polite manner.

We were speechless and aghast at the intrusion of this insufferable and altogether unpleasant bore, spoiling our golden hour!

Presently 'Abdu'l-Bahá rose and, making a sign to the man to follow Him, went to His own private room.

We looked at one another. The bore had gone, yes, but alas! so had the Master!

Can nothing be done? Being the hostess, I was perturbed and perplexed. Then I went to the door of the audience room, and said to the secretary: 'Will you kindly say to 'Abdu'l-Bahá that the ladies with whom the appointment has been made are awaiting His pleasure.'

I returned to the guests and we awaited the result.

Almost immediately we heard steps approaching along the corridor. They came across the hall to the door. The sound of kind farewell words reached us. Then the closing of the door, and the Beloved came back.

'Oh, Master!' we said.

Pausing near the door, He looked at us each in turn, with a look of deep, grave meaning.

'You were making that poor man uncomfortable, so strongly desiring his absence; I took him away to make him feel happy.'

Truly 'Abdu'l-Bahá's thoughts and ways were far removed from ours![8] *Lady Blomfield*

4

A. Can you give a good definition of courtesy without consulting a dictionary? Does a dictionary help? Is this what Bahá'u'lláh means by courtesy?

B. How can one offend a heart or hurt a soul? Why is the last quotation in section 2 so strongly worded?

C. How is it possible to be courteous and not let yourself be used by others?

D. Why does Bahá'u'lláh describe courtesy as a 'great bounty'?

E. What station is given to courtesy in the preceding quotations? Why do you suppose that this particular virtue is so highly honoured? Why do you think Bahá'u'lláh called it 'the prince of virtues'?

A last thought about courtesy: 'We, verily, have chosen courtesy, and made it the true mark of such as are nigh unto Him.'[9]

Bahá'u'lláh

F. And a last question: What has sincerity to do with courtesy?

Criticism

1

'One should not pry into the faults of others, things left done and undone by others, but one's own deeds done and undone.'[1]
Dhammapada

'. . . overlook the faults of one another for My name's sake . . .'[2]
Bahá'u'lláh

'And why beholdest thou the mote that is in thy brother's eye, but perceivest not the beam that is in thine own eye?'[3] *New Testament*

'. . . and magnify not the faults of others that thine own faults may not appear great . . .'[4] *Bahá'u'lláh*

2

'O Son of Being! How couldst thou forget thine own faults and busy thyself with the faults of others? Whoso doeth this is accursed of Me.'[5] *Bahá'u'lláh*

3

The disciples of Jesus, passing along the road and seeing a dead dog, remarked how offensive and disgusting a spectacle it was. Then Christ, turning to them said, 'Yes, but see how white and beautiful are his teeth.'

'Abdu'l-Bahá told this story to some pilgrims who had visited him in 'Akká. He used the story, as Jesus did, to teach that there is some good in everything, and that it is better to look at the good qualities in a person rather than find fault.[6] *Grundy*

Two pilgrims were at the Master's luncheon table one day in 1908. He asked them if they were glad to be in 'Akká and if they were happy. They replied that they were very happy to be there with Him, but unhappy when they thought of their own faults. 'Think not of yourselves,' He said, 'but think of the Bounty of God. This will always make you happy.' Then with a smile He referred to an Arabic saying about the peacock, who 'is contented because he never looks at his feet – which are very ugly – but always at his plumage which is very beautiful.'[7] *Honnold*

Johnny was a young boy who lived near many other children but who never seemed to have any friends. Do you know why? I'll tell you. He was always making others feel bad by saying something to hurt them.

'Hello, four-eyes,' he would say to his little sister who wore glasses.

'Oh, look! Here comes cauliflower-ears,' he would say when the little boy next door, whose ears were rather big and fat, would walk by. He would laugh if he heard someone try to sing, or pull faces when he did not like the look of someone's new clothes. It seemed that everything he saw and heard was for him to find fault with, and, of course, for that reason other children did not like to be around him very much.

One day Johnny was in the garden playing alone with his new red bicycle. The bicycle had a loud bell and shone beautifully in the sunlight. As he rode out of the garden gate into the street he saw a boy from the bazaar happily riding his rather old, rusty bike. Johnny laughed.

'Look at your old crock compared to my new red bike,' he called out rudely.

Sensibly the boy was too happy to feel bad about Johnny's cruel words. Still Johnny wanted to show the boy his bicycle was better. He peddled as fast as he could and rang his bell loudly behind the boy. At last he overtook him, shouting with glee, 'Old bikes like yours should not be on the road. Why don't you try and sell it and buy a donkey. Ha! Ha! Ha!'

Unfortunately all that unkind chatter meant that Johnny forgot to concentrate on what he was doing. He was going very fast down a slope and he began to lose control. He wobbled from side to side. Suddenly, to his horror, he saw a huge truck looming in front of him. Johnny had no choice but to swerve into the side of the road. He hit a tree and fell into a muddy ditch. His bicycle was twisted and the wheels buckled; all the lovely red paint was scratched away. Johnny was hurt too. He felt his mouth and realised that his two front teeth were missing! There they were, lying in the ditch looking at him!

4

A. Why should we overlook the faults of others, especially when the fault might be hurting us?

'If any differences arise amongst you, behold Me standing before your face, and overlook the faults of one another for My name's sake and as a token of your love for My manifest and resplendent Cause.'[8] *Bahá'u'lláh*

B. Would we find fault with people so often if we knew God was standing before us?
C. What is one of the ways in which we can show our love for God?

'Judge not, that ye be not judged, For with what judgement ye judge, ye shall be judged; and with what measure ye mete, it shall be measured to you again. And why beholdest thou the mote that is in thy brother's eye, but considerest not the beam that is in thine own eye? . . .

Thou hypocrite, first cast out the beam out of thine own eye; and then shalt thou see clearly to cast out the mote out of thy brother's eye.'[9] *New Testament*

D. Why does Jesus call fault-finders hypocrites?
E. What is the reason why Jesus says we should not judge another's actions?
F. How do we react to those who criticise?

'As an elephant in the battlefield withstands the arrows shot from a bow, even so will I endure abuse; verily most people are undisciplined.'[10] *Dhammapada*

G. How can looking at the good points of others help us overcome any tendency we have to be critical?

H. When is it good to be critical (of ourselves, of injustice, etc.)?

For younger children

I. Ask the children to finish the story of Johnny.

J. Discuss whether the accident would have happened had Johnny been silent.

K. Discuss what will remind him not to be critical of others.

Deeds not Words

1

'Let deeds, not words, be your adorning.'[1]   *Bahá'u'lláh*

'Let your acts be a guide unto all mankind . . .'[2]   *Bahá'u'lláh*

'. . . be ye doers of the word, and not hearers only . . .'[3]
                                                    New Testament

'In the actions of the best men others find their rule of action. The path that a great man follows becomes a guide to the world.'[4]   *Gita*

'And whosoever does deeds of righteousness, be it male or female, believing – they shall enter Paradise, and not be wronged a single date spot.'[5]   *Muḥammad*

'The essence of faith is fewness of words and abundance of deeds; he whose words exceed his deeds, know verily his death is better than his life.'[6]   *Bahá'u'lláh*

2

'Do men gather grapes of thorns, or figs of thistles? Even so every good tree bringeth forth good fruit; but a corrupt tree bringeth forth evil fruit. A good tree cannot bring forth evil fruit, neither can a corrupt tree bring forth good fruit. Every tree that bringeth not forth good fruit is hewn down, and cast into the fire. Wherefore by their fruits ye shall know them.'[7]   *New Testament*

'Set thy heart upon thy work, but never on its reward. Work not for a reward; but never cease to do thy work.'[8]   *Gita*

'As a flower that is lovely and beautiful, but is scentless, even so fruitless is the well-spoken word of one who does not practise it.'[9]
                                                    Dhammapada

'A man who does great good, and talks not of it, is on the way to perfection. The man who has accomplished a small good and magnifies it in his speech is worth very little.'[10]   *'Abdu'l-Bahá*

'Surely God shall not wrong as much as the weight of an ant; if it be a good deed He will double it, and give from Himself a mighty wage.'[11]   *Muḥammad*

'Despise not merit, saying, "It will not come nigh unto me"; even by the falling of drops a water-jar is filled; likewise the wise man, gathering little by little, fills himself with good.'[12]   *Dhammapada*

3

The Shoemaker and the Elves

Once upon a time there lived a shoemaker who worked as hard as he could, but he had such a lot of bad luck that every day he grew poorer and poorer. At last everything he had was gone except one small piece of leather – enough for only one pair of shoes. The shoemaker cut out the leather, got it ready to stitch together in the morning, and left it on his workbench. He said his prayers and went to bed, trusting that he could finish the shoes the next day and sell them.

Bright and early the next morning he rose, said his prayers again, and went to his workbench. There to his great surprise stood a pair of new shoes beautifully made and the leather he had left gone!

The shoemaker and his wife were amazed and did not know what to think.

'Who could have made these lovely shoes?' asked the shoemaker's wife. 'Look, not a stitch is crooked.'

The first customer who saw the shoes was so pleased with them that he paid enough for the shoemaker to buy two pieces of leather.

Happily the shoemaker cut out the leather for two pairs of shoes, left the leather on his bench, said his prayers and went to bed.

When he awoke the next morning he found two pairs of perfectly made shoes on the bench, just as beautiful as before. Two customers

paid enough for these shoes to pay for four pieces of leather. The shoemaker cut out the leather, said his prayers and went to sleep. In the morning, exactly the same thing had happened.

And so it went for some time. Each night the shoemaker cut out leather and each morning he found the neatest pair of shoes possible. This continued until the shoemaker and his wife became thriving, prosperous people.

One night the shoemaker and his wife decided that they would stay up and watch what happened to the pieces of leather left on the workbench. They both hid behind a curtain. Just as the clock struck twelve, two tiny elves, about the size of your hand, came leaping in through the window. Although the shoemaker and his wife thought the elves looked very funny with their pointed ears, they were sad to see that the elves had no clothes to wear.

The elves immediately started to work on the leather. Tip, tap, tip, tap went their little hammers; stitch, stitch, stitch went their needles. They worked hard. The shoemaker had never seen anyone work as quickly. They finished their work, danced around the shoes and at two o'clock left.

'How can we thank those kind elves for helping us?' asked the shoemaker.

'Well,' said his wife, 'they must be cold, for they haven't any clothes. Let's stitch new suits for them. I'll make such pretty clothes.'

So she made two tiny waistcoats, two tiny pairs of trousers, two tiny caps, and two woollen scarves. The shoemaker made them some tiny shoes.

That night the clothes were left on the workbench instead of the leather. When the elves saw the clothes they danced, sang and clapped their hands. They quickly put on their new clothes and ran away. They never came back, but they had brought such good luck to the shoemaker and his wife that the two never again needed any help.   *Adapted by Wendi Momen*

The Dutch Boy and the Dyke

Peter was a small boy who lived a long time ago with his mother and father in Holland. Holland is a country in northern Europe which is flat and where beautiful tulips grow.

Peter loved his home and the tulips, and he loved looking beyond them to the slowly turning windmills and beyond them to the sea.

In some parts of Holland the land is lower than the sea, and water could easily come and cover the land. The Dutch have built high walls called dykes to keep the water out. It is the job of many men in Holland to watch these walls and repair them as soon as they see a hole. Even little children are taught to watch the dykes because they know how quickly a small hole can become a big one and how dangerous it would be if the water came pouring in.

One evening Peter was hurrying home along the top of the dyke. He had spent the day with his grandmother and it was quite late. Suddenly Peter heard the sound of water trickling and he saw a tiny hole in the dyke wall. He ran down to take a closer look. Peter would have loved just to run home, but he knew how serious the hole was. It would soon get bigger, and then the wall would collapse and his country would be flooded.

Peter looked around for someone but no one was about. He had to do something, so he put his finger in the hole. It soon became cold and numb, so he tried another finger, then another. Each time he changed fingers water poured through the dyke. Finally he put in his thumb and he did not dare take it out even for a minute.

Even though he shouted, 'Help! Help!' many times, no one came along. His mother and father thought that he was staying with his grandmother, so they did not worry. They never dreamed that he needed help.

Peter spent a painful, cold, lonely and frightening night with his thumb in that hole because he knew that if he didn't the roaring sea would flood the land.

It wasn't until early morning that a man walking along the road heard him and rushed to help him.

Everyone praised Peter for his great deed and called him 'the hero of Holland'. Peter was taken home to hot food and a warm bed by his proud and loving parents. He said just before he went to sleep, 'I would do it again if I had to. I am glad I could do something to help my country.'

All this happened long ago, but we still remember Peter's great deed today. *Adapted by Wendi Momen*

4

A. What is right action?
B. Do our deeds always conform to what we know is right action?
C. Can you think of a time when your actions did not conform to what you knew was right?
D. How do we learn what is right action?
E. What is better, to think good thoughts or to do good deeds?
F. Freddie always said that it was wrong to take and keep what did not belong to him, but he kept his favourite library book under his pillow and didn't return it to the library. Did his deeds conform to his words?

Detachment

1

'O Friends! Abandon not the everlasting beauty for a beauty that must die, and set not your affections on this mortal world of dust.'[1] *Bahá'u'lláh*

'O My Servant! Free thyself from the fetters of this world, and loose thy soul from the prison of self. Seize thy chance, for it will come to thee no more.'[2] *Bahá'u'lláh*

'He that seeketh to be a helper of God in this Day, let him close his eyes to whatever he may possess, and open them to the things of God.'[3] *Bahá'u'lláh*

'Verily, the thing that deterreth you, in this day, from God is worldliness in its essence.'[4] *Bahá'u'lláh*

'And as the human heart, as fashioned by God, is one and undivided, it behoveth thee to take heed that its affections be, also, one and undivided.'[5] *Bahá'u'lláh*

'Whoso in the world overcomes this base unruly craving, from him sorrows fall away, like water-drops from a lotus-leaf.'[6]

Dhammapada

'When all desires are in peace . . . the mind, withdrawing within, gathers the multitudiness straying sense into the harmony of recollection . . .'[7] *Gita*

'Behold the universe in the glory of God . . . Leaving the transient, find joy in the Eternal; set not your heart on another's possession.'[8] *Isa Upanishad*

'I know that treasures pass away and that the Eternal is not reached by the transient.'[9] *Katha Upanishad*

'The essence of detachment is for man to turn his face towards the courts of the Lord, to enter His Presence, behold His Countenance, and stand as witness before Him.'[10] *Bahá'u'lláh*

'Two paths lie in front of man. Pondering on them, the wise man chooses the path of joy; the fool takes the path of pleasure.'[11]

Katha Upanishad

2

'If we suffer, it is the outcome of material things, and all the trials and troubles come from this world of illusion.

'For instance, a merchant may lose his trade and depression ensues. A workman is dismissed and starvation stares him in the face. A farmer has a bad harvest, anxiety fills his mind. A man builds a house which is burnt to the ground and he is straightway homeless, ruined, and in despair.

'All these examples are to show you that the trials which beset our every step, all our sorrow, pain, shame and grief, are born in the world of matter: whereas the spiritual Kingdom never causes sadness. A man living with his thoughts in this Kingdom knows perpetual joy. The ills all flesh is heir to do not pass him by, but they only touch the surface of his life, the depths are calm and serene.'[12]

'Abdu'l-Bahá

3

En route to Fort Ṭabarsí

As soon as Mullá Ḥusayn had determined to pursue the way that led to Mázindarán, he, immediately after he had offered his morning prayer, bade his companions discard all their possessions. 'Leave behind all your belongings,' he urged them, 'and content yourselves only with your steeds and swords, that all may witness your renunciation of all earthly things, and may realize that this little band of God's chosen companions has no desire to safeguard its own property, much less to covet the property of others.' Instantly they all obeyed, and unburdening their steeds, arose and joyously followed him. The father of Badí' was the first to throw aside his satchel which contained a considerable amount of turquoise which he had brought with him from the mine that belonged to his father. One word from Mullá Ḥusayn proved sufficient to induce him to fling by the roadside what was undoubtedly his most treasured possession, and to cling to the desire of his leader.[13]   *Nabíl*

The Bábís in the Síyáh-Chál

One day, there was brought to Our prison a tray of roasted meat which they informed Us the Sháh had ordered to be distributed among the prisoners. 'The Sháh,' We were told, 'faithful to a vow he made, has chosen this day to offer to you all this lamb in fulfilment of his pledge.' A deep silence fell upon Our companions, who expected Us to make answer on their behalf. 'We return this gift to you,' We replied, 'we can well dispense with this offer.' The answer We made would have greatly irritated the guards had they not been eager to devour the food we had refused to touch. Despite the hunger with which Our companions were afflicted, only one among them, a certain Mírzá Husayn-i-Mutavallíy-i-Qumí, showed any desire to eat of the food the sovereign had spread before us. With a fortitude that was truly heroic, Our fellow-prisoners submitted, without a murmur, to endure the piteous plight to which they were reduced. Praise of God, instead of complaint of the treatment meted out to them by the Sháh, fell unceasingly from their lips – praise with which they sought to beguile the hardships of a cruel captivity.

Every day Our gaolers, entering Our cell, would call the name of one of Our companions, bidding him arise and follow them to the foot of the gallows. With what eagerness would the owner of that name respond to that solemn call! Relieved of his chains, he would spring to his feet and, in a state of uncontrollable delight, would approach and embrace Us. We would seek to comfort him with the assurance of an ever-lasting life in the world beyond, and, filling his heart with hope and joy, would send him forth to win the crown of glory. He would embrace, in turn, the rest of his fellow-prisoners, and then proceed to die as dauntlessly as he had lived. Soon after the martyrdom of each of these companions, We would be informed by the executioner, who had grown to be friendly with Us, of the circumstances of the death of his victim, and of the joy with which he had endured his sufferings to the very end.[14]   *Bahá'u'lláh*

For younger children

Whilst children are small they are often fiercely possessive about the things they own. When teaching about detachment, try to direct their thoughts to the fact that physical possessions do not last – they break, get lost, wear out, and so on; but spiritual possessions like love, kindness, trustworthiness last forever and ever. The following stories will help you illustrate this.

Fujita

When 'Abdu'l-Bahá came to America, H. S. Fujita was a medical student at the University of Michigan. Like his famous forerunner who was short of stature, he climbed a sycamore tree to see the Master pass by. 'Come down, Zachias, for this day I would sup with thee,' called the flute-like voice of 'Abdu'l-Bahá, and Fujita relinquishing every human tie followed Him back to Mount Carmel to become a helper in the household.' Fujita, who passed away quite recently, spent most of his time, since that day in 1912, in the Holy Land.[15]   *Honnold*

Bahá'u'lláh and the Egyptian Merchant

Bahá'u'lláh spent many years of His life in prison because people did not understand Him. But finally He was allowed to live in a house outside the walls of the old city of 'Akká. Now there was a merchant in Egypt who longed to visit Bahá'u'lláh, so he wrote and asked if he might come. Bahá'u'lláh told him that he could make a visit only when he no longer owed money to anyone.

The merchant had an important business. His caravans crossed the desert laden with riches. He was quite wealthy, but he also owed a great deal of money to different people. If he paid back all this money, he would not be nearly so rich. But he felt that this did not matter, for more than anything else in the world he wanted to see Bahá'u'lláh. So be began to pay his debts. It took him five years to pay everything. And when he had finished, he had only enough money left to take care of his family while he was away and to pay for a steamer ticket. He could not even pay for a bed on the boat. He would have to sleep on the deck.

But he was very happy when he got on the boat. He did not even worry when his shawl, which would help keep out the winds at night, slipped into the water and disappeared. He was on his way to see Bahá'u'lláh and nothing else mattered.

On the day when the boat was to arrive in Haifa, Bahá'u'lláh sent a man with a horse and carriage to meet the merchant. He told this servant that He was expecting a very noble guest. So the servant went to the boat and looked for someone who appeared very rich and grand. He found no such person, so he drove back to Bahá'u'lláh and told Him that the visitor had not come.

But Bahá'u'lláh knew better. He knew that the servant had not recognised His guest. So this time He sent 'Abdu'l-Bahá. The Master went to Haifa and He found only a shabby, sad-looking little man sitting quietly on a bench. He hurried to his side and welcomed him.

The merchant had been disappointed that no one had met him and thought Bahá'u'lláh had forgotten all about him. Now here was 'Abdu'l-Bahá and he felt very ashamed for thinking that Bahá'u'lláh had failed him.

The Master suggested that they drive to 'Akká. But the merchant said he could not go yet. He must first pray and beg God's forgiveness for his lack of faith. He had not a single penny and he could not let 'Abdu'l-Bahá pay for a room at a hotel, so they decided to spend the night praying on the little bench.

'Abdu'l-Bahá unbuttoned His long, wide cloak and wrapped it around them both. He put His arm around the merchant. And so they sat and prayed together all through the night.

In the morning they drove to 'Akká. Now the merchant felt that his heart was at last pure enough to come to Bahá'u'lláh and talk with Him about God. He must have felt rich indeed. He was rich in the love of God. It did not matter that he was a poor man without money. *Adapted from M. H. Ford*

Lucky Hans

Hans had served his master for seven long years. 'My time is up now,' he said to his master. 'Give me my wages, for I want to go home to my mother.'

'You have served me well and faithfully,' replied his master. 'Your reward shall be as good as your service.' With these words he gave Hans a huge lump of gold as big as his head. Hans pulled his handkerchief out of his pocket, wrapped up the lump of gold, lifted it on his shoulder, and set out for home.

The way was long and exhausting. His eyes lit up when he suddenly saw a man on horseback, trotting merrily along, at ease with the world. 'How wonderful it must be to ride!' he exclaimed.

'There you sit, just as if you were in an armchair. You don't stub your toes against stones, you save your shoe leather, and you cover the ground at a fine rate.'

The horseman heard his words, and pulled up. 'Hullo, Hans!' he called. 'If that's what you think, why are you walking?'

'I have to,' Hans explained sadly. 'I have this heavy old lump to carry around with me. It is pure gold, it's true, but it is so heavy that I cannot stand upright.'

'I know,' said the horseman. 'Let us make an exchange. I will give you my horse, and you give me your lump.'

'Delighted!' cried Hans. 'But I must warn you that you will soon be tired out with carrying it.'

So the horseman dismounted and took the bundle. He helped Hans upon the horse and put the reins in his hands. 'If you want it to go faster,' he explained, 'you simply click your tongue and say, "Hup, hup".'

Hans was very pleased with himself as he sat on the horse's back and rode along without having to exert himself at all. After a while he thought he would like to go faster, so he clicked his tongue and cried, 'Hup, hup'. At once the horse broke into a brisk canter, and before Hans knew what was happening he flew over the horse's head and landed in a muddy ditch. The horse would have run away, had it not been caught by a farmer who was passing by, driving a cow before him. After making sure that no bones were broken, Hans stood up and said sulkily, 'A fine game, this riding, when the horse does its best to break your neck! That's the last time you'll ever catch me riding a horse!'

'Well,' said the farmer, 'if it suits you, I shall be pleased to exchange my cow for your horse.' Hans agreed gladly, and the farmer leapt into the saddle and rode off.

Hans drove the cow quietly along, and thought how lucky he had been. As long as I have bread, he said to himself, I can have bread with butter and cheese on it as often as I want! If I am thirsty, all I have to do is to milk the cow. What else could I possibly ask for?

When he came to a wayside inn he halted and ate all the food he had with him, and bought a small glass of beer for a few pence. Then he drove his cow on towards his mother's village.

As midday approached the heat became more and more oppressive, and Hans found himself crossing a wide heath. He grew so hot and thirsty that he stopped to milk the cow in order to quench his thirst. He tethered her to a tree trunk and, as he had no bucket, he laid his leather cap on the ground beneath her. But no matter how hard he tried, not a single drop of milk appeared. He was so clumsy that the poor beast lost patience with him and gave him a powerful kick on the head with her hind leg, which sent him sprawling on the ground.

For a few moments Hans did not know where he was, but luckily for him a butcher chanced to pass that way, pushing before him a young pig in a wheelbarrow. 'What's the trouble, Hans?' he called. Hans told him what had happened and the butcher gave him a drink from his water-bottle. 'That cow will never give you much milk,' he said. 'She is far too old and is fit only for ploughing or for meat.'

'Who would have thought it?' said Hans, rubbing his head. 'I suppose I could use her for meat, but I don't like beef! It is too dry for me. But a young pig like yours, that would taste fine, and you could have sausages, too.'

'Listen, Hans,' said the butcher. 'If you like, I will help you by exchanging my little pig for your old cow.'

'Many thanks indeed for your generosity,' cried Hans, and he handed over his cow, leading the pig away in exchange.

He continued on his way, well contented with his lot. Whenever anything happened to annoy him, something always turned up to put matters right. Before long he met a young fellow who was carrying a plump goose under his arm. Hans told him all about his good fortune, and how he had made so many favourable exchanges. The young fellow told him that he was taking the goose to a christening feast. 'Just feel how heavy it is!' he said, holding it up by the wings. 'I've been fattening it for eight weeks. It will make a tasty roast.'

'Yes,' said Hans, weighing the goose in his hands. 'It's quite heavy. But so is my pig.'

Meanwhile the young fellow was looking about suspiciously and shaking his head doubtfully at the pig. 'You know,' he said 'the mayor of our village has just had a pig stolen, and I'm afraid – I'm very much afraid – that it's the one you have here. He has sent people out to look for it, and it would be a sad thing for you if you were caught. They would certainly lock you up in the dungeon.'

Poor Hans was scared out of his wits. 'What can I do?' he cried. 'Would you exchange your goose for my pig?'

'Well,' said the lad, 'it's a little risky, but I hate to think of you getting into trouble.' So he set the goose down, seized the pig, and made off quickly down another track.

Freed of his worries, Hans took the goose under his arm and plodded on towards his mother's cottage. 'Another good exchange!' he said to himself. 'I shall have a wonderful roast and plenty of goose dripping for my bread for several months, and I shall have all the beautiful soft feathers besides. I think I will make a pillow with the feathers so that I shall be able to sleep comfortably at nights. How pleased my mother will be!'

As he walked through the last village on his way home, he came across a grinder with his grindstone on a barrow. As he turned the grindstone, the grinder sang,

       'I sharpen scissors and knives all day
       My stone drives all the rust away.'

Hans paused to watch him at work. 'You seem to have a very happy job.'

'Yes indeed,' replied the grinder. 'This trade is a great money-spinner. A good grinder will find money whenever he puts his hand in his pocket. But where did you buy that fine goose?'

'I didn't buy it,' said Hans, 'I exchanged my pig for it.'

'And your pig?'

'Oh, I was given that in exchange for my cow.'

'And the cow?'

'I was given that in exchange for my horse.'

'And the horse?'

'I exchanged my lump of gold for that – a lump as big as my head.'

'And the gold?'

'That was my wages for seven years' service.'

'You seem to have done very well for yourself,' he said. 'How would you like to hear the money jingle in your pocket every time you stand up or sit down?'

'How could I do that?' asked Hans.

'By becoming a grinder, like me. All you need is a grindstone – the rest is easy. You could have mine, if you like. It is a little worn, so I will let you have it in exchange for your goose, if you like.'

'Will you really?' said Hans. 'I am the luckiest person in the whole world. What shall I have to worry about, if I have money whenever I put my hand in my pocket?' So he handed over his goose, and took the grindstone.

'And here,' said the grinder as he picked up a heavy boulder from the roadside, 'is another useful stone, which you can use for hammering straight all your bent nails. Take this too, and look after it well!'

Hans picked up his two stones, and went happily on his way. His eyes sparkled with joy. 'I must have been born under a lucky star,' he said. 'Everything I could possibly wish for seems to come true!'

He had been on his feet all day, and by this time he was tired. He was also beginning to feel very hungry, for he had eaten all his food in his joy at having the cow. Soon he was stumbling along a few yards at a time, pausing every few minutes to rest. His two stones weighed him down painfully, and he thought how good it would be if only he did not have to carry them. He crawled at a snail's pace to a spring by the side of the track to take another rest and refresh himself with a drink of cool water. He laid his stones carefully by the edge of the spring so that they would not be damaged as he sat down, and then he bent to drink. But as he stretched he knocked against the stones and they fell into the spring with a great splash.

When he watched them sink right to the bottom, Hans jumped for joy, and then knelt with tears in his eyes to thank God for delivering him from his troublesome burden, which was all that had prevented him from being perfectly happy.

'There's no one under the sun as lucky as I,' he cried. With a light heart and free of every burden, he ran lightly on his way and was soon home in his mother's cottage. *Folk Tale*

4

A. How can we be detached and still live a 'normal' life in this world? Should we live like a 'holy' man in the forest away from the real world?

'By the world is meant that which turneth you aside from Him Who is the Dawning-Place of Revelation, and inclineth you unto that which is unprofitable unto you.'[16]   *Bahá'u'lláh*

B. What sort of things do you think could turn you away from God?

C. Consider very carefully what things are profitable to you in the long run, throughout eternity, and what people think are valuable for a shorter length of time.

D. Do we only need to be detached from material things?
   'As a solid rock is not shaken by the wind, even so the wise are not ruffled by praise or blame.'[17]   *Dhammapada*

E. Must we also be detached from love?
   'He must so cleanse his heart that no remnant of either love or hate may linger therein, lest that love blindly incline him to error, or that hate repel him away from the truth.'[18]   *Bahá'u'lláh*

F. How can love lead us to make mistakes?

G. Is it human love or divine love that God asks us to be detached from?

Distinction

1

'In the love of God you must become distinguished from all else.'[1]

'Abdu'l-Bahá

'Indulge not in heedlessness . . .'[2] *Dhammapada*

'. . . Ye must conduct yourselves in such a manner that ye may stand out distinguished and brilliant as the sun among other souls.'[3] *'Abdu'l-Bahá*

'You must become distinguished for loving humanity, for unity and accord, for love and justice.'[4] *'Abdu'l-Bahá*

2

'I do not desire for you financial distinction. It is not an ordinary distinction I desire; not scientific, commercial, industrial distinction. For you I desire spiritual distinction – that is, you must become eminent and distinguished in morals.'[5] *'Abdu'l-Bahá*

3

Maid in the Mirror

Lu was a young man who lived in China in days long gone by. His family was not rich but they had determined that their son should be given as much schooling as any other youth in their city. They saved every penny in order that he might have the best teachers, and they watched each step he took along the road to where the Emperor's examinations were held.

Now Lu was young and Lu sometimes was lazy. And there came a time when he did not work very hard over his books and his brushes. No matter how earnestly his father explained that once the examinations were passed he would be given a high position, Lu was not interested. He let his books lie closed and he spent his whole time in games with his friends or walking under the trees along the bank of the river.

One summer day as this idle young man strolled there with his bird cage in his hand, he met a maiden who said her name was Feng Hsien. She was of such shining beauty that both the sun and the moon seemed dim beside her. Feng Hsien smiled shyly at Lu. They exchanged words of greeting. And straightaway the young man knew that he would have her for his wife or he would never be wed.

Again and again Feng Hsien and Lu met on the river bank, and sweet were the hours they spent talking together. But one day, when it was time for them to part, the maiden grew sorrowful. 'Our meetings must end,' she said to the youth. 'You are wasting your days. You do not open a book. You do not lift the brush or the pen. The paste is dry on your ink stone. I shall not come again until you have passed your examinations. But I have brought you a present by means of which you sometimes may see me.'

And she handed Lu a shining mirror. There was so little glass in those days that most of the Chinese mirrors were made of polished metal like this one. When she put the round mirror into his hand, Feng Hsien said, 'My honourable friend, you will see my poor self in the face of this mirror. But you will see it there only when you have done well with your books and your writing brush.' And with that she was gone.

Lu sadly turned his steps towards home. When he had shut himself in the room which his family had given him for his study, he examined the mirror. He looked first at its back with the graceful bamboo leaves carved deep in its metal. Then he turned it around and peered at its smooth, polished, silvery face. There indeed he could see the figure of the lovely Feng Hsien. But the maid's back was turned, and she seemed to be moving away from him.

'Only when you have done well will you see me.' Lu repeated to himself the words Feng Hsien had said to him and he sat down at his table and opened his books. His parents were overjoyed at the change in their son. From dawn until dark he worked in his study. He would not receive visitors. He no longer went forth to play games with his friends. His teachers had nothing but good to report of him. And each morning and each evening when Lu looked in the mirror he saw there the smiling face of Feng Hsien.

But summer does not last forever, and in climbing a hill the last step must be as firm as the first. In time Lu became weary of his well-doing. He began to go about once more with his friends. His books were seldom opened. His teachers shook their grey heads.

Then one day the young man looked in the mirror and saw the fair maid with tears on her cheeks. She turned her back and began to move away as she had done on the day when Lu had first found her in the mirror. A wave of regret swept over the youth. He felt greatly ashamed, and he hurried to open his books. Once more he worked from dawn until dark. He hung the mirror where he could not fail to see when Feng Hsien was pleased and when she was sorrowful. His love for her grew so great, and he worked so well, that in just a few years he was ready to take the Emperor's examinations.

Three times he went in and out of the rooms where the tests were given. Three times he passed and three times he returned in triumph to the house of his parents.

What excitement there was in Lu's neighbourhood when the red official notice of his final success was pasted upon his gate! Fire-crackers were set off. Candles and incense burned in the Hall of the Ancestors so that they might know of the good fortune that had come to the family. Flags flew and friends streamed in through the gate to congratulate the young man. Lu, dressed in a splendid new gown, rode about in a sedan chair to visit his friends and there was a fine feast and a procession in honour of the occasion. Women strewed flowers along the way, musicians played, and red banners tied upon leafy bamboo poles were carried before the young scholar.

While the family celebration was still going on, there came a knock at the gate of Lu's house, and there was announced a go-between who had been sent by the wealthiest man in the whole city to discuss the matter of a marriage between Lu and his daughter. Such is the power of learning that this man wished to bestow his fairest child and many rich gifts with her, upon the son of this modest household.

The young man's parents were overcome with joy at such good fortune. But to their surprise, Lu himself would not listen to the go-between's words. 'I do not care how fair the young maiden may be, I will not wed her,' he said to his father. And he went into his study and closed the door.

There he turned to the mirror to seek his beloved Feng Hsien. He found the maid's face wreathed in smiles, and as he looked, it seemed to him that she stepped down out of the mirror and stood close beside him. 'Go back to the go-between, O youth of goodness and wisdom,' the mirror-maid said. 'Consent to the marriage he offers. Do not ask my reason, for I may not tell it. But believe me, all will be just as you most desire.'

Before Lu could ask her one question the maiden had vanished.

Try as he would he could not find even her shadow on the silvery face of the mirror. There was nothing for him to do but to follow her wishes and, to his parents' great joy, the marriage was arranged.

Lu's heart was sad, for he could not yet understand why his beloved Feng Hsien should wish him to marry another. And it was with downcast eyes that he met the bridal chair at the gate. However, his sorrow was soon turned to joy. For when the bride stood before him, he found that she was not a stranger but Feng Hsien herself!

Never again did Lu see her face in the mirror. And never would she tell him what fairy had sent her spirit to meet him there on the river bank. As a matter of fact, he had no need to know that, and he had no need to look for her again in the mirror since all through his life she stood by his side.

High position and riches and a beautiful bride! All these came to Lu because he paid attention to his books and his brush. And such good luck may come also to all who work hard in the court of learning. *Folk Tale*

4

A. What is the distinction that 'Abdu'l-Bahá wishes us to have? How is this different from the common idea of a 'distinguished' person? Is a person distinguished only because he or she is more wealthy than others?
B. Does this mean that we should not aim for distinction and perfection in human endeavours?

'. . . the acquisition of sciences and the perfection of arts are considered acts of worship.'[6]   *'Abdu'l-Bahá*

'Would . . . the development of useful arts and sciences . . . be harmful things? For such endeavour lifts the individual within the mass and raises him out of the depths of ignorance to the highest reaches of knowledge and human excellence.[7]

'Abdu'l-Bahá

C. Can we attain excellence in any subject or occupation if we do not love the work?
D. What harm is there if we do not strive for excellence and distinction in: our work? our spiritual life?
E. Do we all have the same capacities?
F. Is it necessary for us all to be excellent at the same things?
G. How can we come to know the things at which we are good?
H. Is there any point in feeling frustrated with our own inability to do a particular thing that our friend does well? What should we do instead?

'Let each morn be better than its eve and each morrow richer than its yesterday. Man's merit lieth in service and virtue and not in pageantry of wealth and riches.'[8]   *Bahá'u'lláh*

For younger children

We can explain distinction to younger children as 'doing our best' and that to do our best we need both will-power and determination. We can ask:

I. What are goals?
J. What sort of goals should we have in our lives? Can we make our own or should we let others make them for us?
K. Why should we try to do our best in everything we do?
L. Do you really feel satisfied when you have done something half-heartedly?
M. Is it only in our studies that we should do our best?

The story 'The Maid in the Mirror' can help the children understand the rewards of striving for excellence in study. It can be used as a starting point for discussing the concept of striving for excellence in other things.

Education

1

'Bend your energies to whatever may foster the education of men.'[1]   *Bahá'u'lláh*

'Regard man as a mine rich in gems of inestimable value. Education can, alone, cause it to reveal its treasures, and enable mankind to benefit.'[2]   *Bahá'u'lláh*

'They all attain perfection when they find joy in their work.'[3]   *Gita*

'Are they equal – those who know and those who know not?'[4]

Muḥammad

2

'. . . sloth is the taint of beauty . . . stinginess is the taint of a donor . . . A worse taint than these is Ignorance, the greatest taint. Abandoning this taint be taintless . . .'[5]   *Dhammapada*

3

George Washington Carver

In 1860 a little Black boy was born. In those days, slaves were often taken away from their children. George's mother was soon separated from him but the child was treated kindly by his master, Mr Carver, whose name George took as his own.

Even when George was a little boy, he loved plants and could make anything grow. Neighbours called him 'plant doctor' because he would look at a plant that seemed to be dying and could tell how to make it green and strong again. He was always studying plants and flowers. George longed to know why flowers of many colours grew from the same piece of moss. Off in the bushes, this little boy built a secret garden where he could plant different seeds and watch how they grew.

All his life, George wanted to learn about many things and to use what he learned to help others. He had no parents to help him, no money for schooling, and besides, he was a Black. In those days coloured boys were not taken in most schools and colleges. Because he had no one to help him, he decided to help himself.

First he learned to do housework. At the age of ten he could wash, iron, and scrub floors as well as any woman. He did this work to earn his way so that he could live near a school. Any work that George did, he did beautifully. He was never satisfied with doing any task 'about' right. He said, 'If it's only about right, it's wrong.'

When he grew older and had to pay for his schooling, he would work hard and save money, then go to school until the money was spent. He never allowed anyone to give him anything except the chance to work. The reason George wanted an education was to learn all about everything so he could help people. He seemed to know that God gave man more power than the animal so that he could make the world better and happier.

By the time he had finished college, he knew a great deal about plants. Farmers asked him to tell them how to have better crops. He used to take trips into the country to help farmers who did not know what was the matter with their gardens. Then he became a teacher in a Black college called Tuskegee. Sometimes people were rude to Mr Carver because he was a Black. He told his coloured students in college that they should not be angry when people criticised the Blacks. He said they should try to correct their faults.

George Carver studied plants because he wanted to understand what God created. He always prayed while working and said he could not have learned so much without the help of God. One day

he asked God how he could learn about everything that God had made. He said God told him to start by studying the peanut. After a while Carver discovered four hundred uses for the peanut!

When studying the wonders of nature, Carver was always talking with God. If you had been there, you could not have heard him, because he talked silently or in his heart. He said he wanted to understand the mineral, vegetable, and animal kingdoms because God created them. He wanted to learn how each kingdom worked and how one helped the other.

Carver lived to be an old man. All his life he was working, and learning, and helping people. No wonder he was so loved and respected![6]   *Janet Lindstrom*

4

A. What is education? Does it take place only when you are sitting in the classroom receiving instruction, or is it something more?

'Man is the Supreme Talisman. Lack of a proper education hath, however, deprived him of that which he doth inherently possess.'[7]   *Bahá'u'lláh*

B. What is a talisman?
C. What do we all inherently possess?
D. What should our attitude be towards our own education?
     '. . . man should know his own self and recognise that which leadeth unto loftiness or lowliness, glory or abasement, wealth or poverty.'[8]   *Bahá'u'lláh*
E. Discuss why this statement is true: 'Furthermore, the education of woman is more necessary and important than that of man.'[9]   *'Abdu'l-Bahá*
F. Consider this also: 'The mothers are the first educators of mankind; if they be imperfect, alas for the condition and future of the race.'[10]   *'Abdu'l-Bahá*

Environment

1

'Wings that are besmirched with mire can never soar.'[1]   *Bahá'u'lláh*

'. . . although bodily cleanliness is a physical thing, it hath, nevertheless, a powerful influence on the life of the spirit.'[2]

'Abdu'l-Bahá

'And it is God who sends down out of heaven water, and therewith revives the earth after it is dead. Surely in that is a sign for a people who have ears.'[3]   *Muḥammad*

2

'May sky be peaceful.
May atmosphere be peaceful.
May earth be peaceful.
May waters be peaceful . . .
May plants be peaceful . . .
May all the objects be peaceful.
May peace itself be peaceful.
May that peace come unto me.'[4]

Yajur Veda

3

The Wonderful World

Great, wide, beautiful, wonderful world,
With the wonderful water round you curled,
And the wonderful grass upon your breast, –
World, you are beautifully drest!

William Brighty Rands

Happy Thought

The world is so full of a number of things,
I'm sure we should all be as happy as kings.

Robert Louis Stevenson

Snow in the City

Snow is out of fashion,
   But it still comes down,
To whiten all the buildings
   In our town;
To dull the noise of traffic;
   To dim each glaring light
With star-shaped feathers
   Of frosty white.
And not the tallest building
   Halfway up the sky;
Or all the trains and buses,
   And taxis scudding by;
And not a million people,
   Not one of them at all,
Can do a thing about the snow
   But let it fall.

Rachel Field

April Rain Song

Let the rain kiss you.
Let the rain beat upon your head with silver liquid drops.
Let the rain sing you a lullaby.

The rain makes still pools on the sidewalk.
The rain makes running pools in the gutter.
The rain plays a little sleep-song on our roof at night –

And I love the rain.

Langston Hughes

Boats Sail on the Rivers

Boats sail on the rivers,
And ships sail on the seas;

But clouds that sail across the sky
Are prettier far than these.

There are bridges on the rivers,
As pretty as you please;
But the bow that bridges heaven,
And overtops the trees,
And builds a road from earth to sky,
Is prettier far than these.

Christina Rossetti

4

Much is written in the newspapers about ecology, the study of the environment. People are paying serious attention to the pollution of our air, our water and our land. You might consider discussing the environment on World Environment Day, June 5th.

A. What examples come to your mind of the types of pollution that are destroying the natural balance of nature on our planet?

B. Why is it significant that every country observes World Environment Day? What can we do here to improve our surroundings?

C. How do our surroundings affect the way we feel?

D. Do you feel like having a picnic in a spot that is littered with rusty cans, dirty papers and broken bottles? Can you enjoy the rest of the scenery when these things are in front of your eyes?

E. Do you study well in a classroom littered with paper?

F. Do you feel self-confident when your clothes look grubby?

G. Not many people realise that the beautiful Taj Mahal in India and the Parthenon in Greece are gradually being destroyed by atmospheric pollution. Why is it important for us to preserve such buildings? What can we do about the pollution that is destroying them?

H. Do you know that many birds die because their wings are covered by oil lost by oil-tankers? They are no longer able to fly. Do you think Bahá'u'lláh was only referring to nature when He gave this warning? 'Wings that are besmirched with mire can never soar.'

I. We feel sorry for birds caught in oilslicks and spend a lot of time trying to save them. In the same way, now people are waging a constant battle against the pollution of the water, air and earth that is affecting the health of the people of the world. They are waging a battle of life.

Shoghi Effendi has said, 'Ultimately, all the battle of life is within the individual.'[5] What do you think this means?

J. We must consider carefully the quality of our inner life, as well as the environment around us. If you like, we can say that there are two types of pollution that are affecting humanity: one is inside us and one is outside us.

Can you think of some examples of the pollution within the hearts of people? Shoghi Effendi gives us many examples: 'The recrudescence of religious intolerance, of racial animosity, and of patriotic arrogance; the increasing evidences of selfishness, of suspicion, of fear and of fraud; the spread of terrorism, of lawlessness, of drunkenness and of crime; the unquenchable thirst for, and the feverish pursuit after, earthly vanities, riches and pleasures; the weakening of family solidarity; the laxity in parental control; the lapse into luxurious indulgence; the irresponsible attitude towards marriage and the consequent rising tide of divorce; the degeneracy of art and music, the infection of literature, and the corruption of the press . . .'[6]

There are many more examples, but you may like to start by discussing these. For examples you have only to pick up a newspaper.

K. How can what we are affect our surroundings?

M. The kingdom of God on earth is something which is promised to mankind. How can this vision become a reality?

For younger children

N. When you look at your school and at other places, can you see anything put there by us that you think spoils the place where you work and play? Are any of these unwanted things dangerous to us or to animals?

O. How can we stop our surroundings being spoilt by others?

P. Another word for our surroundings is environment. The word meaning the spoiling of our surroundings is pollution. Is it important to think about the pollution of our environment?

Q. How will a polluted planet affect us all?

Faith

1

'The essence of faith is fewness of words and abundance of deeds
. . .'[1] *Bahá'u'lláh*

'Amity and rectitude of conduct, rather than dissension and mischief, are the marks of true faith.'[2] *Bahá'u'lláh*

'He who has faith has wisdom . . .'[3] *Gita*

'For as the body without the spirit is dead, so faith without works is dead also.'[4] *New Testament*

2

'Say: This is the Day when every ear must needs be attentive to His voice. Hearken ye to the Call of this wronged One, and magnify ye the name of the one true God, and adorn yourselves with the ornament of His remembrance, and illumine your hearts with the light of His love. This is the key that unlocketh the hearts of men, the burnish that shall cleanse the souls of all beings. He that is careless of what hath poured out from the finger of the Will of God liveth in manifest error. Amity and rectitude of conduct, rather than dissension and mischief, are the marks of true faith.'[5]

Bahá'u'lláh

3

Lua's Mission to the King

Lua Getsinger was a wonderful Bahá'í teacher. She loved 'Abdu'l-Bahá very much and wanted to please him by serving the Cause.

One day a letter came from 'Abdu'l-Bahá to Lua. Enclosed with it was a second letter. This was addressed to the Sháh, the King of Persia. 'Abdu'l-Bahá asked that Lua carry this second letter to Persia and deliver it to the King in person.

The letter to the Sháh explained that religious fanatics in Persia were once again persecuting the followers of the Bahá'í Faith. Many men, women and children were being killed for their beliefs. 'Abdu'l-Bahá asked the S͟háh to protect the Bahá'ís. The letter was so important that 'Abdu'l-Bahá wanted to be sure that the S͟háh received it. This was why he asked Lua to deliver it herself.

The S͟háh was in Paris at that time, so Lua went there. She tried to meet the Prime Minister of Persia, but she was turned away at the door. She was told he would not see anyone because his son was seriously ill and was not expected to live.

But Lua was not to be defeated. 'Abdu'l-Bahá had trusted her, and she had faith that his desire would be carried out. So she said to the official's secretary, 'Would you take a message from me to His Excellency, and permit me to wait for his answer?'

'There is no purpose in your waiting for his answer,' the secretary insisted. 'He will see no one.'

Lua was persistent. 'Will you ask him if I may see him tomorrow should his son be healed in the meantime?'

The secretary was not pleased, but Lua was patient. Eventually he went into the next room. Lua began to pray quietly to herself and put her faith in God that her mission would be accomplished.

Soon the secretary returned. 'The Minister will see you tomorrow. But only on your own conditions!'

Lua thanked him. Her faith had been rewarded.

That night Lua gathered together as many of the Bahá'ís in Paris as possible. She explained her mission to them and asked for their help. She asked them to put their trust in God.

'Let us sit up all night and pray for the little boy,' she urged. She told them how 'Abdu'l-Bahá had taught her that any difficulty could be solved through prayer and faith. All that was necessary was to be sincere.

The Bahá'ís were happy to help Lua. A vigil was held all through the night, each one praying that the little boy should become well again.

The next morning Lua went back to the Prime Minister's office. The secretary greeted her with a welcoming smile. He said simply, 'The Prime Minister will see you right away.'

Lua smiled back. 'Is the little boy better?' she asked.

The secretary nodded. 'The crisis is passed. He is well on his way to recovery.'

The secretary then showed her in to the Prime Minister's office.

Thus Lua, through faith in God and prayer, was able to present 'Abdu'l-Bahá's letter through the official channels, and it eventually reached the S͟háh. After this letter was received by the S͟háh, there was a remarkable cessation of persecution of Bahá'ís in Persia.

Adapted from William Sears and Robert Quigley

4

A definition of faith: trust, strong belief, unquestioning confidence.

A. How old is faith?

'. . . the conception of faith hath existed from the beginning that hath no beginning, and will endure till the end that hath no end . . .'[6]   *Bahá'u'lláh*

B. How can we show that we have faith?

C. What is the power of faith?

'If ye have faith as a grain of mustard seed, ye shall say unto this mountain, Remove hence to yonder place; and it shall remove; and nothing shall be impossible unto you.'[7]

New Testament

'If ye had faith as a grain of mustard seed, ye might say unto this sycamine tree, Be thou plucked up by the root, and be thou planted in the sea; and it should obey you.'[8]   *New Testament*

D. What makes us different from animals?

'. . . the life of the flesh is common to both men and animals, whereas the life of the spirit is possessed only by the pure in heart who have quaffed from the ocean of faith and partaken of the fruit of certitude.'[9]   *Bahá'u'lláh*

E. How can faith be like an ocean? What do you think is the fruit of certitude?

F. Why do you think Bahá'u'lláh gave this advice to a king? 'Gather around thee those ministers from whom thou canst perceive the fragrance of faith and justice . . .'[11]

For younger children

Faith is a difficult concept for small children to grasp but we can talk about having trust and confidence in God. For instance, in the same way that we are sure the sun will rise tomorrow, we can be sure that God will continue to help us if we obey His laws and show by our deeds our love for Him. The story *The Gift* by Cynthia Walcott is good to read to young children on this subject. The rabbit is an example of someone with faith having great courage.

Family

1

'If love and agreement are manifest in a single family, that family will advance, become illumined and spiritual.'[1]   *'Abdu'l-Bahá*

'It is not for the love of children that children are dear; but for the love of the Soul in children that children are dear.'[2]
                                        Brihad-Aranyaka Upanishad

'And have we not heard that hell is waiting for those whose [family] rituals are no more?'[3]   *Gita*

'Thy Lord has decreed you shall not serve any but Him, and to be good to parents . . .'[4]   *Muḥammad*

2

'According to the teachings of Bahá'u'lláh the family, being a human unit, must be educated according to the rules of sanctity. All the virtues must be taught the family. The integrity of the family bond must be constantly considered, and the rights of the individual members must not be transgressed, none of them must be arbitrary. Just as the son has certain obligations to his father, the father, likewise, has certain obligations to his son. The mother, the sister and other members of the household have their certain prerogatives. All these rights and prerogatives must be conserved, yet the unity of the family must be sustained. The injury of one shall be considered the injury of all; the comfort of each, the comfort of all: the honour of one, the honour of all.'[5]   *'Abdu'l-Bahá*

3

Five Chinese Brothers

Once upon a time there lived in a Chinese village near the sea, an old woman and her five grown sons. These sons looked as much alike as peas in a pod.

But they were not really exactly alike, for they could do different things. The eldest brother could gulp up the whole ocean in one mouthful. The second brother had a neck made of steel. The third brother had legs that could stretch out as far as he wanted them to. The fourth brother was so made that he was never hurt by fire, and the fifth brother could live without breathing. They all hid their strange gifts and no one in the village guessed the brothers were odd.

The eldest brother took care of the family by fishing. He used to go alone to the seashore and bring home loads of fine fish every day. The neighbours begged and begged him to teach their sons to fish as well as he did. He would always refuse, but one day, not able to say any longer, 'I cannot', and, 'I won't', he took the boys along with him so that they might learn his art.

When they reached the seashore, he sucked the sea into his mouth in one huge gulp. Then he motioned the boys out to the dry sea bottom to gather in all the fish they could carry. The boys ran out, delighted by the strange seashells, and beautifully coloured pebbles. They ran about picking up as many of them as they could hold in their hands.

After a while the eldest brother grew tired of holding the water so be began beckoning to the boys to return to the shore. But they were so enchanted with the treasures that lay all around them that they paid no attention to him and kept going farther and farther out.

Frantically he motioned to them to come back. They pretended not to notice him. Finally the eldest brother felt he was near to bursting. He could no longer hold the sea in his mouth! He had to let it flow back into its usual place, and the boys were covered by the sea.

As he was returning home, the eldest brother passed his neighbours' houses. They asked him how many fish their sons had caught and how soon they would be back. With great sorrow, he told the neighbours what had happened and assured them that he was not to blame. They had begged him to take their sons with him, and he had agreed only after much pleading on their part.

'Truly, I tried to get the boys to come back to me ashore, but they wouldn't listen to me. I had to return the water to the sea basin, for no other place would hold it,' he pleaded in his own defence.

Nevertheless, the neighbours dragged him before the village judge. 'You took the boys away and have not brought them back,' said he. 'For this your head will be cut off,' the judge decided.

On the day before his execution, the eldest brother asked leave of the judge to visit his mother for the last time. The judge consented. The eldest brother went home alone and told his brothers of the doom about to befall him.

The second brother, the one whose neck was made of steel, said, 'Let me go in your stead. No one will know I am not you, we look so much alike, and they won't be able to cut my head off.'

So the second brother went to court the next day. 'Thank you, judge,' he said, 'for allowing me to see my mother once more. Now I am ready to die.' The second brother placed his head on the block, and the executioner with one swift stroke brought the sword down across the back of his neck. The sword bounced off, and the second brother's neck was left unharmed. A sharper sword was brought, and then another. The same thing happened each time. Each blade was ruined, and the second brother's hard steel neck remained untouched! The angry executioner took the prisoner back to the judge. 'It is impossible to cut his head off, Your Honour,' he said. 'This man's neck must be made of steel!'

The judge then ordered, 'This man shall be drowned in the sea.' When the second brother heard this, he said, 'I bade farewell to my mother expecting that I was to be beheaded. If I am to be drowned, may I not go to receive her blessing once more?'

The judge granted permission for the visit, and the second brother returned home to tell his brothers what had happened. At this, the third brother, the one who could stretch his legs to any length he wanted, offered to take the second brother's place.

So the third brother went to court and no one noticed the substitution. He was put into a boat and taken out to sea. Some distance from the shore he was thrown overboard. But instead of drowning, he stretched his legs until they touched the bottom of the sea, and still his head rose high above the water. He was hauled aboard the boat and taken farther and farther out to the deepest part of the sea. But his ever-stretching legs kept getting longer and longer. He could not be drowned.

Taken before the judge again, he was condemned to die by being boiled in oil. While the oil cauldron was being heated, the third brother begged for permission to tell his mother once more that he was still alive. The judge agreed.

When the brothers heard the latest decree of the judge, the fourth brother, the one who could not be touched by fire, offered to bear this latest penalty of the law.

As the kettle of oil began to boil, the fourth brother was lowered into it. He began to swim about in it as if he were in a lukewarm pool.

'Stir up the fire,' he ordered the executioners, 'it's barely warm enough for me in here!' Finding that he could not be boiled no matter how hot the fire was, the executioners took him back to the judge.

Now all the villagers, the neighbours who had lost their boys by drowning, and the judge all joined together to find a sure way of executing the prisoner. Sword, water and fire had failed. The only thing left they could think of was to smother him in a huge cream cake.

The whole countryside made contributions of flour, sugar and filling. Bricks were collected for a huge oven and it was set up outside the village walls.

Once more the prisoner was allowed to pay a farewell visit to his mother. This time, the fifth brother, the one who could live without breathing, took the fourth brother's place.

The huge cake was baked and a great crowd of people watched as the prisoner was placed inside it. As he could live without air, he rested quite comfortably in the cake till the next midnight. By that time the crowds had departed, satisfied at last that justice had been done.

When all was peaceful and quiet, the fifth brother crawled out of the huge cream cake and returned to his home. There he lived happily for many years with his mother and his four other remarkable brothers. *Folk Tale*

4

A. Why should we have special love for the members of our own family? What is it about our family members that is special to us?

'In truth, it is not for the love of a husband that a husband is dear; but for the love of the Soul in the husband that a husband is dear. It is not for the love of a wife that a wife is dear; but for the love of the Soul in the wife that a wife is dear. It is not for the love of children that children are dear; but for the love of the Soul in children that children are dear.'[6]   *Brihad-Aranyaka Upanishad*

B. What does family loyalty mean?

C. How can a family solve a problem that faces one, or all, of its members?

D. What are the positive results that come from a family that is united?

E. Why is the family such an important unit in our society?

F. How true today is this quotation from the *Bhagavad Gita*, written many thousands of years ago? 'The destruction of a family destroys its rituals of righteousness, and when the righteousness rituals are no more, unrighteousness overcomes the whole family . . . This disorder carries down to hell the family and the destroyers of the family.'

For younger children

G. If we are obedient to our parents' wishes and kind to our brothers and sisters, who will benefit?

Forbearance

1

'Show forbearance and benevolence and love to one another.'[1]

Bahá'u'lláh

'Forbearing patience is the highest devotion . . .'[2]   *Dhammapada*

'And be patient; yet is thy patience only with the help of God.'[3]

Muḥammad

'I . . . beseech you that ye walk worthy of the vocation wherewith ye are called, With all lowliness and meekness, with long-suffering, forbearing one another in love . . .'[4]   *New Testament*

'Those virtues that befit [man's] dignity are forbearance, mercy, compassion and loving-kindness towards all the peoples and kindreds of the earth.'[5]   *Bahá'u'lláh*

2

'Hearken unto my voice that calleth from My prison . . . that thou mayest perceive how great hath been My patience, notwithstanding My might, and how immense My forbearance, notwithstanding My power.'[6]   *Bahá'u'lláh*

'It behoveth, likewise, the loved ones of God to be forbearing towards their fellow-men, and to be so sanctified and detached from all things, and to evince such sincerity and fairness, that all the peoples of the earth may recognise them as the trustees of God amongst men.'[7]   *Bahá'u'lláh*

'Show forbearance and benevolence and love to one another. Should any one among you be incapable of grasping a certain truth, or be striving to comprehend it, show forth, when conversing with him, a spirit of extreme kindliness and good-will.'[8]   *Bahá'u'lláh*

'Say: Let truthfulness and courtesy be your adorning. Suffer not yourselves to be deprived of the robe of forbearance and justice, that the sweet savours of holiness may be wafted from your hearts upon all created things. Say: Beware, O people of Bahá, lest ye walk in the ways of them whose words differ from their deeds.'[9]   *Bahá'u'lláh*

'He Who is the Eternal Truth knoweth well what the breasts of men conceal. His long forbearance hath emboldened His creatures, for not until the appointed time is come will He rend any veil asunder. His surpassing mercy hath restrained the fury of His wrath, and caused most people to imagine that the one true God is unaware of the things they have privily committed.'[10]   *Bahá'u'lláh*

3

On one occasion an unfriendly Governor, hating these peaceful honest Bahá'ís, thought of a plan for destroying their means of livelihood. He gave orders to the police: 'There are fifteen shops owned by Bahá'ís; go tomorrow morning early, lock them up and bring the keys to me.'

The Master called the Bahá'ís to Him that same evening and said:

'Do not open your shops tomorrow, but wait and see what God will send to us.'

The next morning the Governor waited for the keys. Again he sent for the police. 'Go,' he said to the police, 'and see if the shops are open.' The police announced that the shops were closed.

He waited and waited; at ten o'clock all the shops were still unopened, those shops which were always accustomed to open and be ready for trade at seven o'clock. The Governor was greatly perplexed. His plan did not seem to be working as he had schemed.

The Muftí (the chief mullá) came to the Governor whilst he waited.

'How are you?' said the Governor.

'Quite well,' was the reply, 'but very sad; because of a telegram from Damascus, I am full of sorrow.'

'Show it to me,' said the Governor.

To his consternation he saw that the telegram was from the Vali of Damascus, deposing him from his place as Governor, and directing that he be conducted by the police to Damascus.

In fear, sorrow, and amazement he went to his own house to make such preparation as was possible for the hurried and unlooked-for journey.

The shops of the friends were saved.

'Abdu'l-Bahá, hearing of the misfortune which had befallen the Governor, went to visit him.

'You must not be sad because of this; everything in this world changes. Can I do anything for you?' He asked of the erstwhile Governor.

'Now that I am being taken away from them, there will be none to care for those I love. My dear family will be sad, lonely, and helpless, with nobody to counsel and aid them in their sore need.'

'Do not be filled with grief, but tell me where you wish your family to go.'

'If only they could go to Damascus.'

'Now, trust in me, and let your heart be lightened of its distress; I will gladly send an honourable escort with your wife and children to Damascus; you will find that they will be there soon after your own arrival.'

The Master sent the family with a trustworthy escort, providing mules and everything needed for the comfort of the journey, quite a formidable undertaking in those days.

The command was worded: 'Take these persons safely and with great respect to join the Governor at Damascus.' A telegram was despatched after they had set out: 'I have sent your family to Damascus. They will very soon arrive in safety.'

When they arrived in Damascus, the Governor, being greatly rejoiced, enquired of the escort as to the cost of the journey.

'It is nothing: I am but obeying the command of the Master.'

The Governor then wished to give the escort a present for himself.

'I desire no recompense; I am but obeying the Master's command. I can accept nothing.'

When invited to stay the night for rest and refreshment, the reply was:

'I obey the Master's command to return without delay.'

'Then I pray you take a letter, which I will write at once to the Master.'

'O 'Abdu'l-Bahá,' the letter read, 'I pray you pardon me. I did not understand. I did not know you. I have wrought you great evil. You have rewarded me with great good.'

Thus was this enemy, who had indeed wrought great evil to the prisoners, repaid by being loaded with benefits.[11] *Lady Blomfield*

4

A. How can forbearance lead nations to knowledge?
B. Why do you think calamity awaits those persons or nations who lack restraint?
C. How does being forbearing make a man more dignified?

'To act like the beasts of the field is unworthy of man. Those virtues that befit his dignity are forbearance, mercy, compassion and loving-kindness . . .'[12]   *Bahá'u'lláh*

D. When you lack restraint in speech or action are you behaving like a true human being?
E. Why do you think Buddha refers to forbearance as the 'highest devotion'?
F. What negative thoughts or feelings must we give up if we wish to develop the quality of forbearance?

'"He abused me, he beat me, he defeated me, he robbed me," the hatred of those who do not harbour such thoughts is appeased.'[13]   *Dhammapada*

For younger children

Forbearance is a very difficult virtue for young children to understand and practise since childhood is usually the time when being restrained is very difficult. You could give one or two examples such as:

Everyone teases Ramkin because he has a strange-sounding name. However, he never loses his temper but turns away and waits until they have become tired of goading him.

Every time Anita borrows Shamin's eraser or sharpener she seems to lose it. Shamin does not want to quarrel with her friend over this. What can she do to be kind and yet look after her property?

The main idea is for children not to fight back immediately in words or deeds when someone else has hurt them, but to try to be patient.

Forgiveness

1

'. . . let them pardon and forgive. Do you not wish that God should forgive you? God is All-forgiving, All-compassionate.'[1]

Muḥammad

'Conquer anger by love . . .'[2] *Dhammapada*

'For if ye forgive men their trespasses, your heavenly Father will also forgive you . . .'[3] *New Testament*

'[Man must] not only forgive, but also, if possible be of service to his oppressor.'[4] *'Abdu'l-Bahá*

2

'Cast, then, upon me, O my God, the glances of Thy mercy, and forgive me my trespasses and the trespasses of them that are dear to Thee, and which come in between us and the revelation of Thy triumph and Thy grace. Cancel Thou, moreover, our sins which have shut off our faces from the splendours of the Day-Star of Thy favours. Powerful art Thou to do Thy pleasure.'[5] *Bahá'u'lláh*

3

Shaykh Maḥmúd of 'Akká

It is related of Shaykh Maḥmúd of 'Akká that he hated the Bahá'ís. While many of his fellow-townsmen had gradually come to realise how very wrong they had been and were speaking of the prisoners in terms of appreciation and praise, Shaykh Maḥmúd remained adamant in his hatred. One day he was present at a gathering where people were talking of 'Abdu'l-Bahá as a good man, a remarkable man. The Shaykh could bear it no longer and stormed out, saying that he would show up this 'Abbás Effendi for what He was. In blazing anger he rushed to the mosque, where he knew 'Abdu'l-Bahá could be found at that hour, and laid violent hands upon Him.

The Master looked at the Sh̲ay̲kh̲ with that serenity and dignity which only He could command, and reminded him of what the Prophet Muḥammad had said: 'Be generous to the guest, even should he be an infidel.' Sh̲ay̲kh̲ Maḥmúd turned away. His wrath had left him. So had his hate. All that he was conscious of was a deep sense of shame and bitter compunction. He fled to his house and barred the door. Some days later he went straight into the presence of 'Abdu'l-Bahá, fell on his knees, and besought forgiveness: 'Which door but thine can I seek; whose bounty can I hope for but thine?' He became a devoted Bahá'í.[6]   *Honnold*

4

A. Why should we forgive people whom we feel have wronged us?
B. What is the reward for those people who forgive others?
C. Jesus Christ said, '. . . whosoever shall smite thee on thy right cheek, turn to him the other also.'[7] How is Jesus asking us to behave?

   'Abdu'l-Bahá explains these words very clearly. He says: '. . . it was for the purpose of teaching man not to take personal revenge. He did not mean that if a wolf should fall upon a flock of sheep and wish to destroy it, the wolf should be encouraged to do so. No, if Christ had known that a wolf had entered the fold and was about to destroy the sheep, most certainly He would have prevented it.'[8]
D. In this day we are asked to do a little more than 'turn the other cheek'. How does 'Abdu'l-Bahá ask us to treat those who have wronged us?

Friendliness

1

'We love to see you at all times consorting in amity and concord
. . .'[1]   *Bahá'u'lláh*

'Ah, happily do we live without hate amongst the hateful; amidst
hateful men we dwell unhating.'[2]   *Dhammapada*

'A man that hath friends must show himself friendly.'[3]
                                                    Old Testament

'Be worthy of the trust of thy neighbour, and look upon him with a
bright and friendly face.'[4]   *Bahá'u'lláh*

> 'To make the world a friendly place
> One must show it a friendly face.'
>   *James Whitcomb Riley*

2

'Your behaviour towards your neighbour should be such as to
manifest clearly the signs of the One true God . . .'[5]   *Bahá'u'lláh*

'We love to see you at all times consorting in amity and concord
within the paradise of My good-pleasure, and to inhale from your
acts the fragrance of friendliness and unity, of loving-kindness and
fellowship.'[6]   *Bahá'u'lláh*

'It is incumbent upon everyone to show the utmost love . . . and
sincere kindliness unto all the peoples and kindreds of the world, be
they friends or strangers.'[7]   *'Abdu'l-Bahá*

3

The Lion and the Mosquitoes

Once in summertime the lion was very thirsty. But the sun had
taken all the water near the lion's home and he went to many places

seeking for it. In time he found an old well but the water was not fresh. As the lion was very thirsty, he said, 'I must drink even though the water is stale.' But when he reached down into the old well, he found that it was the home of all the mosquitoes of the wilderness. The mosquitoes said to the lion, 'Go away, we do not want you. This is our home and we are happy. We do not wish the lion, the fox or the bear to come here. You are not our friend. Why do you come here?'

The lion roared and said, 'Weak and foolish things! I am the lion. It is you that should go away, for I have come to drink. This is my wilderness and I am the king. Do you know, weak things, that when I come out from my place and send forth my voice, all the creatures of the wilderness shake like leaves and bow their heads to me? What are you, that you should have a place you call your home and tell me that I may or I may not come?'

Then the mosquitoes answered. 'You are only one. You speak as if you were many. Our people had this old well for a home before your roar was heard in the wilderness. And many generations of ours have been born here. This home is ours and we are they that say who shall come or go. And yet you come and tell us to go out of our own door. If you do not leave us, we will call our people and you shall know trouble.'

But the lion held his head high with pride and anger and said, 'What are you, oh, small of the small? I will kill every one of your useless people. When I drink, I will open my mouth only a little wider, and you shall be swallowed like the water. And tomorrow, I shall forget that I drank today.'

'Boastful one,' said the mosquitoes, 'we do not believe that you have the power to destroy all our people. If you wish battle, we shall see. We know your name is great and that all animals bow their heads before you; but our people can kill you.'

The lion jumped high in his rage and said, 'No other creature in the wilderness has dared to say these things to me, the king. Have I come to learn wisdom from the silly mosquitoes?' And he held his head high and gave the mighty roar of battle and made ready to kill all the mosquitoes.

Then the mosquitoes, big and little, flew around him. Many went into his ears and the smallest ones went into his nose, and the big ones went into his mouth to sting. A thousand and a thousand hung in the air just over his head and made a great noise, and the lion soon knew that he could not conquer.

He roared and jumped, and two of his front feet went down into the well. The well was narrow and deep and he could not get out, for his two hind feet were in the air and his head hung downward. And as he died, he said, 'My pride and anger have brought me this fate.

Had I used gentle words, the mosquitoes might have given me water for my thirst. I was wise and strong in the wilderness and even the greatest of the animals feared my power. But I fought with the mosquitoes and I die, not because I have not strength to overcome, but because of the foolishness of anger.'   *Folk Tale*

St Francis of Assisi

A rich Italian merchant of Assisi had a son called Francis. He was so rich that he could give the boy whatever he wanted. In the summer Francis wore clothes made of soft fine silk embroidered in gold and silver, and in winter he had velvet coats lined with fur. If he asked for jewels, his father brought him a tray piled high with every sort of delicacy. He had horses and money, and he led a gay happy life.

One night, when Francis was lying in bed under a silken canopy, his head began to ache and his body to burn with fever. The next day he was very ill, and for a long while he lay on his couch suffering great pain. The best doctors came to see him and he was tenderly nursed.

While he was still too weak to leave his bed, Francis began to compare his own gay life with the lives of all the poor and the sick who lived in Assisi. He thought, 'It is wrong of me to waste my youth and my strength seeking pleasure. I must try to help people who are as ill as I have been, yet have no one to care for them.'

When he was well, Francis sold his jewels and his fine clothes and gave the money to the beggars he met at the roadside.

When his father saw that his son was living like a beggar, he was very angry. He seized Francis and shut him up in prison, thinking, 'When I set him free he will come back and live in this fine house. He will be afraid to disobey me.'

But Francis was not afraid. When he came out of prison he went back to the poor. He even went and lived with the lepers, who had such a terrible illness that people feared to touch them.

One day Francis sold a piece of cloth from his father's warehouse and gave the money to a poor priest who was repairing a shrine. His father was angry and took Francis before the judge.

'Francis,' said the judge, 'you wish to help God by repairing this shrine, but God cannot accept from you something which is not yours. You have no right to your father's money.'

Francis bowed. 'I understand, sir,' he answered. 'All that I have belongs to my father. I will give it back to him.' Then he took off his clothes and gave them back to his father and left the court, wearing only a hair shirt.

So Francis went away from his father's grand house, and put on a coarse, brownish-grey coat, like those worn by the poor country people, and he made friends with the sick and the needy, sitting up with them all night and washing their wounds. He remembered how Jesus had washed the feet of the poor and he wanted to be like Him.

Very soon all the friends who used to dance and hunt with him began to desert him. They thought he was a madman, and they pelted him with mud and stones. But Francis took no notice. He wandered about the country, caring for the sick, making friends with the poor, and teaching everyone about the goodness of God. He had neither money nor food, but because he was always so kind and so cheerful people began to love him. When they saw him coming along the road barefooted and bareheaded, they came to meet him and gave him bread. Then Francis would sing to them the old happy songs that he had learned as a boy and talk to them about the love of God. And the people would look at him gently and say, 'He is our brother and a friend of all the world.'

Francis was a friend of all the world. Indeed, his heart was so full of love that he called everyone and everything his brother or his sister. The flowers in the fields were his 'little sisters', the animals in the woods his 'little brothers'. In summer when the weather was hot and Francis was parched with thirst, Brother Wind and Sister Water refreshed him. In winter, when snow lay on the ground, Brother

Fire warmed his shivering body. At night, Sister Moon gave him light, and in the morning when he awoke he used to sing, 'Praised be Thou, Lord, for all Thy creatures, especially for my Brother Sun which gives us the day.'

He was so well loved that people wanted to be like him. One day a rich nobleman called Bernard and a famous lawyer called Peter gave up all they had and followed Francis. 'Let us be your brothers too,' said they. Then Brother Bernard, Brother Peter and Brother Francis built a hut out of branches and mud and lived together, praying, preaching, and doing good.

Not long afterwards, Francis was walking through the forest when he came to a little patch of bare ground, and there he saw a ploughboy kneeling at prayer. When he heard Francis coming, the ploughboy rose and said, 'My name is Giles. Will you have me too?' And Francis took him by the hand.

They all sat under a tree, the wealthy merchant's son, the young nobleman, the famous lawyer, and the poor ploughboy, and each called the other 'Brother'.

Little by little many people gave up everything and followed Francis and his three friends. Men called them the Francis-can friars, which means the Brothers of Francis. Barefooted and dressed in the coarse, grey-brown robes, with ropes knotted around their waists, they wandered into the dirtiest parts of the town where people were suffering from fevers, and they nursed the sick. They were never weary of helping and serving, for they believed that 'God is love', and this made them happy.

One day, when Francis was walking through the woods, he saw all sorts of birds gathered together, so he ran to the spot and greeted them. The birds were not afraid. They waited till he drew near, and those which were on the ground gazed upwards, and those which had perched on branches bowed their little heads and looked down at him. Then Francis preached them a sermon. He said, 'My Bird Brothers, you ought to praise God who has clothed you with feathers, granted you wings to fly, and given over to you the pure air.' While he was speaking, the little birds all began to stretch their necks and open their beaks and look intently at him. He walked among them and touched them, and not one of them moved away until he had blessed them all. Then they flew singing and twittering above the tops of the trees.

Once, one of the brothers brought Francis a little lame hare which

they had rescued from a trap. 'Come to me, Brother Hare,' said
Francis, and when the little creature loped towards him, he picked it
up and caressed it. But when he put it on the ground so that it might
run away, it returned again and again.

As time passed, Francis gathered more and more friends round
him and he made rules for when he was with them and when he was
away. Because of these rules his brotherhood was called the
Franciscan Order.

One day, when the sun was shining brightly, Francis went on a
journey.

'Where are you going?' asked the people along the way.

'To Rome,' said Francis, 'to ask the Pope to read our rules and
bless our Order.'

People say that when the Pope saw the shabby, grey-brown robe
which Francis was wearing, his dirty hands and dusty naked feet, his
shaggy hair and beard, he was very much astonished. He read the
rules and he thought that they were almost too difficult for any man
to obey. 'Brother,' said he, smiling at the barefooted, untidy man
who stood so humbly before him, 'go to the pigs, for you are more
like them than a man. Read them your rules.'

And Francis went out into the fields. He saw the pigs wallowing
in the mud, and he sat among them and read them his rules. Then he
went back to the Pope and said, 'Father, I have done as you have
commanded. I pray you, grant me now your blessing.'

Francis now began to think that he ought to help other countries
besides Italy, for he knew that everywhere he would find the sick

and poor. So he divided his brothers into little companies and sent them far and wide to carry their message of healing and love into different parts of the world.

The brothers set out bravely. Sometimes people treated them unkindly and mocked them because they were barefooted and poor, but gradually they made friends and, little by little, men came to them and said, 'Let us be brothers too.'

And so it happened that in many different lands there were groups of Franciscan friars tending the sick and caring for the poor. At first they lived in little huts, but after a while people who loved them began to give them land, and they built themselves monasteries where they could live and churches where they could worship.

But Francis stayed in Italy. Year after year he and the brothers who were with him wandered about, doing good and preaching the word of God, until Francis began to grow old and blind. Day by day the brothers watched him growing weaker, until at last his strength failed. He gave them his last sweet smile, and murmuring, 'Welcome, Sister Death,' he died.

With the tears falling from their eyes, the brothers knelt by his bed and prayed. 'Amen,' whispered one, and as he did so the air was filled with sweet music. It was as though soft bells were ringing and heavenly voices were singing. The brothers stole to the door and looked out. On the roof of the hut, in the trees and bushes, on the rocks and among the reeds were birds of all kinds, piping, singing and twittering. These 'little brothers' whom St Francis had loved were still praising God, although their old friend could no longer tell them to do so.

Many years later, people remembered how good and loving Francis had been, and they made him a saint.

A Traditional Story

4

A. How do our own acts of friendliness help us to be happy?
B. How do the Manifestations of God teach us how to behave towards our neighbours?
C. Why is it sometimes difficult for us to be friendly towards strangers? How can we overcome these difficulties?
D. How can you make a new student in your class feel welcome? What might make him feel unwelcome?

Friendship

1

'. . . if We inhale the perfume of your fellowship, Our heart will assuredly rejoice, for naught else can satisfy Us.'[1]   *Bahá'u'lláh*

'Cleave unto that which draweth you together and uniteth you.'[2]
Bahá'u'lláh

'If you get a prudent companion (who is fit) to live with you, who behaves well and is wise, you should live with him, joyfully and mindfully overcoming all dangers.'[3]   *Dhammapada*

'. . . associate with good friends, associate with noble men.'[4]
Dhammapada

'Give us for great friendship, for great delight . . .'[5]   *Yaçna*

'Greater love hath no man than this, that a man lay down his life for his friends.'[6]   *New Testament*

2

'O God, the Dispeller of ignorance and darkness, strengthen me. May all beings regard me with the eye of a friend. May I regard all beings with the eye of a friend. With the eye of a friend do we regard one another.'[7]   *Yajur Veda*

'O well-beloved ones! The tabernacle of unity hath been raised; regard ye not one another as strangers. Ye are the fruits of one tree, and the leaves of one branch.'[8]   *Bahá'u'lláh*

'O Friend! In the garden of thy heart plant naught but the rose of love, and from the nightingale of affection and desire loosen not thy hold. Treasure the companionship of the righteous and eschew all fellowship with the ungodly.'[9]   *Bahá'u'lláh*

3

Androcles and the Lion

In Rome, many centuries ago, there lived a poor slave whose name was Androcles. His master was a cruel man and so unkind to him that one day Androcles ran away.

He hid himself in a wild wood for many days. There was no food to be found and so Androcles became weak and sick, so much so that he thought he would die. He crept into a cave and fell asleep.

After a while a great noise woke him up. A lion had come into the cave and was roaring loudly. Androcles was badly frightened, for he felt sure the beast would kill him. However, he soon saw that the beast was not angry, but that he limped as though his foot hurt him.

Then Androcles wasn't afraid any more. He lifted the lion's paw from the ground and saw there was a long sharp thorn sticking into it. He gave the thorn a strong quick pull and out it came. The lion

was much relieved and very grateful. He jumped about like a dog and licked the hands and feet of his new friend.

Androcles was not at all afraid after this and when night came the lion and Androcles slept side by side.

For a long time the lion brought food to Androcles every day and the two became such good friends that Androcles found his new life a very happy one.

One day soldiers were passing through the wood. They captured Androcles and dragged him back to Rome.

It was the law at that time that any slave who ran away from his master should be made to fight a hungry lion. So a fierce lion was shut up in a cage for a while and a time was set for a fight. Thousands of people gathered to see Androcles fight the lion, but when the lion rushed into the arena Androcles gave a cry of gladness, not fear, for the lion was his old friend. The people expected to see him killed. Instead they saw him hugging a lion who lay down at his feet. Androcles said, 'I am a man, but no man has befriended me. This lion is my brother.' They were then set free and lived together for many happy years. *Traditional*

4

A. Are you a good mixer?
B. Can the expression on your face win a friend?
C. Is it easy to be friendly with someone who shows off?
     '. . . show all meekness to all men.'[10]   *Bahá'u'lláh*
D. Can you keep a secret?
     'Be worthy of the trust of thy neighbour . . .'[11]   *Bahá'u'lláh*
E. Who should we choose as friends?
     'When a man turns his face to God he finds sunshine every where. All men are his brothers.'[12]   *'Abdu'l-Bahá*
     '. . . drive away . . . the tormentor of men like fire, and cast aside the sinners.'[13]   *Yajur Veda*
     'Have for friends those whose soul is beautiful; go with men whose soul is good.'[14]   *Dhammapada*
F. Why should we be careful about choosing our friends?
     'O My Son! The company of the ungodly increaseth sorrow, whilst fellowship with the righteous cleanseth the rust from off the heart.'[15]*Bahá'u'lláh*
G. Why should we not quarrel with each other?
     'O ye beloved of the Lord! In this sacred Dispensation, conflict and contention are in no wise permitted. Every aggressor deprives himself of God's grace.'[16]   *'Abdu'l-Bahá*

Generosity

1

'The poor in your midst are My trust; guard ye My trust, and be not intent only on your own ease.'[1]   *Bahá'u'lláh*

'O Children of Dust! Tell the rich of the midnight sighing of the poor, lest heedlessness lead them into the path of destruction, and deprive them of the Tree of Wealth.'[2]   *Bahá'u'lláh*

'. . . the wise man rejoices in giving and thereby becomes happy thereafter.'[3]   *Dhammapada*

'The man who eats alone brings troubles upon himself alone.'[4]
                                                            Rig Veda

2

'They will question thee concerning what they should expend. Say: "Whatsoever good you expend is for parents and kinsmen, orphans, the needy, and the traveller; and whatever good you may do, God has knowledge of it."'[5]   *Muḥammad*

'To give and to be generous are attributes of Mine; well is it with him that adorneth himself with My virtues.'[6]   *Bahá'u'lláh*

'Now is the time to cheer and refresh the down-cast through the invigorating breeze of love and fellowship, and the living waters of friendliness and charity.'[7]   *Bahá'u'lláh*

3

One Car or *Gifts for the Poor*

When 'Abdu'l-Bahá was almost seventy years old, He decided to travel to Europe and to America to tell people about Bahá'u'lláh's plan for love and peace. It was a hard trip for so old a man, who had spent so many years of his life in prison. As He travelled, people came to love Him very much. And they loved what He was doing to help the world.

One day when He was in London, a woman came to Him and happily handed Him a cheque. She said, 'I have here a cheque for you from a friend who wants you to buy a good car for your work in England and Europe.'

The Master, 'Abdu'l-Bahá, in His kind way, answered, 'I accept with grateful thanks the gift of your friend.' Then He took the cheque into His hands. He seemed to bless it. But He handed it back to the lady and said, 'I return it to be used for gifts to the poor.' The friends had never before seen such unselfishness.'[8]

Adapted from 'The Chosen Highway'

4

A. How do you feel when you receive an unexpected gift? How do you feel when you give someone a gift?

B. Is it only with material things that we should be generous? Can we also be generous with our time or with our love?

The Intercalary Days are days when Bahá'ís especially consider other people. Bahá'ís visit each other and exchange gifts. They also consider the needs of the poor and sick. It is a time of hospitality and friendship. The Intercalary Days fall on February 26th to March 1st.

C. What activities could you arrange for Intercalary Days that would demonstrate generosity?

D. Who will benefit from your generosity?

Giving

1

'Charity is pleasing and praiseworthy in the sight of God and is regarded as a prince among goodly deeds.'[1] *Bahá'u'lláh*

'. . . let thy aim be the good of all, and then carry on thy task in life.'[2] *Gita*

'And now abideth faith, hope, charity, these three; but the greatest of these is charity.'[3] *New Testament*

'Whatsoever good you expend is for parents and kinsmen, orphans, the needy, and the traveller; and whatever good you may do, God has knowledge of it.'[4] *Muḥammad*

2

'Blessed is he who with all his affections hath turned to the Dawning-Place of Thy Revelation and the Fountain-Head of Thine inspiration. Blessed is he that hath expended in Thy path what Thou didst bestow upon him through Thy bounty and favour.'[5]

Bahá'u'lláh

'Protect . . . O my Beloved, through Thy love for them and through the love they bear to Thee, this servant, who hath sacrificed his all for Thee, and expended whatsoever Thou hast given him in the path of Thy love and Thy good pleasure, and preserve him from all that Thou abhorrest . . .'[6] *Bahá'u'lláh*

3

The Miraculous Pitcher

Long, long ago a good man and his wife lived in a little cottage on a hilltop. Their names were Philemon and Baucis. They were old and very poor, and they worked hard to earn their living, but they were happy all day long for they loved one another dearly.

They lived on their hilltop looking after their small garden and their beehives and tending their cow. They seldom had anything more to eat than bread and milk and vegetables, with sometimes a little honey from their beehives, or a few ripe pears or apples from the garden.

They were two of the kindest old people in the world, and would gladly have gone without their dinner any day rather than refuse a slice of bread or a cupful of milk to any hungry traveller who might stop at their cottage.

A beautiful village lay in the valley below the hilltop where the cottage of Philemon and Baucis stood. The valley, shaped like a bowl, was fertile with green meadows, gardens and orchards, but sad to say, the people living in this pleasant fertile valley were selfish and hard-hearted, with never a thought of pity or kindness for the friendless or needy.

These villagers taught their children to be just as unkind as they were. They kept large fierce dogs, and whenever unfortunate strangers appeared in the village, the dogs would rush out barking and snarling at them. The children, too, were encouraged to run after them pelting them with stones and jeering at their shabby clothes.

What made it even worse was that if the strangers were rich people attended by servants, the villagers would be extra polite and would bow and scrape before them. If the children happened to be rude to these wealthy visitors, they had their ears boxed. As for the dogs, if a single dog dared as much as to growl at anyone who was rich, that dog was beaten and tied up without any supper.

One evening, Philemon and Baucis were sitting on a bench outside their doorway, talking quietly about their garden and enjoying the sunset.

Suddenly they were interrupted by the shouts of children and the angry barking of dogs in the village. The noise grew louder and louder until Philemon and Baucis could hardly hear each other speak.

'I have never heard the dogs bark so savagely,' said Baucis.

'Nor the children shout so rudely,' answered old Philemon.

They sat shaking their heads sorrowfully as the noise came nearer and nearer until they saw two strangers coming along the road on foot. Both travellers were very plainly dressed and looked as if they had no money for food or a night's lodging. Close behind them came the fierce dogs snarling at their heels and a little farther off ran a crowd of children who screamed shrilly and flung stones at the strangers.

'Good wife,' said Philemon to Baucis, 'I will go to meet these poor people while you prepare something for them to eat. Perhaps they feel too heavy-hearted to climb the hill.'

And he hastened forward saying heartily, 'Welcome, strangers! Welcome!'

'Thank you,' answered the younger of the two travellers. 'Yours is a kind welcome, very different from the one we just got in the village.'

Philemon took a good look at him and his companion. The younger of the two strangers was slim and dressed in an odd kind of way.

Though the evening was mild, he wore his cloak wrapped tightly about him. He had a cap on with a brim that stuck out over his ears. There was something queer, too, about his shoes, but as it was growing dark, Philemon could not see exactly what they were like.

Another thing struck Philemon. The younger stranger was so wonderfully light and active that it seemed as if his feet sometimes rose from the ground of their own accord and could be kept on the ground only with difficulty. He carried, besides, a staff which was the oddest Philemon had ever seen. It was made of wood and had a little pair of wings near the tip. Two snakes carved in wood were twisting around the staff and these were so finely made that the old man almost thought he could see them wriggling.

The elder of the two strangers was very tall and walked calmly along. He seemed not to have noticed the barking dogs or the screaming children.

When they reached the cottage, Philemon said, 'We are poor folk and haven't much to offer, but all we have is yours.'

The strangers sat down on the bench and the younger one dropped his staff on the grass. And then a strange thing happened. The staff seemed to get up by itself and, spreading its little pair of wings, half-hopped and half-flew to lean itself against the wall of the cottage.

Before Philemon could ask any questions, the elder stranger said, 'Was there not a lake long ago that covered this place where the village now stands?'

'Not in my time,' said Philemon, 'nor in my father's or grandfather's. There have always been meadows and gardens just as there are now and I suppose there always will be.'

'That I am not so sure of,' answered the stranger. 'Since the people of that place have forgotten how to be kind, it might be better perhaps if a lake should be rippling over that village again.' He looked sad and stern.

Philemon was sure now that he was not an ordinary wanderer. His clothes were old and shabby. Perhaps he was a learned man who wandered about the world seeking wisdom and knowledge.

Philemon turned to the younger traveller. 'What is your name, my friend?' he asked.

'I am called Mercury,' he said.

'Does your companion have as strange a name?' asked Philemon.

'You must ask the thunder to tell you,' replied Mercury. 'No other voice is loud enough.'

Philemon did not quite know what to make of this, but the strangers appeared to be so kind and friendly that he began telling them about his good wife Baucis, and what fine butter and cheese she made. He told them how happy they were in their little cottage and how they hoped that when they died, they might die together. The elder of the travellers listened to all this with a gentle smile on his stern face.

Now Baucis had the supper ready and called her husband to invite their guests to come in. 'Had we known you were coming,' she said, 'my husband and I would have been happy to have gone without our supper, to give you a better one.'

'Do not trouble yourself about that,' said the elder of the strangers. 'A cordial welcome is better than the best food and we are so hungry that whatever you have to offer will be a feast.'

Then they all went into the cottage. As they turned into the doorway, that staff of Mercury's that had been leaning against the cottage wall opened its small wings and hopped up the steps and tapped across the floor. It stopped behind the chair where Mercury sat. But Baucis and Philemon did not notice this. They were too busy attending to their guests.

On the table was half a loaf of brown bread and a bit of cheese, a pitcher with some milk, a little honey, and a bunch of purple grapes. Baucis filled two bowls with milk from the pitcher. 'What delicious milk, Mother Baucis!' exclaimed Mercury. 'May I have more? This has been such a warm day I am very thirsty.'

'I am so sorry,' said Baucis, 'but there are barely a few drops left in the pitcher. If only we hadn't used so much milk for our supper before!'

'Let me see,' said Mercury picking up the pitcher. 'Why, there certainly is more milk here.' And he poured out a bowlful for himself and another for his companion.

Baucis could hardly believe her eyes. In a few moments Mercury said, 'Your milk is really the most delicious I have ever tasted. I must have just a little more.'

As Baucis lifted the pitcher to pour out what she thought would be the very last drop of milk into the stranger's bowl, a wonderful stream of rich, fresh milk fell bubbling into it and overflowed onto the table. The more Baucis poured, the more milk remained. The pitcher was always filled to the brim.

And so it was with the bread. Though it had been rather dry when Philemon and Baucis had had it for their supper, it was now as fresh and tasty as if it had just come from the oven. Baucis could hardly believe this was the loaf she had baked with her own hands.

Baucis sat down beside Philemon. 'Did you ever hear of anything so wonderful?' she whispered.

'No, I never did,' answered Philemon. 'Perhaps you are imagining all this, my dear.'

'Just one more bowl of milk, please,' Mercury asked. This time Philemon lifted the pitcher himself and peeped into it. There wasn't a drop in it. Then all at once a little white fountain of milk gushed up from the bottom and soon the pitcher was filled again to its very brim.

In his amazement Philemon nearly dropped the miraculous pitcher. 'Who are you?' he cried, gazing wide-eyed at the wonder-working strangers.

'We are your guests and your friends, my good Philemon,' replied the elder traveller in his deep voice. 'May that pitcher never be empty for yourselves or for any needy wayfarer.'

The old people did not like to ask any more questions. They gave their beds to the strangers and they themselves lay down to sleep on the hard kitchen floor. In the morning they rose with the sun to help their guests make ready to continue their journey.

'If the villagers only knew what a pleasure it is to be kind to strangers, they would tie up their dogs and never allow their children to fling another stone,' said Philemon.

'It is a sin and a shame for them to behave that way, and I mean to tell them so this very day,' declared Baucis firmly.

'I'm afraid,' said Mercury smiling, 'that you will find none of them home.' And he pointed to the foot of the hill.

The old people looked at the elder traveller. His face had grown very grave and stern. 'When men do not feel towards the poorest stranger as if he were a brother,' he said in his deep voice, 'they do not deserve to remain on earth.'

Philemon and Baucis turned towards the valley where just the evening before they had seen meadows, houses, gardens and streets. But now there was not a sign of the village, or even of the valley.

'Alas! What has become of our poor neighbours?' asked the kind-hearted old people.

'They are not men and women any longer,' answered the elder traveller in a voice like thunder. 'Those wicked people of the valley have had their punishment. As for you, good Philemon and Baucis, your reward shall be anything you may wish for.'

Philemon and Baucis looked at one another and whispered together for a moment. Then Philemon spoke to the gods. 'Our wish, O great gods from high Olympus,' the old man said slowly, 'is that we may live the rest of our lives together. Neither of us wishes to live without the other.'

'So be it,' said the elder stranger who was the god Jupiter. As he spoke, he and his companion vanished from sight like mist in the morning sun.

When Baucis and Philemon turned to go back to their little cottage, it had disappeared. In its place stood a white marble palace with a beautiful park around it. The kind old people lived there for many years, and to every traveller who passed that way they offered a drink from the bubbling pitcher.

Baucis and Philemon grew very very old. Then one summer morning when guests came to visit them, neither Baucis nor Philemon could be found. The guests looked everywhere but it was of no use. Suddenly one of them noticed two large beautiful trees in the garden just in front of the doorway of the palace. One was an oak tree and the other a linden, and their branches were entwined so that they seemed to be embracing one another.

No one could remember having seen them before. While the guests wondered how such fine trees could possibly have grown up in one night, a gentle wind blew up that set the branches stirring.

A mysterious voice whispered from the oak, 'I am Philemon.' And from the linden came, 'I am Baucis.' Then the voices seemed to speak together.

Now the people knew that the good couple would live on for many many years in the lovely trees. They would cast a pleasant shade for the weary traveller who rested under their branches, and they seemed to be forever saying, 'Welcome, dear travellers, welcome.' *Nathaniel Hawthorne*

4

A. What is true charity?

'The essence of charity is for the servant to recount the blessings of His Lord, and to render thanks unto Him at all times and under all conditions.'[7] *Bahá'u'lláh*

B. 'They who are possessed of riches . . . must have the utmost regard for the poor . . .'[8] *Bahá'u'lláh.* What does it mean to 'have regard for the poor'?

C. Is charity only giving money away?

D. There is a saying, 'What you keep is lost. What you give is forever yours.' What does this mean?

E. Is a selfish person ever really happy for long?

For younger children

In your family you wouldn't like to see your father, mother, brothers or sisters hurt, sad, hungry, sick or lonely. You would try to do something for them, wouldn't you? When we feel this way about all people then it is God-like charity.

F. Why is it important for us to be generous to other people?

G. Whom should we be generous towards?

Good Conduct

1

'The sword of a virtuous character and upright conduct is sharper than blades of steel.'[1] *Bahá'u'lláh*

'There is the path of joy, and here is the path of pleasure. Both attract the soul. Who follows the first comes to good; and who follows pleasure reaches not the End.'[2] *Katha Upanishad*

'Though one should live a hundred years, without wisdom and control, yet better, indeed, is the single day's life of one who is moral and meditative.'[3] *Dhammapada*

'Whoso makes the mind better, and performs good works, He (acts) according to the law with word and deed . . .'[4] *Yaçna*

'O you who believe, wherefore do you say what you do not?'[5]
Muḥammad

2

'This people need no weapons of destruction, inasmuch as they have girded themselves to reconstruct the world. Their hosts are the hosts of goodly deeds, and their arms the arms of upright conduct, and their commander the fear of God.'[6] *Bahá'u'lláh*

'Whoso ariseth, in this Day, to aid Our Cause, and summoneth to his assistance the hosts of a praiseworthy character and upright conduct, the influence flowing from such an action will, most certainly, be diffused throughout the whole world.'[7] *Bahá'u'lláh*

'. . . he whose words exceed his deeds, know verily his death is better than his life.'[8] *Bahá'u'lláh*

'O Son of My Handmaid! Guidance hath ever been given by words, and now it is given by deeds. Everyone must show forth deeds that are pure and holy, for words are the property of all alike, whereas such deeds as these belong only to Our loved ones. Strive then with

heart and soul to distinguish yourselves by your deeds. In this wise
We counsel you in this holy and resplendent tablet.'[9]   *Bahá'u'lláh*

3

Some years ago in the city of St Louis, USA, there was a huge
Bahá'í Conference attended by twelve thousand people. This meant
that there were fourteen hundred Bahá'í children, for whom special
classes were arranged.

After one of the morning classes some of the children were taken
by special buses to collect their packed lunch at a restaurant. Because
of the parking restrictions necessary in the centre of the busy town,
the buses were not allowed to wait outside the restaurant at any
time.

All the children got off their buses, patiently waited until they
received their lunch packets, and then walked quietly and with
dignity through the busy streets until they came to a park where
they could sit and have their lunch. There were not ten or twenty
children in this group but several bus loads, so you can imagine that
they numbered nearly three hundred.

It so happened that a newspaper reporter was observing all these
children and was astonished to see so many young people behaving
so patiently. He wrote a long report about the incident for his
newspaper praising the children for their good conduct. This must
have brought much happiness to the parents, teachers and others at
the conference; but most of all, it must have brought happiness to
the children themselves.

'Abdu'l-Bahá said, 'I desire distinction for you.'[10]

4

A. Why is it so important to arm ourselves with good conduct?
B. What is our purpose in life?
C. What is the responsibility on the shoulders of the young people in this day which is different from any other time?
D. How can we decide which is the right and which is the wrong way to behave?
E. Who benefits most when you conduct yourself properly?
F. What is the difference between behaving the right way and just talking about it?

Good Language

1

'. . . the tongue is for mentioning what is good; defile it not with unseemly talk.'[1] *Bahá'u'lláh*

'Defile not your tongues with cursing . . .'[2] *Bahá'u'lláh*

'Speak not harshly to anyone; those thus addressed will retort . . .'[3] *Dhammapada*

'And find not faults with one another, neither revile one another by nicknames.'[4] *Muḥammad*

'Let all bitterness, and wrath, and anger, and clamour, and evil speaking, be put away from you . . .'[5] *New Testament*

2

'It behoveth every man to blot out the trace of every idle word from the tablet of his heart. Defile not the tongue with cursing or execrating and guard your eyes against that which is not worthy . . . the tongue is for mentioning what is good, defile it not with unseemly talk. God hath forgiven what is past. Henceforth everyone should utter that which is meet and seemly and should refrain from slander, abuse and whatever causeth sadness in men.'[6] *Bahá'u'lláh*

3

Toads and Diamonds

There was once a widow who had two daughters. The elder was so like her mother in face and disposition that to have seen one was to have seen the other. They were both so disagreeable that it was impossible to live with them. The younger, who was the exact image of her dead father, was as beautiful a girl as one could see, and she was as kind and sweet-natured as she was pretty.

The widow doted on the daughter who was so like herself. But she had no love for the other, whom she compelled to work hard all day and to live on what her older sister had left over.

Among her other hard tasks, the poor girl was forced to go twice a day to fetch water from a place more than a mile from home and carry back a large jug filled to the brim.

One day when she had just filled the jug at this spring, a poor old woman came up to her and asked the girl to give her some water to drink.

'With all my heart', replied the lovely girl. Glad to show a kindness to one who was old and weak, she held the jug while the woman quenched her thirst.

Now, the old woman was not really a trembling old peasant, as she appeared to be, but a fairy who rewarded good deeds.

'Your face is pretty and your heart is gentle,' said she. 'For your kindness to a poor old woman, I will make you a gift. With every word you speak, either a flower or a precious stone will fall from your mouth.'

The girl had no sooner reached home than her mother began scolding her for coming back so late. 'I am sorry, Mother,' she said gently, 'that I was away so long', and as she spoke, there dropped from her mouth six roses, two pearls, and two large diamonds.

'What is this I see!' exclaimed the astonished widow. 'Pearls and diamonds seem to be dropping from your mouth! How is this, my daughter?' It was the first time she had called the girl her daughter.

The poor girl was so happy to be called daughter by her mother that she eagerly related her experiences with the old woman at the spring, and while she spoke, precious stones and roses continued to drop from her lips.

The widow immediately called her favourite daughter to her. 'Look!' she said. 'See what falls from your sister's mouth when she speaks! Wouldn't you like to receive such a gift too? All you have to do is to go and fetch water from the spring and if an old woman asks you for some to drink, give it to her nicely and politely.'

'I'd like to see myself going to the spring,' answered the girl crossly.

'I insist on your going,' the mother went on, 'and at once!'

The elder girl went off, still grumbling and sullen, taking with her the handsomest silver tankard she could find.

She had no sooner arrived at the spring than she saw a handsomely dressed lady walking towards her from the wood. She asked for some water to drink.

It was the same fairy who had appeared to the sister, but she had now put on the airs and garments of a princess, in order to see how far her rudeness would go.

'Do you think I came here just to draw water for you?' answered the unmannerly girl. 'But if you want some, take the pitcher and help yourself. I'd have you know I am as good as you are!'

'You are scarcely polite,' said the fairy, without losing her temper, 'and to equal your discourtesy and ill-breeding, I will make you a gift. With every word you speak, a snake or a toad shall fall out from your mouth.'

The girl ran home to her mother, who met her at the door. 'Well, daughter,' she said, impatient to hear her speak.

'Well, mother,' replied the ill-tempered girl, spitting out as she spoke two snakes and a toad.

'Alas!' cried the horrified mother. 'This is the fault of your wretched sister.' She ran towards the poor younger daughter intending to beat her. The unhappy girl fled from the house to a neighbouring forest to escape the cruel blows, and threw herself upon the green grass, weeping bitterly.

The King's son, who was returning from a hunting trip, found her, and seeing how beautiful she was, asked her what she was doing there all alone and why she was crying.

'My mother has driven me to run away from home,' she told him sadly. The girl was so lovely that the King's son fell in love with her at once and begged her to tell him more. She then related the whole story, while pearls and diamonds and roses kept dripping from her lips. Enraptured, he took her to the King, who gave his consent to their immediate marriage.

As for her sister, she made herself so hateful and disagreeable that even her own mother turned against her and drove her from the house. The miserable girl, after finding that no one would take her in, crept into the woods and died.   *Charles Perrault*

4

A. Why should we avoid hurtful expressions when speaking to others, even when we are angry because others have hurt our feelings themselves?
B. What is wrong with using nicknames? Why do you think Muḥammad forbade the use of nicknames?
C. What does 'defile' mean? Why does Bahá'u'lláh teach us not to defile our tongues?
D. Why should we not speak harshly to anyone?

'Do not speak harshly to anyone; those thus addressed will retort; painful, indeed, is vindictive speech; blows in exchange may bruise you.'[7]   *Dhammapada*

For younger children
E. What are the rewards for people who always use good language?
F. If we use bad language when we talk to other children will they really think of us as a good friend?

Gratitude

1

'My God, my Adored One, my King, my Desire! What tongue can voice my thanks to Thee?'[1]   *Bahá'u'lláh*

'Be generous in prosperity, and thankful in adversity.'[2]
Bahá'u'lláh

'. . . the best way to thank God is to love one another.'[3]
'Abdu'l-Bahá

'And let the peace of God rule in your hearts . . . and be ye thankful.'[4]   *New Testament*

'. . . We pardoned you . . . that haply you should be thankful.'[5]
Muḥammad

2

'. . . mere verbal thanksgiving is without effect. But real thankfulness is a cordial giving of thanks from the heart. When man in response to the favours of God manifests susceptibilities of conscience, the heart is happy, the spirit exhilarated. These spiritual susceptibilities are ideal thanksgiving.
    '. . . To express his gratitude for the favours of God man must show forth praiseworthy actions. In response to these bestowals he must render good deeds, be self-sacrificing, loving the servants of God, forfeiting even life for them, showing loving kindness to all the creatures. He must be severed from this world, attracted to the Kingdom of Abhá, the face radiant, the tongue eloquent, the ear attentive, striving day and night to attain the good pleasure of God. Whatsoever he wishes to do must be in harmony with the good pleasure of God. He must observe and see what is the will of God and act accordingly. There can be no doubt that such commendable deeds are thankfulness for the favours of God.'[6]   *'Abdu'l-Bahá*

3

Pelle's New Suit

There was once a little Swedish boy whose name was Pelle. Now Pelle had a lamb which was all his own and which he took care of all by himself.

The lamb grew and Pelle grew. And the lamb's wool grew longer and longer, but Pelle's coat only grew shorter!

One day Pelle took a pair of shears and cut off all the lamb's wool. Then he took the wool to his grandmother and said: 'Granny dear, please card this wool for me!'

'That I will, my dear,' said his grandmother, 'if you will pull the weeds in my carrot patch for me.'

So Pelle pulled the weeds in Granny's carrot patch and Granny carded Pelle's wool.

Then Pelle went to his other grandmother and said: 'Grandmother dear, please spin this wool into yarn for me!'

'That I will gladly do, my dear,' said his grandmother, 'if while I am spinning it you will tend my cows for me.'

And so Pelle tended Grandmother's cows and Grandmother spun Pelle's yarn.

Then Pelle went to a neighbour who was a painter and asked him for some paint with which to colour his yarn.

'What a silly little boy you are!' laughed the painter. 'My paint is not what you want to colour your wool. But if you will row over to the store to get a bottle of turpentine for me, you may buy yourself some dye out of the change from the shilling.'

So Pelle rowed over to the store and bought a bottle of turpentine for the painter, and bought for himself a large sack of blue dye out of the change from the shilling.

Then he dyed his wool himself until it was all, all blue.

And then Pelle went to his mother and said: 'Mother dear, please weave this yarn into cloth for me.'

'That I will gladly do,' said his mother, 'if you will take care of your little sister for me.'

So Pelle took good care of his little sister, and Mother wove the wool into cloth.

Then Pelle went to the tailor. 'Dear Mr Tailor, please make a suit for me out of this cloth.'

'Is that what you want, you little rascal?' said the tailor. 'Indeed I will, if you will rake my hay and bring in my wood and feed my pigs for me.'

So Pelle raked the tailor's hay and fed his pigs.

And then he carried in all the wood. And the tailor had Pelle's suit ready that very Saturday evening.

And on Sunday morning Pelle put on his new suit and went to his lamb and said: 'Thank you very much for my new suit, little lamb.'

'Ba-a-ah,' said the lamb, and it sounded almost as if the lamb were laughing.   *Elsa Beskow*

4

A. What is true thankfulness?

B. How can we show our gratitude to God for His favours?

C. Can having a 'thankful heart' help us be happy, can it guarantee us happiness?

D. To which people in this life should we show gratitude?

Guidance

1

'Surely God is my Lord and your Lord, so serve Him. This is a straight path'.[1] *Muḥammad*

'And the Lord shall guide thee continually . . .'[2] *Old Testament*

'. . . when he, the Spirit of truth, is come, he will guide you into all truth'.[3] *New Testament*

'Let your acts be a guide unto all mankind.'[4] *Bahá'u'lláh*

2

'Hold Thou my right arm, O God! and dwell continually with me. Guide me to the fountain of Thy knowledge, and encircle me with Thy glory. Set Thine angels on my right hand, and open mine eyes to Thy splendour. Let mine ears hearken to Thy melodious tone, and comfort me with thy Presence. For Thou art the strength of my heart, and the trust of my soul, and I desire none other beside Thee.'[5] *Bahá'u'lláh*

'Our Lord, make not our hearts to swerve after that Thou hast guided us; and give us mercy from Thee; Thou art the Giver.'[6]

Muḥammad

'Should one see a wise man, who, like a revealer of treasures, points out faults and reproves, let one associate with such a wise person; it will be better, not worse, for him who associates with such a one. Let him advise, instruct, and dissuade one from evil . . .'[7]

Dhammapada

3

Mrs Peterkin Wishes to go to Drive

One morning Mrs Peterkin was feeling very tired, as she had been having a great many things to think of, and she said to Mr Peterkin, 'I believe I shall take a ride this morning!'

And the little boys cried out, 'Oh, may we go too?'

Mrs Peterkin said that Elizabeth Eliza and the little boys might go.

So Mr Peterkin had the horse put into the carryall, and he and Agamemnon went off to their business, and Solomon John to school; and Mrs Peterkin began to get ready for her ride.

She had some currants she wanted to carry to old Mrs Twomly, and some gooseberries for somebody else, and Elizabeth Eliza wanted to pick some flowers to take to the minister's wife; so it took them a long time to prepare.

The little boys went out to pick the currants and the gooseberries, and Elizabeth Eliza went out for her flowers, and Mrs Peterkin put on her cape bonnet, and in time they were all ready. The little boys were in their india-rubber boots, and they got into the carriage.

Elizabeth Eliza was to drive; so she sat on the front seat, and took up the reins, and the horse started off merrily, and then suddenly stopped, and would not go any farther.

Elizabeth Eliza shook the reins, and pulled them, and then she clucked to the horse: and Mrs Peterkin clucked; and the little boys whistled and shouted; but still the horse would not go.

'We shall have to whip him,' said Elizabeth Eliza.

Now Mrs Peterkin never liked to use the whip; but, as the horse would not go, she said she would get out and turn her head the other way, while Elizabeth Eliza whipped the horse, and when he began to go she would hurry and get in.

So they tried, but the horse would not stir.

'Perhaps we have too heavy a load,' said Mrs Peterkin, as she got in.

So they took out the currants and the gooseberries and the flowers, but still the horse would not go.

One of the neighbours, from the opposite house, looking out just then, called out to them to try the whip. There was a high wind, and they could not hear exactly what she said.

'I have tried the whip,' said Elizabeth Eliza.

'She says "whips", such as you eat,' said one of the little boys.

'We might make those,' said Mrs Peterkin, thoughtfully.

'We have got plenty of cream,' said Elizabeth Eliza.

'Yes, let us have some whips,' cried the little boys, getting out.

And the opposite neighbour cried out something about whips; and the wind was very high.

So they went into the kitchen, and whipped up the cream, and made some very delicious whips; and the little boys tasted all round, and they all thought they were very nice.

They carried some out to the horse, who swallowed it down very quickly.

'That is just what he wanted,' said Mrs Peterkin; 'now he will certainly go!'

So they all got into the carriage again, and put in the currants, and the gooseberries, and the flowers; and Elizabeth Eliza shook the reins, and they all clucked; but still the horse would not go!

'We must either give up our ride,' said Mrs Peterkin mournfully, 'or else send over to the lady from Philadelphia, and see what she will say.'

The little boys jumped out as quickly as they could; they were eager to go and ask the lady from Philadelphia. Elizabeth Eliza went with them, while her mother took the reins.

They found that the lady from Philadelphia was very ill that day, and was in her bed. But when she was told what the trouble was she very kindly said they might draw up the curtain from the window at the foot of the bed, and open the blinds, and she would see. Then she asked for her opera glass, and looked through it, across the way, up the street, to Mrs Peterkin's door.

After she had looked through the glass she laid it down, leaned her head back against the pillow, for she was very tired, and then said, 'Why don't you unchain the horse from the horse post?'

Elizabeth Eliza and the little boys looked at one another, and then hurried back to the house and told their mother. The horse was untied, and they all went to ride.   *Lucretia P. Hale*

4

A. What is a guide?

B. How many different guides do you have?

C. Who are the greatest sources of guidance to mankind?

D. How do these divine guides help us to be happy?

'But the man who rejects the words of the Scriptures and follows the impulse of desire attains neither his perfection, nor joy, nor the Path Supreme.'[8] *Gita*

E. Does divine guidance change?

'Likewise confirming the truth of the Torah that is before me, and to make lawful to you certain things that before were forbidden unto you. I have come to you with a sign from your Lord; so fear you God, and obey you me.'[9] *Muḥammad*

F. If we follow the guidance given by God can we be a guide to others?

'Let your acts be a guide unto all mankind . . .' Why?

'. . . for the professions of most men, be they high or low, differ from their conduct. It is through your deeds that ye can distinguish yourselves from others. Through them the brightness of your light can be shed upon the whole earth.'[10] *Bahá'u'lláh*

G. How can we guide our own actions?

Happiness

1

'Happy is association with the wise . . .'[1]   *Dhammapada*

'Here he rejoices, hereafter he rejoices; in both states the well-doer rejoices . . .'[2]   *Dhammapada*

'Happy is the man that findeth wisdom, and the man that getteth understanding.'[3]   *Old Testament*

'O Son of Spirit! With the joyful tidings of light I hail thee, rejoice!'[4]   *Bahá'u'lláh*

2

'. . . he that hath mercy on the poor, happy is he.'[5]   *Old Testament*

'. . . and whoso trusteth in the Lord, happy is he.'[6]   *Old Testament*

'. . . and that keepeth the law, happy is he.'[7]   *Old Testament*

'Ah, happily do we live without hate amongst the hateful . . . Ah, happily do we live without yearning amongst them who yearn . . . Ah, happily do we live, we who have no impediments, feeders of joy shall we be even as the gods of the Radiant Realm.'[8]
Dhammapada

'. . . the foundation of Bahá'u'lláh is love . . . The people must be so attracted to you that they will exclaim, "What happiness exists among you!" and will see in your faces the lights of the Kingdom; then in wonderment they will turn to you and seek the cause of your happiness . . . I want you to be happy . . . to laugh, smile and rejoice in order that others may be made happy by you.'[9]
'Abdu'l-Bahá

3

The Happy Prince

High above the city, on a tall column, stood the statue of the Happy
Prince. He was gilded all over with thin leaves of fine gold; for eyes
he had two bright sapphires, and a large red ruby glowed on his
swordhilt. He was very much admired indeed.

One night there flew over the city a little Swallow. He saw the
statue on the tall column.

'I will put up there,' he cried; 'it is a fine position, with plenty of
fresh air.' So he alighted just between the feet of the Happy Prince.

'I have a golden bedroom,' he said softly to himself as he looked
round, and he prepared to go to sleep; but just as he was putting his
head under his wing a large drop of water fell on him. 'What a
curious thing,' he cried; 'there is not a single cloud in the sky, the
stars are quite clear and bright, and yet it is raining. The climate in
the north of Europe is really dreadful.'

Then another drop fell.

'What is the use of a statue if it cannot keep the rain off?' he said; 'I
must look for a good chimneypot,' and he determined to fly away.

But before he had opened his wings, a third drop fell, and he
looked up, and saw – Ah! what did he see?

The eyes of the Happy Prince were filled with tears, and tears
were running down his golden cheeks. His face was so beautiful in
the moonlight that the little Swallow was filled with pity.

'Who are you?' he said.

'I am the Happy Prince.'

'Why are you weeping then?' asked the Swallow. 'You have quite
drenched me.'

'When I was alive and had a human heart,' answered the statue, 'I
did not know what tears were. In the daytime I played with my

companions in the garden, and in the evening I led the dance in the Great Hall. Round the garden ran a very lofty wall, but I never cared to ask what lay beyond it, everything about me was so beautiful. My courtiers called me the Happy Prince, and happy indeed I was, if pleasure be happiness. So I lived, and so I died. And now that I am dead they have set me up here so high that I can see all the ugliness and all the misery of my city, and though my heart is made of lead yet I cannot choose but weep.'

'What! is he not solid gold?' said the Swallow to himself. He was too polite to make any personal remarks out loud.

'Far away,' continued the statue in a low musical voice, 'in a little street there is a poor house. One of the windows is open, and through it I can see a woman seated at a table. Her face is thin and worn, and she has coarse, red hands, all pricked by the needle, for she is a seamstress. She is embroidering passion-flowers on a satin gown for the loveliest of the Queen's maids-of-honour to wear at the next Court-ball. In a bed in the corner of the room her little boy is lying ill. He has a fever and is asking for oranges. His mother has nothing to give him but river water, so he is crying. Swallow, Swallow, little Swallow, will you not bring her the ruby out of my sword-hilt? My feet are fastened to this pedestal and I cannot move.'

'I am waited for in Egypt,' said the Swallow. 'My friends are flying up and down the Nile, and talking to the large lotus-flowers. Soon they will go to sleep in the tomb of the great King.'

'Swallow, Swallow, little Swallow,' said the Prince, 'will you not stay with me for one night, and be my messenger? The boy is so thirsty, and the mother so sad.'

'I don't think I like boys,' answered the Swallow. 'Last summer when I was staying on the river, there were two rude boys, the miller's sons, who were always throwing stones at me.'

But the Happy Prince looked so sad that the little Swallow was sorry. 'It is very cold here,' he said, 'but I will stay with you for one night, and be your messenger.'

'Thank you, little Swallow,' said the Prince.

So the Swallow picked out the great ruby from the Prince's sword and flew away with it in his beak over the roofs of the town.

He passed by the cathedral tower, where the white marble angels were sculptured. He passed by the palace and heard the sound of dancing. He passed over the river, and saw the lanterns hanging to the masts of the ships. He passed over the Ghetto, and saw the old

Jews bargaining with each other, and weighing out money in copper scales. At last he came to the poor house and looked in. The boy was tossing feverishly on his bed and the mother had fallen asleep, she was so tired. In he hopped and laid the great ruby on the table beside the woman's thimble. Then he flew gently round the bed, fanning the boy's forehead with his wings. 'How cool I feel!' said the boy. 'I must be getting better,' and he sank into a delicious slumber.

Then the Swallow flew back to the Happy Prince, and told him what he had done. 'It is curious,' he remarked, 'but I feel quite warm now, although it is so cold.'

'That is because you have done a good action,' said the Prince. And the little Swallow began to think, and then he fell asleep. Thinking always made him sleepy.

When day broke he flew down to the river and had a bath. 'Tonight I go to Egypt,' said the Swallow, and he was in high spirits at the prospect.

When the moon rose he flew back to the Happy Prince. 'Have you any commissions for Egypt?' he cried. 'I am just starting.'

'Swallow, Swallow, little Swallow,' said the Prince. 'Will you not stay with me one night longer?'

'I am waited for in Egypt,' answered the Swallow. 'Tomorrow my friends will fly up to the Second Cataract.'

'Swallow, Swallow, little Swallow,' said the Prince, 'far away across the city I see a young man in a garret. He is leaning over a desk covered with papers, and in a tumbler by his side there is a bunch of withered violets. His hair is brown and crisp, and his lips are red as a pomegranate, and he has large and dreamy eyes. He is trying to finish a play for the Director of the Theatre, but he is too cold to write any more. There is no fire in the grate, and hunger has made him faint.'

'I will wait with you one night longer,' said the Swallow, who really had a good heart. 'Shall I take him another ruby?'

'Alas! I have no ruby now,' said the Prince. 'My eyes are all that I have left. They are made of rare sapphires which were brought out of India a thousand years ago. Pluck out one of them and take it to him. He will sell it to the jeweller, and buy firewood, and finish the play.'

'Dear Prince,' said the Swallow, 'I cannot do that', and he began to weep.

'Swallow, Swallow, little Swallow,' said the Prince, 'do as I command you.'

So the Swallow plucked out the Prince's eye, and flew away to the student's garret. It was easy enough to get in, as there was a hole in the roof. Through this he darted and came into the room. The young man had his head buried in his hands, so he did not hear the flutter of the bird's wings, and when he looked up he found the beautiful sapphire lying on the withered violets.

'I am beginning to be appreciated,' he cried. 'This is from some great admirer. Now I can finish my play,' and he looked quite happy.

The next day the Swallow flew down to the harbour. He sat on the mast of a large vessel and watched the sailors hauling big chests out of the hold with ropes. 'Heave a-hoy!' they shouted, as each chest came up. 'I am going to Egypt!' cried the Swallow, but nobody minded, and when the moon rose he flew back to the Happy Prince.

'I am come to bid you goodbye,' he cried.

'Swallow, Swallow, little Swallow,' said the Prince, 'will you not stay with me one night longer?'

'It is winter,' answered the Swallow, 'and the chill snow will soon be here. My companions are building a nest in the Temple of Baalbec, and the pink and white doves are watching them, and cooing to each other. Dear Prince, I must leave you, but I will never forget you, and next spring I will bring you back two beautiful jewels in place of those you have given away. The ruby shall be redder than a red rose, and the sapphire shall be as blue as the great sea.'

'In the square below,' said the Happy Prince, 'there stands a little match girl. She has let her matches fall in the gutter, and they are all spoiled. Her father will beat her if she does not bring home some money, and she is crying. She has no shoes or stockings, and her little head is bare. Pluck out my other eye, and give it to her, and her father will not beat her.'

'I will stay with you one night longer,' said the Swallow, 'but I cannot pluck out your other eye. You would be quite blind then.'

'Swallow, Swallow, little Swallow,' said the Prince, 'do as I command you.'

So he plucked out the Prince's other eye, and darted down with it. He swooped past the match girl and slipped the jewel into the palm of her hand. 'What a lovely bit of glass!' cried the little girl, and she ran home, laughing.

The Swallow came back to the Prince. 'You are blind now,' he said, 'so I will stay with you always.'

'No, little Swallow,' said the poor Prince, 'you must go away to Egypt.'

'I will stay with you always,' said the Swallow, and he slept at the Prince's feet.

All the next day he sat on the Prince's shoulder, and told him stories of what he had seen in strange lands.

'Dear little Swallow' said the Prince, 'you tell me of marvellous things, but more marvellous than anything is the suffering of men and women. There is no Mystery so great as Misery. Fly over my city, little Swallow, and tell me what you see there.'

So the Swallow flew over the great city, and saw the rich making merry in their beautiful houses, while the beggars were sitting at the gates. He flew into dark lanes, and saw the white faces of starving children looking out listlessly at the black streets. Under the archway of a bridge two little boys were lying in one another's arms to try to keep themselves warm. 'How hungry we are,' they said. 'You must not lie here,' shouted the watchman, and they wandered out into the rain.

Then he flew back and told the Prince what he had seen.

'I am covered with fine gold,' said the Prince, 'you must take it off, leaf by leaf, and give it to the poor; the living always think that gold can make them happy.'

Leaf after leaf of the fine gold the Swallow picked off, till the happy Prince looked quite dull and grey. Leaf after leaf of the fine gold he brought to the poor, and the children's faces grew rosier, and they laughed and played games in the street. 'We have bread now!' they cried.

Then the snow came, and after the snow came the frost. The streets looked as if they were made of silver, they were so bright and glistening everybody went about in furs, and the little boys wore scarlet caps and skated on the ice.

The poor little Swallow grew colder and colder, but he would not leave the Prince. He loved him too well. He picked up crumbs outside the baker's door when the baker was not looking, and tried to keep himself warm by flapping his wings.

But at last he knew that he was going to die. He had just enough strength to fly up to the Prince's shoulder once more. 'Goodbye dear Prince!' he murmured. 'Will you let me kiss your hand?'

'I am glad that you are going to Egypt at last, little Swallow,' said the Prince, 'you have stayed too long here; but you must kiss me on the lips, for I love you.'

'It is not to Egypt that I am going,' said the Swallow. 'I am going to the House of Death. Death is the brother of Sleep, is he not?'

And he kissed the Happy Prince on the lips, and fell down dead at his feet.

At that moment a curious crack sounded inside the statue, as if something had broken. The fact is that the leaden heart had snapped right in two. It certainly was a dreadfully hard frost.

Early the next morning the Mayor was walking in the square below in the company of the Town Councillors. As they passed the column he looked up at the statue. 'Dear me! how shabby the Happy Prince looks!' he said.

'How shabby, indeed!' cried the Town Councillors, who always agreed with the Mayor, and they went up to look at it.

'The ruby has fallen out of his sword, his eyes are gone, and he is golden no longer,' said the Mayor, 'in fact, he is little better than a beggar!'

'Little better than a beggar,' said the Town Councillors.

'And here is actually a dead bird at his feet!' continued the Mayor. 'We must really issue a proclamation that birds are not to be allowed to die here.' And the Town Clerk made a note of the suggestion.

So they pulled down the statue of the Happy Prince. Then they melted the statue in a furnace, and the Mayor held a meeting of the

Corporation to decide what was to be done with the metal. 'We must have another statue of course,' he said, 'and it shall be a statue of myself.'

'What a strange thing!' said the overseer of the workmen at the foundry. 'This broken lead heart will not melt in the furnace. We must throw it away.' So they threw it on a dust heap where the dead Swallow was also lying.

'Bring me the two most precious things in the city,' said God to one of His Angels; and the Angel brought Him the leaden heart and the dead bird.

'You have rightly chosen,' said God, 'for in my garden of Paradise this little bird shall sing for evermore and in my city of gold the Happy Prince shall praise me.'   *Oscar Wilde*

4

A. How can we be happy?
B. What do you think the 'tidings of light' are?

> Glad Tidings!
> For everlasting life is here.
> O ye that sleep, awake!
> O ye heedless ones, learn wisdom!
> O blind, receive your sight!
> O deaf, hear!
> O dumb, speak!
> O dead, arise!
> Be happy!
> Be happy!
> Be full of joy![10]
>
> *'Abdu'l-Bahá*

C. Why should we try to be happy?
D. What sort of things make us happy?

Health and Healing

1

'Thy name is my healing, O my God . . .'[1]   *Bahá'u'lláh*

'Health is the highest gain . . .'[2]   *Dhammapada*

'If thou art desirous of health, wish thou health for serving the Kingdom.'[3]   *'Abdu'l-Bahá*

2

'If the health and well-being of the body be expended in the path of the Kingdom, this is very acceptable and praiseworthy; and if it is expended to the benefit of the human world in general – even though it be to their material benefit and be a means of doing good – that is also acceptable. But if the health and welfare of man be spent in sensual desires, in a life on the animal plane, and in devilish pursuits – then disease is better than such health; nay, death itself is preferable to such a life. If thou art desirous of health, wish thou health for serving the Kingdom. I hope thou mayest attain a perfect insight, an inflexible resolution, a complete health and spiritual and physical strength in order that thou mayest drink from the fountain of eternal life and be assisted by the spirit of divine confirmation.'[4]

'Abdu'l-Bahá

3

Mírzá Ja'far

Speaking of Mírzá Ja'far, 'Abdu'l-Bahá has recounted the following story:

The Prison was a garden of roses to him, and his narrow cell a wide and fragrant place. At the time when we were in the barracks he fell dangerously ill and was confined to his bed. He suffered many complications, until finally the doctor gave him up and would visit him no more. Then the sick man breathed his last. Mírzá Áqá Ján ran to Bahá'u'lláh, with word of the death. Not only had the patient ceased to breathe, but his body was already going limp. His family were gathered about him mourning him and shedding bitter tears. The Blessèd Beauty said, 'Go; chant the prayer of Yá Shafí – O Thou, the Healer – and Mírzá Ja'far will come alive. Very rapidly, he will be as well as ever.' I reached his bedside. His body was cold and all the signs of death were present. Slowly, he began to stir; soon he could move his limbs, and before an hour had passed he lifted his head, sat up, and proceeded to laugh and tell jokes.

He lived for a long time after that, occupied as ever with serving the friends. This giving service was a point of pride with him: to all, he was a servant. He was always modest and humble, calling God to mind, and to the highest degree full of hope and faith.[5]

'Abdu'l-Bahá

['Abdu'l-Bahá's] kind heart went out to those who were ill. If He could alleviate a pain or discomfort, He set about to do so. We are told that one old couple who were ill in bed for a month had twenty visits from the Master during that time. In 'Akká, He daily sent a servant to inquire about the welfare of the ill, and as there was no hospital in the town, He paid a doctor a regular salary to look after the poor. The doctor was instructed not to tell Who provided this service. When a poor and crippled woman was shunned on contracting measles, the Master, on being informed, 'immediately engaged a woman to care for her; took a room, put comfortable bedding (His own) into it, called the doctor, sent food and everything she needed. He went to see that she had every attention, and when she died in peace and comfort, He it was Who arranged her simple funeral, paying all charges.'[6] *Honnold*

A man, ill with tuberculosis, was avoided by his friends – even his family was fearful and hardly dared enter his room. The Master needed only to hear of it and 'thereafter went daily to the sick man, took him delicacies, read and discoursed to him, and was alone with him when he died.'[7] *Honnold*

While in San Francisco, 'Abdu'l-Bahá visited a black believer, Mr Charles Tinsley, who had been confined to bed for a long time with a broken leg. The Master said to him: 'You must not be sad. This affliction will make you spiritually stronger. Do not be sad. Cheer up! Praise be to God, you are dear to me.'[8] *Honnold*

The Happy Cure

A foolish king lay dying. At least, that's what he said. Yes, he said he
was at death's door. But the truth of the matter was this: the king
was suffering from having nothing to do. He was being bored to
death.

Of course, the king would not admit this. He groaned and
moaned and complained of sharp stabs in every muscle and sticking
pains in every bone in his body. Physicians and surgeons came from
far and wide. They looked down the king's throat, they tapped his
chest, and they felt his pulse. They hemmed and hawed and stroked
their beards. But they could find nothing wrong.

'Physicians and surgeons are dolts,' cried the king. 'Aren't there
any plain ordinary doctors in the kingdom?'

The plain ordinary doctors came from hither and yon. They felt
the king's pulse, tapped his chest, and looked down his throat. They
hawed and hemmed, took off their spectacles, put them on again.
But they could find nothing wrong.

'Plain ordinary doctors are idiots,' cried the king in a rage. 'The
next one who examines me and finds nothing wrong will have his
ears cut off and his nose shortened.'

Well, you would think that would have put a stop to the coming
of the doctors and the surgeons and the physicians. But no. The king
kept sending messengers and couriers to bring them in. The people
were in despair. Such an epidemic of heads without ears and faces
with shortened noses had never been seen.

Finally a simple old woman came to see the king. The exhausted
prime minister brought her into the royal bedchamber.

The simple old woman peered into the king's face for a long time.
Then she said, 'Your Majesty, you are suffering from a strange and
rare disease. So rare and strange, that no name exists for it.'

'There I knew it,' cried the king in glee. 'I kept telling all of them,
the fools, that I'm a sick man.'

'A very sick man,' said the old woman.

The king leaned back among his silken pillows and closed his eyes
and wrinkled his brow as if he were in pain.

'And is there no cure for me?' he asked.

'Oh, yes, your Majesty. You need sleep but one night in the shirt
of a happy man and you will be cured instantly,' said the simple old
woman.

The king summoned the captain of his guard and his bravest

soldiers; the best couriers in the land; and the swiftest messengers and heralds.

'Start off at once,' he commanded them, 'and bring me back the shirt of a happy man. And mind you don't return without it,' he added darkly.

The soldiers and couriers, messengers and heralds travelled far and wide from east to west, from north to south, across seas and deserts, through cities and over mountains, from one end of the kingdom to the other. But nowhere could they find a happy man. They sent long reports to the king. And this is what they said:

The people in the east might be happy if your Majesty didn't tax them so heavily.

And: The people in the west might be happy if they didn't have to work so long and so hard, so they might have a little time to enjoy singing and dancing.

And: The people in the north might be happy if sometimes they could see you and felt you were interested in them.

And: The people in the south might be happy if your Majesty would notice their industry and faithfulness and would reward them.

The king read the reports hastily and flung them away. But as time went by and none of the messengers returned, and more and more reports came to him of a people that might be happy if their king so chose, he began to read more carefully.

One day a little stableboy wandering about the palace grounds

came upon a man sitting under a tree in the royal garden. He was singing lustily.

The little stableboy approached him.

'Good afternoon,' he said politely. 'What makes you sing so merrily?'

'I sing from joy,' said the stranger. 'I love my fellow men. I own but little and want less. I am a happy man and I sing.'

'A happy man!' cried the little stableboy. 'Oh, do you not know then that the whole kingdom is looking for you? Do you not know that the king is very ill and only if he can sleep one night in the shirt of a happy man can he be cured? Quick, quick, take off your shirt! Quick, quick, give it to me.'

The man burst into laughter. 'My shirt,' he gasped. 'Why, you little ragamuffin, I don't possess a shirt.' And jumping to his feet, he gathered his tattered coat about him and walked off.

The little stableboy flew to the palace. Past the guards and the prime minister he sped, right into the royal bedchamber.

'What have we here?' cried the king.

The little stableboy had to wait to recover his breath before he could talk.

'Oh, your Majesty,' he cried. 'The cure was right here all the time – right at hand – right on the palace grounds. I found him – he said he loved his fellow men, owned but little and wanted less. But,' and the little boy's lips trembled, 'but he didn't possess a shirt.'

Then the king hung his head ashamed.

'Yes, the cure has been here all the time,' he murmured. 'Only I can cure my own folly.'

And he resolved then and there to be a good king, to help his people, to rule wisely and well. He never fancied himself ill again for he became too busy for such folly, and so he lived to a ripe old age.

Retold by Rose Dobbs

4

A. What does it mean to be healthy?
B. Good health and cleanliness go together, so we must take care of our bodies. If we do so, whom will we please?
C. How can we keep our bodies clean?
D. How can we help people who have become ill?
E. 'The body should be the servant of the soul, never its master, but it should be a willing, obedient and efficient servant, and should be treated with the consideration which a good servant deserves. If it is not properly treated, disease and disaster result,

with injurious consequences to master as well as servant.'[9]

J. E. Esslemont.

Discuss what you think this means.

F. How do the laws of the Messengers of God help us keep healthy?

'Experience hath shown how greatly the renouncing of smoking, of intoxicating drink, and of opium, conduceth to health and vigour, to the expansion and keenness of the mind and to bodily strength.'[10]   *'Abdu'l-Bahá*

G. How is cleanliness associated with good health and spirituality?

H. Do fear, anger, worry have an effect on health? If so, what about hope, love, joy and so on?

I. How can we assist in the healing of others?

'There are two ways of healing sickness, material means and spiritual means. The first is by the use of remedies, of medicines; the second consists in praying to God and in turning to Him. Both means should be used and practised. Illness caused by physical accident should be treated with medical remedies; those which are due to spiritual causes disappear through spiritual means.'[11]   *'Abdu'l-Bahá*

J. Why should we wish for good health?

K. Is there ever a wisdom in sickness?

'Abdu'l-Bahá at an early age was a victim of consumption. Sixty years later, when speaking of the illness which was keeping Him in the French capital for a period longer than expected, He brought to mind those years of His childhood:

'I have been travelling for two years and a half. Nowhere was I ill except here. Because of that I had to stay a long time. Were it not for this illness I would not have stayed in Paris for more than a month. There is a reason for this . . . It has been so from the early years of my life. The wisdom of whatever has happened to me has become apparent later. While I was a child in Tihrán, seven years of age, I contracted tuberculosis. There was no hope of recovery. Afterwards the wisdom of and the reason for this became evident. Were it not for that illness I would have been in Mazindárán. But because of it I remained in Tihrán and was there when the Blessed Perfection was imprisoned. Thus I travelled to 'Iráq in His company. And when the time came, although physicians had despaired of my recovery, I was suddenly cured. It happened in spite of the fact that all had said a cure was impossible.'[12]   *'Abdu'l-Bahá*

Honesty

1

'Beautify your tongues, O people, with truthfulness, and adorn your souls with the ornament of honesty.'[1] *Bahá'u'lláh*

'And fill up the measure and the balance with justice . . . And when you speak be just . . .'[2] *Muḥammad*

'But that on the good ground are they, which in an honest and good heart, having heard the word, keep it, and bring forth fruit with patience.'[3] *New Testament*

'Truth obtains victory, not untruth.'[4] *Mundaka Upanishad*

'. . . conquer the liar by truth.'[5] *Dhammapada*

'One should utter the truth; one should not be angry; one should give even from a scanty store to him who asks . . .'[6] *Dhammapada*

2

'They who dwell within the tabernacle of God, and are established upon the seats of everlasting glory, will refuse, though they be dying of hunger, to stretch their hands and seize unlawfully the property of their neighbour, however vile and worthless he may be.'[7] *Bahá'u'lláh*

'O ye friends of God in His cities and His loved ones in His lands! This wronged one enjoineth on you honesty and piety. Blessed the city that shineth by their light. Through them man is exalted, and the door of security is unlocked before the face of all creation. Happy the man that cleaveth fast unto them, and recogniseth their virtue, and woe betide him that denieth their station.'[8] *Bahá'u'lláh*

3

Economic justice, even in small matters, was important to the Master. Once in Egypt 'Abdu'l-Bahá obtained a carriage in order that He might offer a ride to an important Páshá, who was to be His luncheon guest. When they reached their destination, the driver asked an exorbitant fee. The Master was fully aware of this and refused to pay the full amount. The driver, big and rough, grabbed His sash and 'jerked Him back and forth', demanding his unfair price. 'Abdu'l-Bahá remained firm and the man eventually let go. The Master paid what He actually owed him and informed him that had be been honest, he would have received a handsome tip instead of only the fare. He then walked away.

Shoghi Effendi, His grandson, was present when this happened. He later admitted to being very embarrassed that this should have happened in front of the Páshá. 'Abdu'l-Bahá, on the other hand, was evidently 'not at all upset', but simply determined not to be cheated.[9] *Honnold*

The Wonderful Mallet

Once upon a time there were two brothers. The elder was an honest and good man, but he was very poor, while the younger, who was dishonest and stingy, had managed to pile up a large fortune. The name of the elder was Kane, and that of the younger was Cho.

Now, one day Kane went to Cho's house, and begged for the loan of some seed-rice and some silkworms' eggs, for he was in want of both.

Cho had plenty of good rice and excellent silkworms' eggs, but he was such a miser that he did not want to lend them. At the same time, he felt ashamed to refuse his brother's request, so he gave him some worm-eaten musty rice and some dead eggs, which he felt sure would never hatch.

Kane, never suspecting that his brother would play him such a shabby trick, put plenty of mulberry leaves with the eggs, to be food for the silkworms when they should appear. Appear they did, and thrived and grew wonderfully, much better than those of the stingy brother, who was angry and jealous when he heard of it.

Going to Kane's house one day, and finding his brother was out, Cho took a knife and killed all the silkworms, cutting each poor little creature in two. Then he went home without having been seen by anybody.

When Kane came home he was dismayed to find his silkworms in this state, but he did not suspect who had done him such a bad turn.

He tried feeding them with mulberry leaves as before. The silkworms came to life again, and doubled their number, for now each half had become a living worm. They grew and thrived, and the silk they spun was twice as much as Kane had expected. So now be began to prosper.

The envious Cho, seeing this, cut all his own silkworms in half, but, alas! they did not come to life again, so he lost a great deal of money, and became more jealous than ever of his brother.

Kane also planted the seed-rice which he had borrowed from his brother, and it sprang up, and grew far better than Cho's had done.

The rice ripened well, and Kane was just ready to cut and harvest it when a flight of thousands upon thousands of swallows came and began to devour it. Kane was much astonished, and shouted and made as much noise as he could in order to drive them away. They flew away, indeed, but came back immediately, so that he kept driving them away, and they kept flying back again.

At last he pursued them into a distant field, where he lost sight of them. He was by this time so hot and tired that he sat down to rest. Little by little his eyes closed, his head dropped, and he fell fast asleep.

Then he dreamed that a merry band of children came into the field, laughing and shouting. They sat down upon the ground in a ring, and one who seemed the oldest, a boy of fourteen or fifteen, came close to the bank on which he lay asleep, and, raising a big stone near his head, drew from under it a small wooden mallet.

Then in his dream Kane saw this big boy stand in the middle of the ring with the mallet in his hand, and ask the children each in turn, 'What would you like the mallet to bring you?'

The first child answered, 'A kite.' The big boy shook the mallet, upon which appeared immediately a fine kite with tail and string all complete.

The next cried, 'A battledore.'

Out sprang a splendid battledore and a shower of shuttlecocks.

Then a little girl shyly whispered, 'A doll.'

The mallet was shaken, and there stood a beautifully dressed doll.

'I should like all the fairy-tale books that have ever been written in the whole world,' said a bright-eyed intelligent maiden, and no sooner had she spoken than piles on piles of beautiful books appeared.

And so at last the wishes of all the children were granted, and they stayed a long time in the field with the things the mallet had given them. At last they got tired, and prepared to go home; but first the big boy carefully hid the mallet under the stone from whence he had taken it. Then all the children went away.

Presently Kane awoke, and gradually remembered his dream. In preparing to rise he turned around, and there, close to where his head had lain, was the big stone he had seen in his dream. 'How strange!' he thought, expecting he hardly knew what. He raised the stone, and there lay the mallet!

He took it home with him and, following the example of the children he had seen in his dream, shook it, at the same time calling out, 'gold' or 'rice', 'silk' or 'sake'. Whatever he called for flew immediately out of the mallet, so that he could have everything he wanted, and as much of it as he liked.

Kane being now a rich and prosperous man, Cho was of course jealous of him, and determined to find a magic mallet which would do as much for him. He came, therefore, to Kane and borrowed seed-rice which he planted and tended with care, being impatient for it to grow and ripen soon.

It grew well and ripened soon, and now Cho watched daily for the swallows to appear. And, to be sure, one day a flight of swallows came and began to eat up the rice.

Cho was delighted at this, and drove them away, pursuing them to the distant field where Kane had followed them before. There he lay down, intending to go to sleep as his brother had done, but the more he tried to go to sleep the wider awake he seemed.

Presently the band of children came skipping and jumping, so he shut his eyes and pretended to be asleep, but all the time he watched anxiously to see what the children would do. They sat down in a ring, as before, and the big boy came close to Cho's head and lifted the stone. He put down his hand to lift the mallet, but no mallet was there.

One of the children said, 'Perhaps that lazy old farmer has taken our mallet.' So the big boy laid hold of Cho's nose, which was rather long, and gave it a good pinch, and all the other children ran up and pinched and pulled his nose, and the nose itself got longer and longer. First it hung down to his chin, then over his chest, next down to his knees, and at last to his very feet.

It was in vain that Cho protested his innocence; the children pinched and pummelled him to their hearts' content, then capered around him, shouting and laughing, and making game of him, and so at last went away.

Now Cho was left alone, a sad and angry man. Holding his long nose painfully in both hands, he slowly took his way towards his

brother Kane's house. Here he related all that had happened to him from the very day when he had behaved so badly about the seed-rice and silkworms' eggs. He humbly begged his brother to pardon him, and, if possible, do something to restore his unfortunate nose to its proper size.

The kind-hearted Kane pitied him, and said, 'You have been dishonest, mean, selfish and envious. That is why you have got this punishment. If you promise to behave better for the future, I will try to see what can be done.'

So saying, he took the mallet and rubbed Cho's nose with it gently, and the nose gradually became shorter and shorter until at last it came back to its proper shape and size. But ever after, if at any time Cho felt inclined to be selfish and dishonest, as he did now and then, his nose began to smart and burn, and he fancied he felt it beginning to grow. So great was his horror of having a long nose again that these symptoms never failed to bring him back to good behaviour.   *An Old Japanese Tale*

He was Disgraced for Telling the Truth

There was once an Italian boy called Galileo Galilei, who liked to sit by himself in a corner and make toys which could be worked by wheels and pulleys.

His father was a clever man who enjoyed doing experiments, but he was sorry his little boy showed such an interest in mechanical toys. 'The child will be a mathematician when he grows up,' sighed he, 'and there's no money in that. I want him to be a merchant.'

To become a merchant Galileo must have a good education, so his father sent him to an excellent school where he worked hard for several years. As the boy's reports were so good, old Galilei decided that the boy would probably never be satisfied with buying and selling, and so he sent him to the university, hoping that Galileo would become a doctor.

One day the young student happened to pass the cathedral and went in to say a prayer. It was beginning to grow dark, and as he rose from his knees, a man came in with a taper and lit a lamp which hung from the roof by a chain. He left it swinging to and fro and passed along with a glance of curiosity at the young student whose eyes were fixed with intense interest on the lamp.

Backwards and forwards swung the lamp, casting strange moving shadows on the walls. At first the swing was quite a long one; but as it began to die, the distance was shorter.

Galileo stared. It seemed to him that the lamp was taking the same length of time to swing a short distance as a long one. He swung it again, determined to make sure. But he had no watch with which to test it, and so he put his fingers on his pulse and counted the beats. He was right. When the lamp was nearly still it took as long to do its little swing as it had taken to do its big one.

Galileo had made a discovery. He had found that the length of time it takes a weight on a string to swing does not depend on the distance it swings, but on the length of its chain or cord. This was Galileo's first discovery and because of it people were able to make cuckoo clocks and grandfather clocks, both of which depend upon this kind of swing of the pendulum.

Soon after this, Galileo made friends with an old teacher of mathematics. The subject fascinated him so much that he gave all his spare time to it. His father scolded him and warned him that he could never grow rich. But it was of no use. At the age of twenty-six, the young man became a professor of mathematics, and instead of taking the salary of a doctor, he earned hardly anything. But he was far more interested in knowledge than in money.

One day he found that a heavy weight and a light one would both fall to the ground at the same moment. When no one would believe him he said, 'Very well, I'll prove it. Meet me in the square by the Leaning Tower.'

Eager young students, grey-bearded professors, and all sorts of people from the town came to the square, shrugging their shoulders and saying, 'What nonsense. Well, it will do him good to make a fool of himself.'

Galileo only smiled. He climbed the stairs of the famous Leaning Tower of Pisa and stood looking down at the crowd. On the edge of the tower he placed two cannon-balls. One weighed a hundred pounds and the other one pound.

'Pooh!' said the people. 'The heavy one will fall a hundred times quicker than the light one.' And they laughed. Just at that moment Galileo pushed the balls over the edge.

They struck the ground at the same moment. The old books, which the professors had believed without trying to prove, were quite wrong.

Meanwhile, Galileo had been thinking deeply. In his day most people believed that the earth was the middle of the universe with the sun moving around it. Galileo could not believe this. He had read about an old monk called Copernicus, who had lived many years earlier. Copernicus had watched the stars and planets and had seen that they were in different parts of the sky at different times. He came to the conclusion that the sun was the centre of all this movement and not the earth. 'The rising and setting of the sun,' said he, 'is due to the spinning of the earth. The earth is a planet like Jupiter or Venus. It spins like a top for day and night, and at the same time it makes the year by slowly circling around the sun.'

'Don't listen to that rubbish!' said the people. 'The earth a planet, indeed! Why, it's dark. It doesn't shine. Just think of the solid earth with us and our houses and the trees and the hills and the seas spinning around and around like a top, and at the same time careering around the sun. What an idea! Ha, ha.' And they continued to laugh for years at the ridiculous notion.

But Galileo did not laugh. He thought Copernicus was right and he wished he could examine the planets and find out more about them. 'If only they were near!' he sighed.

While he was thinking about Copernicus and his ideas, Galileo began to make experiments with spectacle glasses. He had heard that a Dutch boy had been playing about in his master's workshop and had discovered that if he looked through two sorts of spectacle glasses at the same time, holding each at a different distance from his eye, he saw the church spire ever so much nearer and upside down. A general had made use of this discovery for finding out the movements of the enemy. 'I'll make use of it', thought Galileo, 'to find out the movements of the planets. It will bring them nearer and may help me to prove that Copernicus was right.'

He set to work. But none of his experiments were of any use until, one day, he picked up a bit of old organ pipe and, pushing a bulgy spectacle glass into one end and a hollow one into the other, he looked through it. For a minute he said nothing; then his face lit up with a wonderful smile. His queer new instrument had made things look three times nearer and not upside down. Galileo had made the first telescope.

News of his wonderful invention flew all around Italy. Everyone wanted to look through Galileo's spy glass. He became the hero of the hour.

His life was more interesting than ever. He improved his instrument, making it stronger, and be began to explore the sky. He gazed at the Milky Way and found that this strange brightness was made by numbers of stars. He gazed at the moon and found that it was a

world with mountains, valleys, craters, seas and plains like his own country. This had never been known before, and now Galileo could see it. He found that the earth shone like the moon and that what a poet called 'the old moon in the new moon's arms' was really earthshine.

'Rubbish,' said the people who did not like new ideas.

'But Copernicus was right,' said Galileo. 'The earth is a planet.'

One night in January, he made a marvellous discovery about the planet Jupiter. He found that just as the earth has one moon, Jupiter has several moons. Yet, strange to say, there were still people who would not believe him even when they saw the moons through the telescope. Of course Galileo only laughed at them. He had many friends and there was no need to bother himself with folk who did not want to believe their own eyes. And so, for many years, he continued to make new discoveries, and to teach people about Copernicus. 'The earth', said he, 'moves around the sun,' and he explained all the good reasons he had for believing this.

Unfortunately poor Galileo was living at a time when it was not always wise or safe to teach what other men did not believe. And now, when so many people were listening to Galileo, his enemies were alarmed and angry. 'He teaches things which are not in the Bible,' they said. 'His ideas are wicked. The learned churchmen say the earth does not move around the sun.'

Messages were sent to Rome saying that this man and his telescope were doing harm, and so hot and angry were the arguments that at last the Pope asked Galileo to come and explain his ideas. Away went Galileo, telescope and all. He was kindly received, and at first he thought his visit had been successful. But before long the trouble began again.

As time passed, Galileo's life became more and more difficult. He was growing old and weak and he knew that the people who did not want to believe the truth were working against him. In spite of this he wrote a book about the ideas of Copernicus, and a number of people read it with eagerness.

When this book appeared, Galileo was once again summoned to Rome. He was accused of preaching something which was against the teaching of the Church. In vain did his friends plead that he was seventy years old and ill, that the roads were bad, and that there was a quarantine on account of the plague. It was of no use, Galileo was obliged to go to Rome and face the judges.

He was brought before a body of powerful churchmen, known as the Inquisition. They did not put him in prison but they questioned and threatened him until he was ill with weariness. They told him to deny all he had been teaching, to say the sun and planets went around the earth, and that the earth was the centre of the universe.

For a long while Galileo would not give in, for he knew his ideas were right. But at last he could resist no longer. 'I am in your hands,' said he. 'I will say what you wish.'

In the presence of his judges he was made to kneel, clothed in the robe of the penitent, and to swear that what Copernicus had believed was untrue.

Legend tells us that, when he had sworn that the centre of the universe was the earth which could not move, he rose from his knees whispering, 'But it does move! It does move all the same!'

Utterly broken and disgraced, knowing that his enemies would rejoice at his downfall, Galileo went home.

He continued to make experiments and to use his telescope. But life had still to deal him one more blow. He wrote of it, some time later, in a letter to a friend. 'Henceforth this heaven, this universe, which I had enlarged a hundred and a thousand times . . . is shrunk from me into the narrow space which I myself fill in it.' Galileo had become blind.

When he died, no one was allowed to put up a monument to his name, but we, who live hundreds of years later, cannot forget him. We profit every day by the truth he discovered but was not allowed to teach.   *Adapted by Irene Taafaki*

The Wishing Ring

Once upon a time there was a poor farmer who had a very hard time. He was resting at his work one day when an old witch passed him. She asked, 'Why do you work so hard, when you can't get on anyway? I'll tell you what to do. Walk straight ahead until you get to a great pine tree that is taller than all the trees in the forest. Chop it down and your luck will be made.'

The farmer took his axe and started out. After two days he found the pine tree. He chopped at the mighty trunk, and at the moment that the tree fell there fell from its highest tip a great bird's nest with two eggs in it.

The eggs rolled on the ground and broke. Out of one came an eaglet; out of the other fell a gold ring. The eagle grew and grew till he was half as big as the farmer. He tried his wings and as he rose he called out, 'You have delivered me from enchantment. Take the ring that fell from the egg. It is a wishing ring! Turn it on your finger, while you speak aloud your wish, and it will surely come true. But remember – there is only one wish in the ring. When that has been fulfilled, the ring will have lost its power and will be like any ordinary ring. Therefore, consider well before you make your wish, so that you may not repent later.' Then the eagle flew away.

The farmer took the ring and with joy in his heart started homeward. Towards evening he walked through the street of a little town and saw a jeweller standing before his shop, where many precious rings and jewels were shown. The farmer showed him the ring on his finger and said, 'What do you think this ring of mine is worth?' 'Not a handful of straw,' said the jeweller. 'Ha, ha!' laughed the farmer. 'You don't know everything about rings, after all.' He told him that it was a wishing ring, worth more than all the rings in the shop.

The jeweller was a greedy man and he wanted the ring. He invited the farmer to spend the night in his house and offered him supper and wine to make him drowsy. When the farmer was asleep the jeweller tiptoed in and stole the wishing ring from his finger. In its place he slipped an ordinary ring made to look like the magic ring.

The next morning after the farmer had left, the jeweller went into his biggest room, locked the door, closed the windows and drew the curtains. Then standing in the middle of the room, he turned the ring on his finger and called, 'I want a million dollars right away.'

Hardly had the words left his mouth, when it commenced to rain bright hard silver dollars, and they struck him on his head and shoulders, and kept pouring down. He screamed with pain and fright, and tried to run away, but the rain of dollars struck him down. In another minute, the floor broke through from the weight of all the money. The jeweller crashed down into the cellar while the dollars kept beating down until one million dollars had fallen. By that time the poor man was killed, and when the neighbours found him dead under the heap of money, they said, 'It's bad luck when plenty comes in bushels,' and they took the money away.

In the meantime the farmer arrived home and showed his wife the ring. 'Now we shall never want for anything,' he said. 'We have only to consider carefully what we shall wish for.' His wife asked if they could wish for another acre of land? 'Oh no,' answered the farmer. 'If we work hard for one year and have a bit of luck, I believe we can buy it.' And so it turned out. They worked so well that after a good harvest they bought the acre of land, and had some money left.

'Now,' said the farmer's wife, 'it might be good to use that wish for a cow or a horse!'

'Waste the magic wish on such a little thing? Nonsense,' said the farmer. 'We can buy them with our savings after a while.' And at the end of the year they bought the horse and cow. 'See,' said the farmer, gleefully, 'we have saved the wish for another year and still got what we wanted. We are the luckiest people.' And so it went from year to year, until his wife said impatiently, 'Whatever has come over you lately? You always used to long for things, and now when you have them, you work harder than ever. You might be a prince with chests full of gold, if you would decide on your wish.'

'Now,' said the farmer, 'we are still young and life is long. There is but one wish in the ring, and that can be made and lost so easily. Who knows what the future has in store for us, when we may really need the wish? In the meantime, we have prospered so well that all our neighbours wonder at us. So be sensible. You can spend time planning what to wish.'

Blessings had indeed come to the farmer and his people, for the harvests were fine, and the barns and lofts were full of hay and grain year after year.

After a while, the poor farmer had become a rich man who worked side by side with his men in the fields all day and in the evening sat happily with his wife and children under the trees by the door of his house and talked with his neighbours. And comfort and goodwill were about him.

The years went on, and once in a while the wife would remind her husband of the ring and the magic power that still was in it. She would make suggestions for the great wish. But each time the farmer said there was no hurry – one always did think of the best thing last, and they grew to speak less and less of the ring. The farmer himself looked at it almost daily, but he was careful not to speak any wish aloud.

Then thirty years passed and forty. The farmer and his wife grew old and grey, and then passed into a happy old age. They died on the same night within a short time of each other. The wish had not been made. Their children and grandchildren mourned them and brought flowers to lay over them. One of them noticed the ring on the farmer's hand and wanted to take it as a keepsake; but the eldest son said, 'Let us leave this ring on Father's finger. There must have been some dear remembrance connected with it, for he looked at it often.'

So when the old farmer was buried, he wore the ring which was to have been a wishing ring but was not, and which, nevertheless, brought into his home all possible happiness and good fortune.

After all, there is something peculiar about things that are true and things that are false and, in the end, a worthless thing in honest hands will always have much more value than an honest thing in worthless hands. *Folk Tale*

4

A. What does it mean to be dishonest?
B. Paul copied in the exam. Is he acting honestly?
C. Benjamin Franklin said, 'Honesty is the best policy.' What does this mean?
D. Are dishonest people happy?
E. Sam buys a book and is given extra change by mistake. He pockets this money. What do you think of his action?
F. Ravi gets into a bus and the conductor is at the other end. It is time for him to get off, so he calls the conductor and pays the fare, even though he could easily have got off without buying a ticket. What do you think about this?
G. You are doing a problem during a maths exam and just cannot solve it. Your neighbour quietly passes you the answer. What do you do?

Hospitality

1

'Be kind to the strangers . . . Help to make them feel at home
. . .'[1]   *'Abdu'l-Bahá*

'When need arises, happy (is it to have) friends . . .'[2]   *Dhammapada*

'Do not be content with showing friendship in words alone, let your
heart burn with loving kindness for all who may cross your
path.'[3]   *'Abdu'l-Bahá*

'O believers, do not enter houses other than your houses until you
first ask leave and salute the people thereof . . .'[4]   *Muḥammad*

'And above all things have fervent charity among yourselves . . .
Use hospitality one to another without grudging.'[5]
                                                    New Testament

2

'My home is the home of peace. My home is the home of joy and
delight. My home is the home of laughter and exultation.
Whosoever enters through the portals of this home, must go out
with gladsome heart. This is the home of light; whosoever enters
here must become illumined.'[6]   *'Abdu'l-Bahá*

3

Bahá'u'lláh and the Hermit

. . . once when the Blessed Perfection was travelling from one place
to another with His followers He passed through a lonely country
where, at some little distance from the highway, a hermit lived alone
in a cave. He was a holy man, and having heard that Our Lord,
Bahá'u'lláh, would pass that way, he watched eagerly for His
approach. When the Manifestation arrived at that spot the hermit
knelt down and kissed the dust before His feet, and said to Him:
'Oh, my Lord, I am a poor man living alone in a cave near by; but

henceforth I shall account myself the happiest of mortals if Thou wilt but come for a moment to my cave and bless it by Thy Presence.' Then Bahá'u'lláh told the man that He would come, not for a moment but for three days, and He bade His followers cast their tents, and await His return. The poor man was so overcome with joy and gratitude that he was speechless, and led the way in humble silence to his lowly dwelling in a rock. There the Glorious One sat with him, talking to him and teaching him, and towards evening the man bethought himself that he had nothing to offer his great Guest but some dry meat and some dark bread, and water from a spring nearby. Not knowing what to do he threw himself at the feet of his Lord and confessed his dilemma. Bahá'u'lláh comforted him and by a word bade him fetch the meat and bread and water; then the Lord of the universe partook of this frugal repast with joy and fragrance as though it had been a banquet, and during the three days of His visit they ate only of this food which seemed to the poor hermit the most delicious he had ever eaten. Bahá'u'lláh declared that He had never been more nobly entertained nor received greater hospitality and love.[7]   *May Maxwell*

The Hospitality of the Báb

The Youth who met me outside the gate of Shíráz overwhelmed me with expressions of affection and loving-kindness. He extended to me a warm invitation to visit His home, and there refresh myself after the fatigues of my journey . . .

We soon found ourselves standing at the gate of a house of modest appearance. He knocked at the door, which was soon opened by an Ethiopian servant. 'Enter therein in peace, secure,' were His words as He crossed the threshold and motioned me to follow Him . . . Immediately we were seated, He ordered a ewer of water to be brought, and bade me wash away from my hands and feet the stains of travel. I pleaded permission to retire from His presence and perform my ablutions in an adjoining room. He refused to grant my request, and proceeded to pour the water over my hands. He then gave me to drink of a refreshing beverage, after which He asked for the samovar, and Himself prepared the tea which He offered me . . .

At the third hour after sunset, my Host ordered the dinner to be served. That same Ethiopian servant appeared and spread before us the choicest food. That holy repast refreshed alike my body and soul. In the presence of my Host, at that hour, I felt as though I were feeding upon the fruits of Paradise . . . Had my youthful Host no other claim to greatness, this were sufficient – that He received me with that quality of hospitality and loving-kindness which I was convinced no other human being could possibly reveal.[8]

Mullá Ḥusayn

The story of Philemon and Baucis also demonstrates the value of hospitality (see pages 99–105).

4

A. What is hospitality?
    'Be kind to the strangers . . . Help to make them feel at home; find out where they are staying, ask if you may render them any service; try to make their lives a little happier.'[9]   *'Abdu'l-Bahá*

B. Why should we show hospitality?
    'When a man turns his face to God he finds sunshine everywhere. All men are his brothers.'[10]   *'Abdu'l-Bahá*

C. Does our shyness sometimes make us seem inhospitable?
    'Let not conventionality cause you to seem cold and unsympathetic when you meet strange people . . .'[11]   *'Abdu'l-Bahá*

D. What attributes of God are reflected in hospitality, both by hosts and guests? Think of qualities such as service, courtesy, graciousness and gratitude when you answer.

E. Does hospitality only mean providing food and accommodation to guests?

F. Do you have to be rich to be hospitable?

Humility

1

'Transgress not thy limits, nor claim that which beseemeth thee not.'[1] *Bahá'u'lláh*

'Seek you help in patience and prayer, for grievous it is, save to the humble . . .'[2] *Muhammad*

'Blessed are the meek: for they shall inherit the earth.'[3]

New Testament

'One should give up anger; one should abandon pride . . .'[4]

Dhammapada

'Be . . . a fruit upon the tree of humility.'[5] *Bahá'u'lláh*

2

'Humility exalteth man to the heaven of glory and power, whilst pride abaseth him to the depths of wretchedness and degradation.'[6] *Bahá'u'lláh*

'. . . man must become evanescent in God. Must forget his own selfish conditions that he may thus arise to the station of sacrifice. It should be to such a degree that if he sleep, it should not be for pleasure, but to rest the body in order to do better, to speak better, to explain more beautifully, to serve the servants of God and to prove the truths. When he remains awake, he should seek to be attentive, serve the Cause of God and sacrifice his own stations for those of God. When he attains to this station, the confirmations of the Holy Spirit will surely reach him, and man with this power can withstand all who inhabit the earth.'[7] *'Abdu'l-Bahá*

3

A man took his son into a beautiful garden where many people had gathered to pray. After an hour of chanting prayers, the boy looked around and observed that many of the worshippers were lost not in prayer but in sleep. He turned to his father and asked, 'Are we not better than those who are sleeping instead of praying?' The father simply replied, 'You might have been better had you not asked this question.' *Traditional*

Isfandíyár

In April 1920, in the garden of the Military Governor of Haifa, 'Abdu'l-Bahá was invested with the insignia of the Knighthood of the British Empire. That knighthood was conferred on Him in recognition of His humanitarian work during the war for the relief of distress and famine. He accepted the honour as the gift of a 'just king', but he never used the title. Lady Blomfield writes:

The dignitaries of the British crown from Jerusalem were gathered in Haifa, eager to do honour to the Master, Whom everyone had come to love and reverence for His life of unselfish service. An imposing motor-car had been sent to bring 'Abdu'l-Bahá to the ceremony. The Master, however, could not be found. People were sent in every direction to look for Him, when suddenly from an unexpected side He appeared, alone, walking His kingly walk, with that simplicity of greatness which always enfolded Him.

The faithful servant Isfandíyár, whose joy it had been for many years to drive the Master on errands of mercy, stood sadly looking on the elegant motor-car which awaited the honoured guest.

'No longer am I needed.'

At a sign from Him, Who knew the sorrow, old Isfandíyár rushed off to harness the horse, and brought the carriage out at the lower gate, whence 'Abdu'l-Bahá was driven to a side entrance of the garden of the Governorate of Phoenicia.

So Isfandíyár was needed and happy.[8] *Lady Blomfield*

The Emperor's Nightingale

Many years ago the great country of China was ruled by a mighty Emperor. The Emperor's palace was the most splendid in the world; it was made entirely of fine porcelain, very costly but so delicate and brittle that one had to take care how one touched it. In the garden were the most exquisite flowers, and to the loveliest of them were tied silver bells which tinkled in the breeze so that nobody should pass by without noticing the flowers.

The Emperor's beautifully arranged garden was so big that the gardener himself did not know where the end was. If a man went on and on, he came into a glorious forest with high trees and deep lakes. The wood extended straight down to the sea, which was blue and deep; and in the trees lived a Nightingale, which sang so splendidly that even the poor fisherman, who had many other things to do, stopped still and listened when he had gone out at night to throw out his nets.

'How beautiful that is!' he said. But he had many tasks to perform and after a while he forgot the bird. But when the bird sang on the next night, the fisherman exclaimed again, 'How beautiful that is!'

From all the countries of the world travellers came to the city of the Emperor and admired it, and the palace, and the garden; but when they heard the Nightingale, they said, 'That is the best of all!'

And the travellers told of it when they came home; and the wise men among them wrote many books about the town, the palace and the garden. But they esteemed the Nightingale highest of all. And those who were poets wrote magnificent poems about the Nightingale in the wood by the deep lake.

The books and poems went through all the world, and once some of them came to the Emperor. He sat on his golden throne and read and read. As he did so, he kept nodding his head, for it made him proud to read the masterly descriptions of the city, the palace and the garden. 'But the Nightingale is the best of all,' said all the books. And the poems extolled the bird in exquisite language.

'What's that?' exclaimed the Emperor. 'I don't know this Nightingale at all! Is there such a bird in my empire and even in my own garden? I've never heard of it. To think that I should have to learn such a thing for the first time from books!'

And hereupon he called his Cavalier. This Cavalier was so grand that if one lower in rank than himself dared to speak to him, or to ask him any question, he answered nothing but 'Tsing-pe!' and that meant nothing.

'There is said to be a wonderful bird here called a Nightingale,' said the Emperor. 'They say it is the best thing in all my great empire. Why have I never heard anything about it?'

'I have never heard him named,' replied the Cavalier. 'He has never been introduced at court.'

'I command that he shall appear this evening and sing before me,' said the Emperor. 'All the world knows what I possess, and I do not know it myself.'

'I have never heard him mentioned,' said the Cavalier. 'But I will seek him. I will find him.'

But where was this Nightingale to be found? The Cavalier ran up and down all the staircases, through halls and passages but no one among all those whom he met had heard talk of the Nightingale. The Cavalier ran back to the Emperor and said it must be a fable invented by the writers of books.

'Your Imperial Majesty cannot believe how much is written that is fiction, besides something they call the black art.'

'But the book in which I read this,' said the Emperor, 'was sent to me by the high and mighty Emperor of Japan. It cannot be falsehood. I will hear the Nightingale! It must be here this evening! It has my imperial favour; and if it does not come, all the court shall be trampled upon after the court has supped!'

'Tsing-pe!' said the Cavalier; and again he ran up and down all the staircases and through all the halls and corridors; and half the court ran with him, for the courtiers did not like the idea of being trampled upon.

Then there was a great inquiry after the wonderful Nightingale, which all the world knew excepting the people at the Emperor's court.

At last they met a poor little girl in the kitchen, who said, 'The Nightingale? I know it well, yes, and it can sing gloriously. Every evening I get leave to carry my poor sick mother the scraps from the table. She lives down by the strand, and when I get back tired, and rest in the wood, then I hear the Nightingale sing. And then the tears come into my eyes, and it is just as if my mother kissed me!'

'Little kitchen girl,' said the Cavalier, 'I will get you a better place in the kitchen, one where you can see the Emperor dine, if you will lead us to the Nightingale, for it is demanded for this evening.'

So they all went out into the wood where the Nightingale was accustomed to sing. Half the court went forth. When they were in the midst of their journey the cows began to moo.

'Oh!' cried the court pages. 'Now we have it! That shows a wonderful power in so small a creature! I have certainly heard it before.'

'No, those are cows mooing!' said the little kitchen girl. 'We are a long way from the place yet.'

Now the frogs began to croak in the marsh.

'Glorious!' said the Chinese court preacher. 'Now I hear it – it sounds just like temple bells.'

'No, those are frogs!' said the little kitchen maid. 'But now I think we shall soon hear it.'

Then the Nightingale began to sing.

'That is it!' exclaimed the little girl. 'Listen, listen! Yonder it sits.' And she pointed to a little grey bird.

'Is it possible?' cried the Cavalier. 'I should never have thought it looked like that! How simple it looks! It must certainly have lost its colour at seeing such grand people around.'

'Little Nightingale!' called the kitchen maid. 'Our gracious Emperor wishes you to sing before him. Will you?'

'With the greatest pleasure!' replied the Nightingale, and began to sing most delightfully.

'It sounds just like crystal bells!' said the Cavalier. 'And look at its little throat, how it's working! It's wonderful that we should never have heard it before. That bird will be a great success at court.'

'Shall I sing once more before the Emperor?' asked the Nightingale, for the bird thought the Emperor was present.

'My excellent little Nightingale,' said the Cavalier. 'I have great pleasure in inviting you to a court festival this evening, when you shall charm his Imperial Majesty with your beautiful singing.'

'My song sounds best in the green wood!' replied the Nightingale. Still it came willingly when it heard what the Emperor wished.

The place was festively adorned. The walls and the floor, which were of porcelain, gleamed in the rays of thousands of golden lamps. The most glorious flowers, which could ring clearly, had been placed in the passages. There was a running to and fro, and all the bells rang so loudly in the breeze that one could not hear oneself speak.

In the midst of the great hall, where the Emperor sat, a golden perch had been placed for the Nightingale. The whole court was there, and the little cook-maid had got leave to stand behind the door, as she had now received the title of a real court cook. All were in full dress, and all looked at the little grey bird.

The Nightingale sang so gloriously that the tears came into the Emperor's eyes and ran down his cheeks. And when the Nightingale sang still more sweetly, the Emperor was so pleased that he said the Nightingale should have his golden slipper to wear around its neck. But the Nightingale declined this with thanks, saying, 'I have seen tears in the Emperor's eyes – that is the real treasure to me. And Emperor's tears have a peculiar power. I am rewarded enough!' Then the Nightingale sang again with a sweet, glorious voice.

'Of all the coquetry!' exclaimed the ladies who stood round about, and they took water in their mouths to gurgle when anyone spoke to them. They thought they would sound like nightingales too. And the lackeys and chambermaids reported they were satisfied too; and that was saying a good deal, for they are the most difficult to please. In short, the Nightingale achieved a real success.

The bird was now to remain at court, to have its own cage, with liberty to go out twice every day and once at night. Twelve servants were appointed when the Nightingale went out, each of whom held a silken string fastened to the bird's leg. There was really no pleasure in an excursion of that kind.

The whole city spoke of the wonderful bird, and when two people met, one said nothing but 'Nightin,' and the other said 'gale'; and then they sighed and understood each other. Eleven pedlars' children were named after the bird, but not one of them could sing a note.

One day the Emperor received a large parcel on which was written 'The Nightingale'.

'This must be a new book about this celebrated bird,' said the Emperor.

It was not a book, however, but a little work of art, contained in a box, an artificial nightingale, which was designed to sing like a natural one, and was brilliantly ornamented with diamonds, rubies, and sapphires. As soon as the artificial bird was wound up, he could sing one of the pieces that the real Nightingale sang, and his tail moved up and down and shone with silver and gold. Around his neck hung a little ribbon, and on it was written, 'The Nightingale of the Emperor of China is poor compared to that of the Emperor of Japan.'

'Is that so!' said they all, and he who had brought the artificial bird immediately received the title Imperial Head-Nightingale-Bringer.

'Now the two must sing together; what a duet that will be!' they said.

And so the two birds had to sing together; but it did not sound very well, for the real Nightingale sang in its own way, and the artificial bird sang in another.

So they tried having the artificial bird sing alone. It had just as much success as the real one, and besides it was much handsomer to look at as it shone like necklaces and bracelets.

Three and thirty times over the bird sang the same song, and yet was not tired. The people would gladly have heard it again, but the Emperor said that the living Nightingale ought to sing something now.

But where was the living Nightingale? No one had noticed that it had flown from its cage, out of the open window, and back to the green wood!

All the courtiers abused the Nightingale and declared that it was a very ungrateful creature.

'We have the best bird, after all,' said they. And the artificial bird had to sing again, and that was the thirty-fourth time they listened to the same piece. And the playmaster praised the bird particularly, declaring that it was better than the real Nightingale, not only because of its plumage and the many beautiful diamonds, but as a singer as well.

'For you see, ladies and gentlemen, and above all, your Imperial Majesty, with the real Nightingale one can never calculate what is coming, but in this artificial bird everything is settled. One can explain it; one can open it and make people understand where the songs come from, how they go, and how one follows another.'

'Those are quite our own ideas,' they all said.

And the speaker received permission to show the bird to the people on the next Sunday. The people were to hear it sing, too, the Emperor commanded; and they did hear it, and were as much pleased as if they had all got tipsy upon tea, for that's quite the Chinese fashion; and they all said 'Oh!' and held up their fore-fingers and nodded. But the poor fisherman, who had heard the real Nightingale, said, 'It sounds well enough, and the melodies resemble each other, but there's something wanting, I know not what!'

The real Nightingale was banished from the country and empire. The artificial bird had its place on a silken cushion close to the Emperor's bed. All the presents it had received, gold and precious stones, were ranged about it. In title it had advanced to be the High Imperial After-Dinner-Singer, and in rank to number one on the left hand; for the Emperor considered that side the more important on which the heart is placed, for even in an Emperor the heart is on the left side. And the playmaster wrote a work of five and twenty volumes about the artificial bird. It was very learned and very long; yet all the people declared they had read it and understood it, for fear of being considered stupid.

So a whole year went by. The Emperor, the court, and all the other Chinese knew every little twitter in the artificial bird's song by heart. But just for that reason it pleased them best: they could sing it themselves, and they did so. The street boys sang, 'Tsi-tsi-tsi-glug-glug!' and the Emperor himself sang it too.

But one evening, when the artificial bird was singing and the Emperor lay in bed listening to it, something inside the bird said 'Whizz!' Something cracked.

'Whirr-r-r!' All the wheels ran round and then the music stopped.

The Emperor immediately sprang out of bed and caused his physician to be called. But what could he do?

Then they sent for a watchmaker and, after a good deal of talking and investigating, the bird was put into something like order. But the watchmaker said the bird must be carefully treated, for the barrels were worn, and it would be impossible to put new ones in so that the music would go. There was a great lamentation; only once in a year was the bird allowed to sing, and that was almost too much. But then the playmaster made a little speech, full of long words, and said the bird was just as good as before and so, of course, it was.

Now five years have gone by, and a real grief came upon the whole nation. The Chinese were really fond of their Emperor; and now he was ill and, it was said, could not live much longer. Already a new Emperor had been chosen, and the people stood out in the street and asked the Cavalier how their old Emperor did.

'Tsing-pe!' said he, and shook his head.

Cold and pale lay the Emperor in his great gorgeous bed. The whole court thought him dead, and each one ran to pay homage to the new ruler.

All about, in all the halls and passages, cloth had been laid down so that no foot-step could be heard, and therefore it was quiet there, very quiet. But the Emperor was not dead yet.

High up, a window stood open, and the moon shone in upon the Emperor and the artificial bird.

The poor Emperor could scarcely breathe; it was as if something lay upon his chest. He opened his eyes, and then he saw that it was Death who sat upon his chest, and had put on his golden crown, and held in one hand the Emperor's sword, and in the other his beautiful banner. And all around, from among the folds of the splendid velvet curtains, strange heads peered forth, a few very ugly, the rest quite lovely and mild. These were the Emperor's bad and good deeds, and they stood before him now that Death sat upon his heart.

'Do you remember this?' whispered one to the other. 'Do you remember that?' and they told him so much that the perspiration ran from his forehead.

In distress the Emperor cried, 'Music! Music!' And to the artificial nightingale he called, 'You little golden bird, sing, sing! I have given you gold and costly presents; I have even hung my golden slipper around your neck – sing for me now, sing!'

But the bird stood still. No one was there to wind him up and he could not sing without that. And Death continued to stare at the Emperor with his great hollow eyes, and it was fearfully quiet.

Then there sounded from the window, suddenly, the most lovely song. It was the little live Nightingale who was sitting outside on a spray. The little grey bird had heard of the Emperor's sad plight and had come to sing to him of comfort and hope. And as it sang the spectres grew paler and paler; the blood ran quicker and more quickly through the Emperor's weak limbs; and even Death listened, and said,

'Sing on, little Nightingale, sing on!'

'But will you, Death, give me the Emperor's golden sword? Will you give me his rich banner? Will you give me his crown?' sang the Nightingale.

Then Death gave up each of these treasures for a song. The Nightingale sang on and on; it sang of the quiet churchyard gardens where white roses grow, where the elder blossom smells sweet, and where the fresh grass is moistened by the tears of those mourning their loved ones. At last Death felt a longing to see his garden, and he floated out of the window in the form of a cold white mist.

'Thank you, thank you!' cried the Emperor. 'You heavenly little bird! I know you well. I banished you from my country and empire, and yet you have charmed away the evil faces from my couch and banished Death from my heart! How can I reward you?'

'You have rewarded me!' replied the Nightingale. 'I drew tears from your eyes when I sang the first time – I shall never forget that. Those are the jewels that rejoice a singer's heart. But now sleep and grow strong again. I will sing you something.'

And the Nightingale sang, and the Emperor fell into a sweet slumber. How refreshing that sleep was! The sun shone upon him through the windows, when he awoke refreshed and restored. Not one of his servants had yet returned, for they all thought he was dead. Only the Nightingale still sat beside him and sang.

'You must always stay with me,' said the Emperor. 'You will sing as you please, and the artificial bird shall be broken into a thousand pieces.'

'Not so,' replied the Nightingale. 'It did well as long it could. Keep it as you have done till now. I cannot build my nest in the palace to dwell in it; I must live in the woods. But let me come when you need me. Then I will sit in the evening on the spray yonder by the window and sing you something so that you may be glad and thoughtful at once. I will sing of those who are happy and of those who suffer. As a little singing bird I fly far around, to the poor fisherman, to the peasant's roof, to everyone who dwells far away from you and from your court. I will come and sing to you. But one thing I beg of you: tell no one that you have a bird who tells you everything.'

The Emperor promised happily, with all his heart, and the Nightingale flew away.

Next morning the servants came in to pay their last respects to their Emperor, who they believed was dead. But there he stood, alive and happy and smiling, and he greeted them with a hearty 'Good morning!'   *Hans Christian Andersen*

4

A. In what way was the Emperor proud?
B. Who taught the Emperor humility?

C. Do you think the Emperor became happier at the end of the story?

D. Meditate upon and discuss: 'O Children of Men! Know ye not why We created you all from the same dust? That no one should exalt himself over the other.'[9]   *Bahá'u'lláh*

E. How are we all created from the same dust? Why is it wrong for us to exalt ourselves over another person?

F. Bahá'u'lláh says, 'Vaunt not thyself over the poor . . .'[10] Is it only the poor over whom we should not vaunt ourselves? How about people from other countries?

Joy

1

'Whoso keepeth the commandments of God shall attain everlasting felicity.'[1]   *Bahá'u'lláh*

'Joy comes from God. Who could live and could breathe if the joy of Brahman filled not the universe?'[2]   *Taitiriya Upanishad*

'Joy gives us wings! In times of joy our strength is more vital, our intellect keener, and our understanding less clouded.'[3]
'Abdu'l-Bahá

'Likewise, I say unto you, there is joy in the presence of the angels of God over one sinner that repenteth.'[4]   *New Testament*

'. . . let the tidings of the revelation of Thine incorruptible Essence bring me joy . . .'[5]   *Bahá'u'lláh*

2

'The honour of man is through the attainment of the knowledge of God; his happiness is from the love of God; his joy is the glad tidings of God; his greatness is dependent upon his servitude to God.'[6]
'Abdu'l-Bahá

'And ye now therefore have sorrow: but I will see you again, and your heart shall rejoice and your joy no man taketh from you.'[7]
New Testament

'O God! Refresh and gladden my spirit. Purify my heart. Illumine my powers. I lay all my affairs in Thy hand. Thou art my Guide and my Refuge. I will no longer be sorrowful and grieved. I will be a happy and joyful being. I will no longer be full of anxiety, nor will I let trouble harass me. I will not dwell on the unpleasant things of life.

'O God! Thou art more friend to me than I am to myself. I dedicate myself to Thee, O Lord.'[8]   *'Abdu'l-Bahá*

In the *Taitiriya Upanishad*, Bhrigu Varuni asks his father to explain the mystery of Brahman, the mystery of the Universe. In the end Bhrigu Varuni sees the truth expressed in these words:

'And then he saw that Brahman is joy: for from joy all beings have come, by joy they all live, and unto joy they all return.'[9]

Taitiriya Upanishad

3

A Little Song of Life

Glad that I live am I;
    That the sky is blue;
Glad for the country lanes,
    And the fall of dew.

After the sun the rain,
    After the rain the sun;
This is the way of life,
    Till the work be done.

All that we need to do,
    Be we low or high,
Is to see that we grow
    Nearer the sky.

Lizette Woodworth Reese

Afternoon on a Hill

I will be the gladdest thing
    Under the sun!
I will touch a hundred flowers
    And not pick one.

I will look at cliffs and clouds
    With quiet eyes,
Watch the wind bow down the grass,
    And watch the grass rise.

And when lights begin to show
    Up from the town,

I will mark which must be mine,
    And then start down.

Edna St Vincent Millay

Barter

Life has loveliness to sell,
    All beautiful and splendid things,
Blue waves whitened on a cliff,
    Soaring fire that sways and sings,
And children's faces looking up
Holding wonder like a cup.

Life has loveliness to sell,
    Music like a curve of gold,
Scent of pine trees in the rain,
    Eyes that love you, arms that hold,
And for your spirit's still delight,
Holy thoughts that star the night.

Spend all you have for loveliness,
    Buy it and never count the cost;
For one white singing hour of peace,
    Count many a year of strife well lost,
And for a breath of ecstasy,
Give all you have been, or could be.

Sara Teasdale

4

A. What are the glad-tidings of God? How can these glad-tidings bring joy?
B. Why are cheerful people usually popular?
C. Anyone can be cheerful when everything is going well. Can we also be joyful when things are not going our way?
D. Cheerful, joyful people are often optimistic. What is an optimist?

Justice

1

'Verily justice is My gift to thee and the sign of My loving-kindness. Set it then before Thine eyes.'[1] *Bahá'u'lláh*

'. . . the path of the just is as the shining light . . .'[2] *Old Testament*

'Surely God bids to justice and good-doing and giving to kinsmen . . .'[3] *Muḥammad*

2

'He is not thereby "just" because he hastily arbitrates. The wise man should investigate both right and wrong. The intelligent man . . . leads others not falsely but lawfully and impartially . . .'[4]
Dhammapada

'O Son of Spirit! The best beloved of all things in My sight is Justice; turn not away therefrom if thou desirest Me, and neglect it not that I may confide in thee. By its aid thou shalt see with thine own eyes and not through the eyes of others, and shalt know of thine own knowledge and not through the knowledge of thy neighbour. Ponder this in thy heart; how it behoveth thee to be. Verily justice is My gift to thee and the sign of My loving-kindness. Set it then before thine eyes.'[5] *Bahá'u'lláh*

3

The Endless Tale

In the Far East, many years ago, there was a great King who had no work to do. Every day, and all day long, he sat on soft cushions and listened to story-tellers telling made-up stories. And no matter what the story was about, he never grew tired of hearing it, even though it was very long.

'There is only one fault that I find with your story,' he often said to a story-teller. 'It is too short.'

All the story-tellers in the world were invited to his palace; and some of them told tales that went on and on and on. But no matter how long a story was, the King was always sad when it ended.

At last he sent a message into every city and town and country place, offering a prize to anyone who would tell him an endless tale.

'To the man who will tell me a story which shall last forever,' he wrote, 'I will give my lovely daughter for his wife; and I will make the man my heir, and he shall be King after me.'

But this was not the whole message. He added a very hard condition: 'If any man shall try to tell such a story and fail, he shall have his head cut off.'

The King's daughter was very pretty, and there were many young men in that country who were willing to do anything to win her. But none of them wanted to lose their heads, so only a few tried for the prize.

One day a stranger came to the Kingdom. He heard of the King's challenge and he decided that he would try his luck. He went to the King's palace.

'Great King,' he said, 'is it true that you offer a prize to the man who can tell a story that has no end?'

'It is true,' said the King.

'And shall this man have your lovely daughter for his wife, and shall he be your heir and become the King after you?'

'Yes, if he succeeds,' said the old King. 'But if he fails, he shall lose his head.'

'Very well, then,' said the stranger. 'I have a pleasant story about locusts which I should like to relate.'

'Tell it,' said the King. 'I will listen to you.'

The story-teller began his tale. This is what he said:

'Once upon a time a certain King seized upon all the corn in his country and stored it away in a strong granary. But a swarm of locusts came over the land and saw where the grain had been put. After searching for many days they found on the east side of the granary a crack that was just large enough for one locust to pass through at a time. So one locust went in and carried away a grain of corn; then another locust went in and carried away a grain of corn; then another locust went in and carried away a grain of corn.'

Day after day, week after week, the strange story-teller kept on saying, 'Then another locust went in and carried away a grain of corn.'

A month passed; a year passed.

At the end of two years, the King said, 'How much longer will the locusts be going in and carrying away corn?'

'O King,' said the story-teller, 'they have as yet cleared only one cubit, and there are many thousand cubits in the granary.'

'Man, man!' cried the King, 'You will drive me mad! I can listen to it no longer. Take my daughter, be my heir, rule my kingdom. But do not let me hear another word about those horrible locusts!'

And so the story-teller married the King's daughter. And he and his bride lived happily in the land for many years. But his father-in-law, the King, did not care to listen to any more stories.

Guinea Fowl and Rabbit get Justice

Somewhere between the Kong mountains and the sea the bird named Guinea Fowl had his farm. It was a good farm. Guinea Fowl worked hard on it and grew fine yams and bananas. He grew beans and okra, millet and tobacco. His farm always looked green and prosperous. Mostly it was because Guinea Fowl was a hard worker. Not very far away Rabbit had a farm. It wasn't a very good farm because Rabbit never worked too hard. He planted at planting time, but he never hoed his crops or pulled out the weeds that grew there. So when harvest time came along there wasn't very much okra or beans or millet.

One day Rabbit was out walking and he saw Guinea Fowl's farm. It looked so much better than his own that he wished he owned it. He thought it over. He became indignant.

'Why is it that it rains over here on Guinea Fowl's land and not on mine so that his crops grow and mine don't?' he asked himself. 'It's not fair!'

He thought all day. And a wonderful idea came to him.

That night he brought out his wife and his children and marched them to Guinea Fowl's farm, then he marched them back again. He did it again. All night his family went back and forth from their house to Guinea Fowl's farm, until by morning they had made a trail. In the morning they started pulling up Guinea Fowl's vegetables and putting them in baskets.

When Guinea Fowl came to work he saw Rabbit there with his family, pulling up all the fine crops he had planted.

'What are you doing with my yams and okra?' Guinea Fowl said. 'And what are you doing on my farm, anyway?'

'Your farm?' Rabbit said. 'There must be some mistake. It's my farm.

'I guess there is a mistake. It's my farm. I planted it and I weeded it and I hoed it,' Guinea Fowl said. 'So I don't see how it can be your farm.'

'How could you plant it and weed it and hoe it when I planted it and weeded it and hoed it?' Rabbit said.

Guinea Fowl was very angry.

'You'd better get off my place,' Rabbit said.

'It's absurd,' Guinea Fowl said.

'It certainly is,' Rabbit said, 'when any old Guinea Fowl can come and claim someone else's property.'

'It's mine,' Guinea Fowl said.

'It's mine,' Rabbit said.

'Well, I'll take the case to the chief,' Guinea Fowl said.

'It's a good idea,' Rabbit said.

So the two of them picked up their hoes and went to the village to the house of the chief.

'This fellow is pulling up my vegetables,' Guinea Fowl said, 'and he won't get off my farm.'

'He's trying to take advantage of me,' Rabbit said. 'I work and work to grow fine yams and then he comes along and wants to own them.'

They argued and argued while the head man listened. Finally they went out together to look the situation over.

'Where is the trail from your house?' the head man asked Rabbit.

'There,' Rabbit said and pointed out the one he had just made.

'And where is the trail from your house?' the head man asked Guinea Fowl.

'Trail? I never had a trail,' Guinea Fowl said.

'Whenever anyone has a farm he has a trail to it from his house,' the head man said.

'But whenever I come to work my farm I fly,' Guinea Fowl said.

The head man thought. He shook his head.

'If a person has a farm he has to have a trail to it,' he said after a while. 'So the land must belong to Rabbit.'

He went away. Rabbit and his family began to pull up more yams. Guinea Fowl went home, feeling very angry.

When Rabbit had a large basket full of vegetables he started off to market with them. But the basket was very heavy. He wasn't used to heavy work because he was lazy. After he had carried his load a little distance along the road he put it down and rested. And while he sat by the roadside Guinea Fowl came along.

'Ah friend Rabbit, your load is very heavy,' Guinea Fowl said sweetly. 'Perhaps I can give you a lift with it.'

Rabbit was touched. Guinea Fowl wasn't angry any more. He was very friendly.

'Thank you,' he said. 'You are a real friend to help me with my vegetables.'

So Guinea Fowl put the load on his head. He smiled at Rabbit. Then he flapped his wings and went off with the load, not on to the market but to his own house.

Rabbit shouted. He ran after Guinea Fowl, but he couldn't catch him. Guinea Fowl soared over the fields and was gone.

Rabbit was angry. He went back to the village to find the head man.

'Guinea Fowl has robbed me!' he shouted. 'He flew away with my basket of vegetables!'

The head man sent for Guinea Fowl.

'They were mine,' Rabbit shouted. 'I harvested them with my own hands!

They argued and argued. The head man thought and thought.

'Well,' he said at last, 'when people carry things a great deal on their heads, after a while the hair gets thin from so much carrying.' The people of the village said yes, that always happened.

'Let me see the top of your head,' the head man said to Rabbit.

Rabbit showed him. The head man clicked his tongue.

'No,' he said to Rabbit, 'your hair is thick and long.'

He turned to Guinea Fowl.

'Let me see yours,' he said, and Guinea Fowl showed him.

Guinea Fowl's head didn't have even a fuzzy feather on it.

'It must belong to you,' the head man said, 'you are absolutely bald.'

'But Guinea Fowl never had any feathers on his head!' Rabbit complained. 'He was always bald!'

'When you carry things on your head the hair becomes thin,' the head man said. 'So the basket belongs to Guinea Fowl.'

They went away. Rabbit prepared another basket of vegetables to take to market. And when he set it down by the side of the road and rested, Guinea Fowl swooped down and took it away. Rabbit prepared another basket, and the same thing happened. It was no use going to the head man any more because Guinea Fowl's head was so bald.

At last Rabbit got tired of pulling up Guinea Fowl's vegetables for him, and he went back to his own farm to work for himself.

That is why people sometimes say, 'The shortest path often goes nowhere.' *Adapted by Irene Taafaki*

4

A. How can we develop a just attitude towards all situations and problems?

B. What is your idea of a problem settled in haste? Is such a settlement usually permanent? What feelings do you usually have towards the person with whom you have had a violent, maybe even physical, quarrel?

C. What is the advantage of seeing 'with thine own eyes and not through the eyes of others'?

D. Can you see why justice is God's gift to us?

E. In what way does happiness and success depend upon good judgement and the ability to make wise decisions?

F. What are some of the dangers of making 'snap' decisions?

Older students may be interested in this system for making reasonable judgements. We cannot expect very skilful evaluations from them at first, but we can try to show what is admissible as evidence and what is not. Preconceived ideas (especially about people from other cultures) and personal wishes look pretty weak in cold black and white.

Method: the idea is to make two lists, one for all the good reasons one can think of for the proposed course of action or way of behaving (depending on the situation) and the other list against it. This should be done thoughtfully without prejudice. Then you balance the importance of one list against the other and decide accordingly.

For younger children

Talk about being fair rather than being just.

G. Is it fair to take away someone's possession just because you need it?

H. Is it fair to strike or abuse a person simply because he annoyed you?

I. Is it fair not to make friends with someone just because they look different from you?

Kindness

1

'A kindly tongue is the lodestone of the hearts of men.'[1]

Bahá'u'lláh

'Honourable words, and forgiveness, are better than a freewill offering followed by injury . . .'[2]   *Muḥammad*

'Conquer anger by love; conquer evil by good . . .'[3]   *Dhammapada*

'With the eye of a friend do we regard one another.'[4]   *Yajur Veda*

'And to godliness [add] brotherly kindness, and to brotherly kindness, charity,'[5]   *New Testament*

2

'In a little wrath I hid my face from thee for a moment; but with everlasting kindness will I have mercy on thee, saith the Lord, thy Redeemer.'[6]   *Old Testament*

'For the mountains shall depart, and the hills be removed; but my kindness shall not depart from thee, neither shall the covenant of my peace be removed, saith the Lord that hath mercy on thee.'[7]

Old Testament

'Let him be cordial in his ways and refined in conduct; thereby full of joy he will make an end of ill.'[8]   *Dhammapada*

'When a man turns his face to God he finds sunshine everywhere. All men are his brothers. Let not conventionality cause you to seem cold and unsympathetic when you meet strange people from other countries. Do not look at them as though you suspected them of being evil-doers, thieves and boors . . .

'I ask you not to think only of yourselves. Be kind to the strangers, whether they come from Turkey, Japan, Persia, Russia, China or any other country in the world.

'Help to make them feel at home; find out where they are staying, ask if you may render them any service; try to make their lives a little happier.

'In this way, even if, sometimes, what you first suspected should be true, still go out of your way to be kind to them – this kindness will help them to become better . . .

'What profit is there in agreeing that universal friendship is good, and talking of the solidarity of the human race as a grand ideal? Unless these thoughts are translated into the world of action, they are useless.'[9] *'Abdu'l-Bahá*

3

[An Afghan] nourished a great enmity against the Master . . . he denounced him with bitter words.

'This man,' he said to all, 'is an imposter. Why do you speak to him? Why do you have dealings with him?' And when he passed the Master on the street he was careful to hold his robe before his face that his sight might not be defiled.

Thus did the Afghan. The Master, however, did thus:

The Afghan was poor and lived in a mosque; he was frequently in need of food and clothing. The Master sent him both. These he accepted, but without thanks. He fell sick. The Master took him a physician, food, medicine, money. These, also, he accepted; but as he held out one hand that the physician might take his pulse, with the other he held his cloak before his face that he might not look

upon the Master. For twenty-four years the Master continued his kindness and the Afghan persisted in his enmity. Then at last one day the Afghan came to the Master's door, and fell down, penitent and weeping, at his feet.

'Forgive me, sir,' he cried. 'For twenty-four years I have done evil to you, for twenty-four years you have done good to me. Now I know that I have been in the wrong.'

The Master bade him rise, and they became friends.[10] *Phelps*

'Let your heart burn with loving-kindness for all who may cross your path.' The above words of the Master during His visit to Paris were exemplified in His life, whether as a prisoner or a free man. As Shoghi Effendi, the Guardian of the Bahá'í Faith, wrote of Him, He was 'incomparable in the spontaneity, the genuineness and warmth of His sympathy and loving-kindness shown to friend and stranger alike, believer and unbeliever, rich and poor, high and low, whom He met, either intimately or casually, whether on board ship, or whilst pacing the streets, in parks or public squares, at receptions or banquets, in slums or mansions, in the gatherings of His followers or the assemblage of the learned, He, the incarnation of every Bahá'í virtue and the embodiment of every Bahá'í ideal . . .' As one of His early admirers in the United States noted, 'He manifested what others mouthed.'[11] *Honnold*

4

A. How is God's kindness shown to us as individuals and to all mankind in general?

B. How is it that when we show kindness to others we can bring joy to ourselves?

C. What are some of the things we might do to show kindness to our family members? to our friends? to strangers?

Knowledge

1

'The source of all learning is the knowledge of God, exalted be His Glory, and this cannot be attained save through the knowledge of His Divine Manifestation.'[1] *Bahá'u'lláh*

'Knowledge is one of the greatest benefits of God. To acquire knowledge is incumbent on all.'[2] *Bahá'u'lláh*

'Whoso makes the mind better, and performs good works, he [acts] according to the law with word and deed, wealth unites itself with him . . .'[3] *Yaçna*

'Are they equal – those who know and those who know not?'[4]
Muḥammad

'. . . knowledge is a veritable treasure for man, and a source of glory, of bounty, of joy, of exaltation, of cheer and gladness unto him.'[5] *Bahá'u'lláh*

'The man of little learning grows old like the bull: his muscles grow, his wisdom grows not.'[6] *Dhammapada*

2

'They lead the trained (horses or elephants) to an assembly. The king mounts the trained; best among men are the trained who endure abuse. Excellent are trained mules, so are thoroughbreds of Sindh and noble elephants, the tuskers; but far more excellent is he that trains himself.'[7] *Dhammapada*

'How great the multitude of truths which the garment of words can never contain! How vast the number of such verities as no expression can adequately describe, whose significance can never be unfolded, and to which not even the remotest allusions can be made! How manifold are the truths which must remain unuttered until the appointed time is come! Even as it hath been said: "Not everything that a man knoweth can be disclosed, nor can everything that he can disclose be regarded as timely, nor can every timely utterance be considered as suited to the capacity of those who hear it. "

'Of these truths some can be disclosed only to the extent of the capacity of the repositories of the light of Our knowledge, and the recipients of Our hidden grace. We beseech God to strengthen thee with His power, and enable thee to recognise Him Who is the Source of all knowledge, that thou mayest detach thyself from all human learning . . . Cleave to the Root of Knowledge . . .'[8]

Bahá'u'lláh

3

Thomas Edison

Samuel Edison came through the kitchen door and spoke to his wife. She was bending over the oven of her big black coal stove, sticking a straw into a cake to see if it was done.

'Nancy,' said Mr Edison, 'I'm bothered about Tommy. I don't think he has good sense.'

Nancy Edison stood up and answered, 'Yes he has. He's a bright child.'

'But listen,' said Tommy's father, 'do you know what he's doing now? He's squatting down on a nest of duck eggs. He expects them to hatch out. And it's mighty cold out there in the barn.'

Nancy flung a shawl over her head and hurried out to the barn. There sat little Tommy, all scrunched up on a nest of eggs. His face was blue with cold, but when his mother made him leave the nest he cried with disappointment. He was only four.

'Why did you sit on those eggs, Tommy?' she asked as she hurried him indoors.

'I wanted to know,' said Tommy. 'I wanted to find out if I would do instead of the duck.' He was saying what he was to say all the rest of his life: 'I want to know.'

The Edisons' kitchen was warm and pleasant. All their friends called it 'a nice kitchen'. It was, too, for a small town in Ohio in 1851. But to a boy or girl of today it would seem very old-fashioned. On a dresser to one side stood a row of kerosene lamps. Tommy watched his mother as she lighted two of the biggest.

'Your father had a time cleaning these out this morning. The chimneys got all smoked up when you turned the wick too high last night.

'Now Tommy, you keep away from those lamps before you set us all on fire. Sit down now. Here's a good hot cup of cocoa to warm you up.'

Tommy sat on a chair drinking the cocoa, but not thinking about it. His bright blue eyes followed his mother as she worked over the big hot iron stove. She lifted a lid, looked at the fire, and said, worried, 'I'm afraid the fire went down too soon. I hope that cake won't fall.'

In a hurry she picked up some coal in a small shovel and poured it through the open lid of the stove. 'Now my hands are all black,' she groaned as she stood and watched the stove to make sure it reached the right heat. 'Better turn up the damper now,' she said, pushing a lever on the chimney.

'Mother,' said Tommy suddenly. 'Why don't you have a longer handle on that coal shovel so you don't have to bend so much?'

Mrs Edison was astonished. 'Why, that would be a good idea,' she smiled. 'I wonder why I never thought of it.'

She could not know that her little boy, with his wide-open blue eyes and his broad smiling face, would think of things, when he grew up, that would astonish a great many people. She could not dream that because of Tommy's ideas mothers would not have to shovel coal into cook stoves, that fathers would not have to spend hours cleaning messy oil lamps. Nancy Edison could not look into the future when women would not have to carry great kettles of hot water from stove to washtub. She could not know that from the brain of that blond head would come electric lights and electric washing machines. And all because Tommy wanted to know, and asked questions, and then figured out a new and better way to do things.

When Tommy was seven, the Edison family moved to Huron, Michigan, where Tommy went to school for the first time. After two months his teacher sent for Mrs Edison.

'This child is stupid,' said the teacher. 'He can't learn. He won't even try. He's not a bad boy, but he sits making drawings – not pretty drawings, but things that look like machines. Only they don't look like anything I ever saw.'

Mrs Edison was used to such remarks about her boy. But she knew better. She answered calmly, 'He is not stupid. But you haven't any way here to teach him what he wants to know. You have a class full of children of all ages and many chores to do. I myself have six children all older than Tom. But I will find the time to teach him.'

The teacher thought Mrs Edison was one of those foolish mothers who spoil their children. 'She'll find out,' she said to herself as Mrs Edison led her boy out of the school.

There was one special thing that bothered many a school teacher at that time. The children, like all children, liked to sing. Some schools had a little organ which the teacher would play. Sometimes the teacher led the singing. But most of the teachers could not play an organ or sing very well and it was hard to teach music to the children. When he became a man this boy who was supposed to be stupid was going to invent the phonograph and phonograph records. Through them he would give everybody music, everywhere and at any time. Today we are so used to the wonders of the record player that it's hard for us to think of a world without music that is available whenever anybody wants to hear it.

After Tommy left that school he never went to another. But with his mother's teaching he learned fast. Besides, he was always learning on his own. He was so curious about everything that by the time he was ten he was reading exciting books about history and science. He was always busy. The cellar of the Edison house was crowded with jars and bottles and queer smells from his experiments. They didn't all turn out well. Once he set the cellar on fire and almost blew himself up. With all his learning he was not solemn. He laughed often, with a great roar of joy.

By the time Tom was twelve years old his experiments were beginning to cost a good deal of money and the Edisons had little to spare. He made up his mind to earn the money he needed and he went to see the superintendent of the Grand Trunk Railroad that ran through his home town.

Tommy got a job as a candy and news 'butcher'. This didn't have anything to do with meat. It is what people called a boy who went through a train selling magazines and newspapers and candy. Tom did well with this 'butcher' job and soon added fruit and vegetables he picked himself. And after a while he got other boys to work for him. He never put on airs with them or acted like a boss and he gave them their fair share of what he got. They all had fun together.

Two very bad things happened to Tom on the train. Once a brakeman, trying to help the boy get on a moving train, pulled him by his ears. The wrench hurt the ears badly and Tom became partially deaf. He never got his hearing back. But he took his deafness well. He said it kept him from hearing things that didn't matter, and made it easy for him to keep his mind on his work.

The other bad thing was this. Tom had set up a laboratory in the baggage car where he tried out experiments while the train was running. One day a jar fell on the floor and broke, and fire swept through the car. The trainman said, 'Goodbye Tom, you're fired,' and that ended his life as a 'butcher' boy on the trains.

But before that, something happened that set him out on his real career as an inventor. It was this way. The railroad telegraph operators were Tom's great friends. He gave them left-over magazines and candy. One day when Tom was talking to Mr Mackenzie at the telegraph office, a baby ran out on the track in front of a freight car that was coming down a hill. Instantly Tom Edison dashed out, grabbed the baby, threw him to safety, and then fell sprawling himself and almost lost a leg. The baby belonged to Mr Mackenzie who was so grateful that he gave Tom the thing he wanted most at that time. He taught Tom how to be a telegraph operator.

That was wonderful. Tom was only sixteen but he studied day and night and got his first job as a telegraph operator on the Grand Trunk Railroad. As always, he kept trying out new things. Samuel Morse had invented the telegraph, but there were more messages than the wires could take because each wire could send only one message at a time. The railroad men said Tom was wasting time on something that didn't make sense. But he eventually found a way to send two messages one way and two messages the other way, all on one wire.

Tom Edison was now eighteen, but even after his great discovery about the telegraph messages, he had trouble getting people to believe in him. One reason was that he never cared how he looked. His coat was usually rumpled and shabby. His hair needed cutting and there were holes in his shoes where the torn stockings showed through. He went from place to place working a little while in each as a telegraph operator, always looking for someone to believe in him. He wound up in Boston.

Though he was partly deaf, he could feel the vibrations coming over the wire. When he got a job in Boston as a telegraph operator, the other men were neat with their stiff high collars and paper cuffs to protect their sleeves. They looked at Edison's hair hanging over his eyes and the holes in his clothes and thought he couldn't be any good at the job. They set out to prove it by giving him the hardest work they could find, work they thought he wouldn't be able to do. They stood around grinning while the fastest operator on the line sent messages at his highest speed. For four hours, without a break, Tom Edison sat and took the messages and wrote them down without a mistake. But Tom liked a joke himself and at the end of the four hours he asked the champion sender if he couldn't go faster. Many a time people started by laughing at Tom Edison and ended in admiration and wonder.

Anyone who thinks up a new invention in America generally sends it to Washington and, if he pays the required fee, the United States government gives him what is called a patent on it. That means that the inventor can pick out the people who will make and sell his invention. But Tom didn't have enough money to pay for a patent and his invention on the telegraph was stolen from him. That was while he was in Boston. He got discouraged then and thought perhaps he would do better in New York.

When he got off the train in New York he didn't have a penny. He slept in a boiler room and walked the streets looking for a job. His clothes got worse and he had nothing to eat except handouts from the engineer in the boiler room. But nothing could stop him. He repaired a broken machine and did it so well and so fast that he got a job as an engineer. The pay was $300 a month. But Tom felt that he could not really work out his own ideas unless he owned his own business.

From that time on, people paid Thomas Edison well for his ideas. But he still went about in shabby clothes and shaggy hair. Whatever he earned went into new experiments.

As the years went on wonders came fast from Thomas Edison. Alexander Graham Bell had invented a kind of telephone, but Edison thought it wasn't good enough. He worked hard on it for two years and made it work for everybody. Then came the phonograph. There was nothing like it in all the world before. It brought Edison fame and great wealth. From that time on, the whole world knew who Thomas Edison was. He was still shy and his dress was still careless, but no one cared any more. People liked his plain simple ways. When he wasn't shut away working on an invention he was friendly with everybody.

In those days the streets were lighted with gas lamps at night. Men would come around with long poles and light the lamps one by one. In the morning they would come around again and turn them off. There was a sort of arc light but it wouldn't stay lighted and wasn't much use. Now Edison and his staff of men worked day and night on a new idea: to make a kind of light that could be used in streets and houses and stay lighted for a long time.

One evening, after five years of effort on Edison's part, a whole section of the city of New York burst into light all at once. Thomas Edison had thrown a switch, that was all. And in the morning he threw another switch and all the lights went out at once.

Now almost everywhere people coming home after dark merely touch a switch at the door and the house lights up. But Edison remembered how, when he was a boy and came home to a dark house, someone had to go in ahead and find an oil lamp and light it with a match and carry it to the door so that the family could come in without falling over something. He was glad his invention would save people so much time and trouble. Everything he invented did that for people, and that was what made him happy.

He went on making even greater inventions. He invented the motion-picture camera. He set up a studio in New Jersey, where he directed and made the first silent movie. He was so fascinated by making moving pictures that for years he could think of little else and gave it his whole time. And because of him we have talking movies today. Indeed, what he did was to make the whole life of people today easier and more pleasant.

He became rich but he always stayed modest and plain and friendly. And when people asked him what made him successful, he said, 'Two per cent inspiration and ninety-eight per cent perspiration.'

On the day Edison died Herbert Hoover, who was then President of the United States, asked everyone to turn off electric lights for one hour as a tribute to the inventive genius of Thomas A. Edison. It is to him that our modern world owes so many of its comforts and conveniences. *Adapted from a story by Will Lane*

4

A. What is the purpose of knowledge?
B. How do we acquire knowledge?
C. Who can teach us?
D. Whom can we teach?

Liberty

1

'Say: True liberty consisteth in man's submission unto My commandments, little as ye know it.'[1] *Bahá'u'lláh*

'He who wishes his own happiness by causing pain to others is not released from hatred, being himself entangled in the tangles of hatred.'[2] *Dhammapada*

'. . . but whosoever submits his will to God, being a good-doer, his wage is with his Lord . . .'[3] *Muḥammad*

'So shall I keep thy law continually for ever and ever. And I will walk at liberty; for I seek thy precepts.'[4] *Old Testament*

2

'Liberty must, in the end, lead to sedition, whose flames none can quench . . . Know ye that the embodiment of liberty and its symbol is the animal. That which beseemeth man is submission unto such restraints as will protect him from his own ignorance, and guard him against the harm of the mischief-maker. Liberty causeth man to overstep the bounds of propriety, and to infringe on the dignity of his station. It debaseth him to the level of extreme depravity and wickedness . . .

'True liberty consisteth in man's submission unto My commandments, little as ye know it. Were men to observe that which we have sent down unto them from the Heaven of Revelation, they would of a certainty, attain unto perfect liberty . . . Say: The liberty that profiteth you is to be found nowhere except in complete servitude unto God, the Eternal Truth. Whoso hath tasted of its sweetness will refuse to barter it for all the dominion of earth and heaven.'[5]

Bahá'u'lláh

'Similarly, with regard to the people who clamour for freedom: the moderate freedom which guarantees the welfare of the world of mankind and maintains and preserves the universal relationships, is found in its fullest power and extension in the teachings of His Holiness Bahá'u'lláh.'⁶ *'Abdu'l-Bahá*

3

The Traveller and His Horse

Imagine a lone rider travelling on his horse across a vast wilderness. He has been riding for many days without seeing a village, house or another person. He has many more days to travel before he reaches his destination. The traveller is a stranger to this country but he has

a map that helps him find his way. As dusk is approaching, the rider decides it is time for him to stop travelling and make camp for the night. Luckily he finds a small stream and halts there. He ties his horse up on a thorny shrub, removes her saddle and his pack and prepares to make a fire by gathering up small dry twigs.

In the meantime, the rider's horse is feeling restless. She takes a long drink of water and nibbles at the straw given her by her master. Then she digs and pulls at the rope which is holding her to the shrub and is pleased to find that it becomes free. With a loud snort the horse takes off at full gallop, away from the camp and her master.

The rider looks up. His horse is gone. Now he is deserted, far away from any other human being. But he does not try to run after the horse. He calmly continues to make his fire and eat his simple meal.

Having eaten, our traveller takes out his blanket and falls into a deep sleep under the starry sky.

When dawn breaks over the mountains, the rider awakens and is not surprised to hear his horse gently whinnying at his side.

Why isn't he surprised? Because the wise rider realises that even though the horse was free to roam all over the wilderness, it is his master, camped by the only stream for miles around, who knows the correct way to their destination. What use was freedom for the animal if this liberty was only to lead the horse to thirst and maybe even death.

The horse looks at her master – she understands. The rider saddles her up and they proceed on their journey together.

The Freedom of 'Abdu'l-Bahá

When people said to 'Abdu'l-Bahá how happy they were that He was now free, He replied:

'Freedom is not a matter of place, but of condition. I was happy in that prison, for those days were passed in the path of service.

'To me prison was freedom.

'Troubles are a rest to me.

'Death is life.

'To be despised is honour.

'Therefore was I full of happiness all through that prison time.

'When one is released from the prison of self, that is indeed freedom! For self is the greatest prison.

'When this release takes place one can never be imprisoned.

'Unless one accepts dire vicissitudes, not with dull resignation, but with radiant acquiescence, one cannot attain this freedom.'[7]

Honnold

The Imprisonment of Bahá'u'lláh in the Síyáh-Chál

Bahíyyih Khánum, the Greatest Holy Leaf, has left us this description of the Síyáh-Chál, where Bahá'u'lláh was imprisoned for four months:

The prison into which my father had been cast was a terrible place, seven steps below the ground; it was ankle-deep in filth, infested with horrible vermin, and of an indescribable loathsomeness. Added to this, there was no glimmer of light in that noisome place. Within its walls forty Bábís were crowded; murderers and highway robbers were also imprisoned there.

My noble father was hurled into this black hole, loaded with heavy chains; five other Bábís were chained to him night and day, and here he remained for four months. Picture to yourself the horror of these conditions.

Any movement caused the chains to cut deeper and deeper not only into the flesh of one, but of all who were chained together; whilst sleep or rest of any kind was not possible. No food was provided, and it was with the utmost difficulty that my mother was able to arrange to get any food or drink taken into that ghastly prison.[8]

[The Blessed Beauty] spoke very little of the terrible sufferings of that time! We, who saw the marks of what he had endured, where the chains had cut into the delicate skin, especially that of his neck, his wounded feet so long untended, evidence of the torture of the bastinado, how we wept with my dear mother.

He, on his part, told of the steadfast faith of the friends, who had gone forth to meet their death at the hands of their torturers, with joy and gladness, to attain the crown of martyrdom.[9]

Bahíyyih Khánum

The Banishment of Bahá'u'lláh to 'Akká

Bahá'u'lláh, referring to His Own suffering during the first nine years of His banishment to the prison-city of 'Akká, has written:

Know thou that upon Our arrival at this Spot, We chose to designate it as the 'Most Great Prison'. Though previously subjected in another land [Ṭihran] to chains and fetters, We yet refused to call it by that name. Say: Ponder thereon, O ye endued with understanding![10] *Bahá'u'lláh*

Again we call upon an interview with the Greatest Holy Leaf for a vivid description of the suffering of the exiles during the first weeks of their imprisonment in the fortress of 'Akká:

When we had entered the barracks the massive door was closed upon us and the great iron bolts thrown home. I cannot find words to describe the filth and stench of that vile place. We were nearly up to our ankles in mud in the room into which we were led. The damp,

close air and the excretions of the soldiers combined to produce horrible odours . . .

The followers [of Bahá'u'lláh] were all brought to the barracks together and lodged on the ground floor. Among them were the women and children, almost dying with hunger and parched with thirst. My brother ['Abdu'l-Bahá] begged to be permitted to go out for food and water. The soldiers replied: 'You cannot put a foot outside of this room. If you do, we will kill you.'. . . Then he asked permission to send out a servant guarded by soldiers. This was refused . . .

The season was summer [1868] and the temperature very high. All our people were huddled together on the damp earth floor of the barracks; with little water to drink, and that very bad, with no water with which to bathe, and scarcely enough for washing their faces. Typhoid fever and dysentery broke out among them. Everyone in our company fell sick excepting my brother, my mother, an aunt, and two others of the believers. We were not allowed a physician; we could not procure medicine. My brother had in his baggage some quinine and bismuth. With these two drugs and his nursing, he brought us all through with the exception of four, who died. These were two months of such awful horror as words cannot picture. Imagine it, if you can. Some seventy men, women and children packed together, hot summer weather, no proper food, bad water, the most offensive odours from purging and excretions, and a general attack of the terrible diseases of dysentery and typhoid.[11]   *Bahíyyih Khánum*

4

A. What is 'perfect liberty'?

B. How is submission to the will of God our protection?

In the Qur'án we read: 'Lo! The true religion with God is Islam.'[12] 'Islam' is an Arabic word meaning 'surrender'; so a follower of Islam is a person who has surrendered to the Will of God.

In the Qur'án we can read a lot about true liberty being servitude to God and obedience to His laws. When you read the following passage, keep in mind that the message of the Qur'án was given to a warring people who lived in a hot desert:

'. . . it is God who has appointed for you coverings of the things He created . . . shirts to protect you from the heat, and shirts to protect you from your own violence. Even so He perfects His blessing upon you, that haply you will surrender.'[13]   *Muḥammad*

C. Can the world attain true liberty?

'The Ancient Beauty hath consented to be bound with chains that mankind may be released from its bondage, and hath accepted to be made a prisoner within this most mighty Stronghold that the whole world may attain unto true liberty.'[14]

Bahá'u'lláh

For younger children

D. If everyone in school did exactly as they wished, could come and go as they pleased, could listen to the teachers or ignore them, do you think your school would be a good place to learn and a happy place to be?

(At first everyone is bound to cry, 'Yes!' but on reflection they will come to realise that the only result will be chaos.)

E. Why is it important that we all obey the rules of our schools and of our countries?

F. Do you have a pet? What would happen to your pet if it escaped from your care? Do you think it would be able to survive for very long?

Love

1

'O Friend! In the garden of thy heart plant naught but the rose of love
. . .'[1] *Bahá'u'lláh*

'In the world of existence there is no greater power than the power
of Love.'[2] *'Abdu'l-Bahá*

'This is my commandment, that ye love one another, as I have loved
you.'[3] *New Testament*

'Only by love can men see me, and know me, and come unto
me.'[4] *Gita*

2

'The foundation of Bahá'u'lláh is love . . . You must have infinite
love for each other, each preferring the other before himself. The
people must be so attracted to you that they will exclaim, "What
happiness exists among you!" and will see in your faces the lights of
the Kingdom; then in wonderment they will turn to you and ask the
cause of your happiness . . . I want you to be happy . . . to laugh,
smile and rejoice in order that others may be made happy by
you.'[5] *'Abdu'l-Bahá*

'Know thou of a certainty that Love is the secret of God's holy
Dispensation, the manifestation of the All-Merciful, the fountain of
spiritual outpourings. Love is heaven's kindly light, the Holy
Spirit's eternal breath that vivifies the human soul. Love is the cause
of God's revelation unto man, the vital bond inherent, according to
Divine creation, in the realities of things. Love is the one means that
ensures true felicity both in this world and the next. Love is the light
that guideth in darkness, the living link that uniteth God with man,
that assureth the progress of every illumined soul. Love is the most
great law that ruleth this mighty and heavenly Cycle, the unique
power that bindeth together the diverse elements of this material
world, the supreme magnetic force that directs the movements of

the spheres in the celestial realms. Love revealeth with unfailing and limitless power the mysteries latent in the universe. Love is the spirit of life unto the adorned body of mankind, the establisher of true civilization in this mortal world, and the shedder of imperishable glory upon every high-aiming race and nation.'[6]   'Abdu'l-Bahá

3

Big Red

Big Red was a beautiful Red Setter.

He was not a house dog or a pet dog.

He was a show dog and lived in the kennels of a very rich man.

His master looked after him carefully, because he wanted Big Red to win first prize in shows.

Every day Big Red was brushed and combed. He had lots to eat and went for walks. But Big Red was unhappy, because he did not have a friend to play with.

He did not *belong* to anybody.

Then one day a boy came to the kennels. His name was Rene. And he and Big Red became friends.

Now Rene brushed Big Red's fine coat.

Rene and Big Red played games together.

Rene fed Big Red and took him for walks.

And in the evenings they sat quietly together while Rene played a song on his harmonica.

Rene and Big Red were friends.

But Big Red was still a show dog.

And one day his master said, 'Big Red, you are not a house dog. You are not a pet dog. You are a show dog. And tomorrow you must go to the big city.'

Sadly, Big Red sat in his cage in the train. The kind guard let Big Red out of his cage.

'There you are, boy, stretch those fine long legs,' said the guard. 'I'll get you some water.'

Suddenly the train went around a curve. The doors of Big Red's car slid open.

And Big Red jumped out.

'That is the end of Big Red,' said his master when he heard the news. 'Big Red does not know how to hunt. He is a show dog. He cannot live in the wild woods.'

'I will find him. I must find him,' said Rene.

'You will never find him,' said the master. 'The woods are big and wild. And you, too, will get lost.'

'My uncle taught me many things about the woods,' said Rene. 'I will go there and look for Big Red.'

Rene got on the train – the same train that had carried Big Red.

'You will never find him, son,' said the same kind guard.

Suddenly the train went around a curve, and Rene saw that the train slowed down.

'Perhaps *this* is where he jumped off,' said Rene. And Rene jumped off too.

Rene wondered which way to go. Then he saw a stream.

'Perhaps Big Red drank some water here,' he thought.

Rene walked along the bank. And sure enough, there was a footprint!

'It's a dog's footprint! It *must* be Big Red's!'

Rene walked and walked, but there were no more footprints. It began to grow dark.

Suddenly Rene stopped. His sharp eyes had seen something caught in a thistle. It was a piece of red hair – Big Red's hair!

'Big Red, Big Red!' called Rene.

But there was no answering bark.

Now the sun was setting. Sadly, Rene unrolled his blanket and lay down.

As soon as morning came, Rene set off again.

'Big Red, Big Red!' he called.

But there was no answering bark.

Rene walked and walked.

He saw a clump of grass that lay flat. Perhaps Big Red had slept there.

'Big Red, Big Red!' called Rene.

But his voice sounded small in the tall mountains.

Tiredly, Rene sat down under a tree. He pulled out his harmonica and began to play a sad little tune.

The music rose sweet and clear in the mountain air. It rose above the treetops. It drifted softly down the valley to a quiet pool.

And Big Red, drinking by the pool, lifted his head.

For a moment the dog stood still, one paw lifted, his whole body quiet and listening.

And then he gave a bark and began to run.

'Big Red, Big Red!' called Rene. He had heard the bark. He began running. He saw a flash of red in the bushes – it was Big Red! It *was*!

The dog leaped at Rene and the two rolled over. Rene laughing and shouting, the dog barking with joy.

'Big Red, you old clown!' gasped Rene. 'I came to find you, and you found me!'

And then he looked more closely at the dog.

'You are thin and hungry, Big Red,' he said. 'Come, I must take you back to your master.'

When the master saw Rene and the dog, he could hardly believe his eyes.

'I never thought I would see either of you again.'

'He found *me*, sir,' said Rene quietly.

'Then he is yours, Rene,' said the master. 'He loves you and you love him. You belong together.'

And so at last Big Red was not just a show dog.

At last he really belonged to somebody.

And at last Big Red was happy.   *Adapted by Kathleen N. Daly*

4

A. How can we show our love for others?

B. Is it only people who are like us who we should love?

'Of old it hath been revealed: "Love of one's country is an element of the Faith of God." The Tongue of Grandeur hath, however, in the day of His manifestation proclaimed: "It is not his to boast who loveth his country, but it is his who loveth the world." '[7]

Bahá'u'lláh

c. How has Bahá'u'lláh changed our ideas of love?
d. How do the words of the Messengers of God help us in our attitude towards strangers?
e. Why should we love everyone? Is it so they will always share with us?
f. How can we overcome feelings of animosity that we may have for someone?

'Hatreds never cease by hatred in this world; by love they cease. This is an ancient law.'[8] *Dhammapada*

Obedience

1

'What mankind needeth in this day is obedience unto them that are in authority, and a faithful adherence to the cord of wisdom.'[1]

Bahá'u'lláh

'The Law must reign, and not the individual; thus will the world become a place of beauty and true brotherhood will be realized.'[2]

'Abdu'l-Bahá

'. . . whoso disobeys God, and His Messenger, and transgresses His bounds . . . for him there awaits a humbling chastisement.'[3]

Muḥammad

2

'O Son of Man! Wert thou to speed through the immensity of space and traverse the expanse of heaven, yet thou wouldst find no rest save in submission to Our command and humbleness before Our Face.'[4] *Bahá'u'lláh*

'Think not that We have revealed unto you a mere code of laws. Nay, rather, We have unsealed the choice Wine with the fingers of might and power. To this beareth witness that which the pen of Revelation hath revealed. Meditate upon this, O men of insight!

'Whenever My laws appear like the sun in the heaven of Mine utterance, they must be faithfully obeyed by all, though my decree be such as to cause the heaven of every religion to be cleft asunder. He doth what He pleaseth.'[5] *Bahá'u'lláh*

3

The Train that would not stay on the Track

Once upon a time there was a train that was tired of staying on the track.

'Why must I run on a track all the days of my life?' asked the train.

'You had much better stay where you are,' said the track. 'I was laid for you to run on and you were made to run on me. Everything is better off in this world if it stays where it belongs.'

But the train would not listen.

'I'm not going to stay here,' he said and he jumped off the track and began to run along the road.

'Keep off!' cried the automobiles. 'This road was made for us. Keep off! Keep off!'

'No such thing!' said the train, 'There's plenty of room on the road for me.'

He ran on down the road. He stopped at the houses for people and trunks and he stopped at the post office for the mail bags. He ran out to the barns for the milk. Everyone was delighted. It was much easier than carrying everything down to the station. But the train took so long that he never got to the end of his trip!

People waited for their trunks and they never came. The letters in the mail bags were so old that no one troubled to read them. The milk was sour and was no good to anyone. People stopped putting their things onto the train and began to send them by automobile instead.

'There now,' said the automobiles, 'no one is using you anymore. You should have stayed on your track as we told you to. The road is no place for you.'

But the train refused to go back to his track. One day he saw a horse running across the fields.

'Why should I stay on the road?' asked the train. 'That looks like fun.'

He left the road and started off across the fields.

'You mustn't come here!' cried the horse, 'This is my field. Keep off! Keep off!'

'No such thing,' answered the train. 'There's plenty of room in this field for me.'

Bump, bump, bump went the train across the field until he came to a brook.

'How do I get over this?' asked the train.

'Jump,' said the horse.

'I never jumped in my life,' said the train 'I always have bridges laid down for me.'

'Bridges?' laughed the horse. 'You'd better go back where you belong. The track is the place for you.'

But the train paid no attention to him for just then he heard an airplane up in the air.

'That looks like fun,' said the train. 'Why should I stay on the ground? I'm going to fly.'

'Silly,' said the horse, 'you, who can't even jump a brook!'

The train tried to fly. He tried with his front wheels. He tried with his back wheels. He tried with all his wheels. He tried until he was tired.

'Well,' said the train, 'there appears to be something wrong. I can't fly. People won't ride on me when I bump across the fields, and they won't send trunks and mail by me when I run on the road. They say I'm too slow. I don't seem to be good for anything! I might as well stay right here and let my fires go out. No one would miss me!'

The train felt lonely and discouraged. He felt he was no longer of any use in the world. Then an idea flashed through his steam pipes.

'I might go back to my tracks,' he thought. 'I wonder if they're still there?'

He crept across the field and down the road to the station. There lay the tracks right where he had left them, stretching off in both directions. They looked so safe and smooth! The train gave a great puff of happiness as he climbed back on.

At the station there were many people waiting and a pile of trunks and mail bags.

'This is just where I belong,' whistled the train cheerfully. And from that time on the little train could be seen every day running happily down the tracks, as smooth as could be.

Adapted by Irene Taafaki

4

A. To whom do we owe obedience? Why?
B. What would happen in school if not one rule was obeyed?
C. What would happen if no one obeyed the traffic laws?
D. What would happen to our social system if no one obeyed the laws of the country?

Parents

1

'A real son is such one as hath branched from the spiritual part of man.'[1] *'Abdu'l-Bahá*

'Be thankful to Me, and to thy parents . . .'[2] *Muḥammad*

'Honour thy father and thy mother . . .'[3] *Old Testament*

'The son shall be devoted to his father, be of the same mind with his mother . . .'[4] *Atharva Veda*

'Be obedient and kind to thy father and mother.'[5] *'Abdu'l-Bahá*

2

'O Lord! In this Most Great Dispensation Thou dost accept the intercession of children on behalf of their parents. This is one of the special, infinite bestowals of this Dispensation. Therefore, O Thou kind Lord, accept the request of this Thy servant at the threshold of Thy singleness and submerge my father in the ocean of Thy grace.'[6] *'Abdu'l-Bahá*

'The [children's] prosperity in this world and in the Kingdom depends upon the good pleasure of parents, and without this they will be in manifest loss.'[7] *'Abdu'l-Bahá*

'It is seemly that the servant should, after each prayer, supplicate God to bestow mercy and forgiveness upon his parents. Thereupon God's call will be raised: "Thousand upon thousand of what thou hast asked for thy parents shall be thy recompense!" Blessed is he who remembereth his parents when communing with God. There is, verily, no God but Him, the Mighty, the Well-Beloved.'[8]

The Báb

3

Her Hands

My mother's hands are cool and fair,
 They can do anything.
Delicate mercies hide them there
 Like flowers in the spring.

When I was small and could not sleep,
 She used to come to me,
And with my cheek upon her hand
 How sure my rest would be.

For everything she ever touched
 Of beautiful or fine,
Their memories living in her hands
 Would warm that sleep of mine.

Her hands remember how they played
 One time in meadow streams, –
And all the flickering song and shade
 Of water took my dreams.

Swift through her haunted fingers pass
 Memories of garden things; –
I dipped my face in flowers and grass
 And sounds of hidden wings.

One time she touched the cloud that kissed
 Brown pastures bleak and far; –
I leaned my cheek into a mist
 And thought I was a star.

All this was very long ago
 And I am grown; but yet
The hand that lured my slumber so
 I can never forget.

For still when drowsiness comes on
 It seems so soft and cool,
Shaped happily beneath my cheek,
 Hollow and beautiful.

Anna Hempstead Branch

Only One Mother

Hundreds of stars in the pretty sky,
  Hundreds of shells on the shore together,
Hundreds of birds that go singing by,
  Hundreds of lambs in the sunny weather.

Hundreds of dewdrops to greet the dawn,
  Hundreds of bees in the purple clover,
Hundreds of butterflies on the lawn,
  But only one mother the wide world over.

George Cooper

Father's Story

We put more coal on the big red fire,
  And while we are waiting for dinner to cook,
Our father comes and tells us about
  A story that he has read in a book.

And Charles and Will and Dick and I
  And all of us but Clarence are there.
And some of us sit on Father's legs,
  But one has to sit on the little red chair.

And when we are sitting very still,
  He sings us a song or tells a piece;
He sings 'Dan Tucker Went to Town,'
  Or he tells us about the golden fleece.

He tells us about the golden wool,
  And some of it is about a boy
Named Jason, and about a ship,
  And some is about a town called Troy.

And while he is telling or singing it through,
  I stand by his arm, for that is my place,
And I push my fingers into his skin
  To make little dents in his big round face.

Elizabeth Madox Roberts

I Know a Secret

I know a secret that the night imparts
　When bedtime ends day's honours and disgraces
And masquerades all stormy little hearts
　With such deceptively angelic faces!

You shan't forget your green and golden youth,
　Lying some day so dim and far behind you:
So, mingling simple fancy, simple truth,
　Here are these little fables to remind you.

You won't forget. And in all joy and pain
　Life offers, dear my urchins, when you're older,
How Daddy'd love to carry once again
　You, and all your world, upon his shoulder!

Christopher Morley

4

A. How do your parents show their love for you?
B. How can you show love for your parents?
C. If we are obedient to our parents, who will benefit?

Patience

1

'He, verily, shall increase the reward of them that endure with patience.'[1] *Bahá'u'lláh*

'O Son of Man! For everything there is a sign. The sign of love is fortitude under My decree and patience under My trials.'[2]

Bahá'u'lláh

'O believers, be patient, and vie you in patience . . . haply so you will prosper.'[3] *Muḥammad*

'Whoso, as a racing chariot, checks his uprisen anger, him I call a charioteer; other folk merely hold the reins.'[4] *Dhammapada*

'. . . on the good ground are they, which in an honest and good heart, having heard the word, keep it, and bring forth fruit with patience.'[5] *New Testament*

'Forbearing patience is the highest devotion . . .'[6] *Dhammapada*

2

'The steed of this Valley [Search] is patience; without patience the wayfarer on this journey will reach nowhere and attain no goal. Nor should he ever be downhearted; if he strive for a hundred thousand years and yet fail to behold the beauty of the Friend, he should not falter.'[7] *Bahá'u'lláh*

3

Bruce and the Spider

A long time ago there lived a King of Scotland named Robert Bruce. He was a greatly troubled man because his country was at war with England and the English were winning. In battle after battle they drove back the Scottish army until at last the King himself had to retreat to the mountains to save his life.

Wandering desperately through the mountain forests, cold and hungry and exhausted, at last the King found a miserable little wooden hut empty and deserted. Glad of any kind of shelter, he lay down on the floor of the hut in deep despair.

'There is no use in going on,' he thought. 'The enemy has thrown back our armies six times. We can never repulse them. I have failed my people. I might as well give up.'

At that moment the King noticed a little grey spider spinning a long thread from one of the rafters. The spider swung along on the thread in an effort to attach the other end to another rafter so he could start spinning his web. But the thread broke and the spider fell to the floor of the hut.

A little dazed perhaps, but with no hesitation at all, the spider climbed up the wall and began spinning again. He kept patiently at it until the thread was long enough. Then he again swung himself to the end of it and tried once more to attach it to the rafter across the corner. But again the spider fell to the floor.

And once more he climbed up and began again.

Six times the spider's thread broke. Six times he fell to the ground. Six times he began. Six times he failed.

Robert Bruce, the King of Scotland, watched in fascination. He became so absorbed in the little spider's efforts that for a time he forgot his own troubles.

The spider did not give up even when he failed for the sixth time. He just tried again, and this time, on the seventh try, he was successful. The end of the thread held! The spider attached it to the far rafter and began spinning his web.

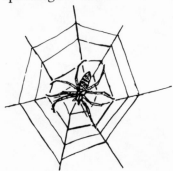

Robert Bruce arose and bowed low to the tiny grey creature. 'O little spider!' he cried. 'You have taught me a wonderful lesson in patience and persistence. You were not ready to give up, as I was.

No matter how often you failed, you were always willing to try again. Perhaps I too shall win if I keep on trying.'

And so, though he was still cold and hungry and weary, he was no longer disheartened. Watching the spider had given him new strength and courage. He buckled on his sword, gathered together his scattered armies and, with the example of the courageous spider to inspire him, King Robert Bruce led his men, on the seventh try, to victory.   *Traditional*

4

A. Can any worthwhile goal ever be achieved without patience?
B. Try and think of some of the advantages of being patient. Is patience a necessity as well as a virtue?
C. Can you think of a situation where you showed patience and your patience was rewarded?
D. Now try to think of a situation where impatience led to trouble.
E. Why do we need patience?
F. Have you heard the expression 'he has the patience of Job'? This comes from a story in the Old Testament where God tested the patience of Job. Read this story and discuss the importance of patience.

Peacefulness

1

'There is no glory for him that committeth disorder on the earth after it hath been made so good.'[1] *Bahá'u'lláh*

'Fighting, and the employment of force, even for the right cause, will not bring good results.'[2] *'Abdu'l-Bahá*

'The others know not that in this quarrel we perish; those of them who realise it have their quarrels calmed thereby.'[3] *Dhammapada*

'Calm is the mind, calm is the speech, and action and right knowledge of him who is wholly freed, perfectly peaceful, and who is such a stable one.'[4] *Dhammapada*

'When a man surrenders all desires that come to the heart and by the grace of God finds the joy of God, then his soul has indeed found peace.'[5] *Gita*

'Let man find the path of the Spirit: who has found this path becomes free from the bonds of evil. Who knows this and has found peace, he is the lord of himself, his is a calm endurance, and calm concentration.'[6] *Upanishads*

2

'I charge you all that each one of you concentrate all the thoughts of your heart on love and unity. When a thought of war comes, oppose it by a stronger thought of peace. A thought of hatred must be destroyed by a more powerful thought of love. Thoughts of war bring destruction to all harmony, well-being, restfulness and content . . . Thoughts of love are constructive of brotherhood, peace, friendship, and happiness.'[7] *'Abdu'l-Bahá*

'How is it possible for men to fight from morning until evening, killing each other, shedding the blood of their fellow-men: And for what object? To gain possession of a part of the earth! Even the animals, when they fight, have an immediate and more reasonable cause for their attacks . . . The highest of created beings fighting to obtain the lowest form of matter, earth! Land belongs not to one people, but to all people. This earth is not man's home, but his tomb.'[8]   *'Abdu'l-Bahá*

3

Ashoka

Ashoka was born in the year 273 BC and was the son of Bindusara who ruled India for many years. According to a story, Bindusara requested King Antiochas I of Syria to send him figs, wine and philosophers. The Syrian King replied that he would be glad to send figs and wine, but philosophers were not for sale.

Though we have fixed Ashoka's birth at 273 BC, we are not quite definite about his early days. The Buddhist tradition says that Bindusara had one hundred and one sons among whom Sumana was the eldest and Ashoka was the second one. According to some accounts, Ashoka was very cruel and blood-thirsty as a young prince. He killed all of his brothers but one and became king. As Ashoka was cruel and blood-thirsty he was called Chandashoka.

In the thirteenth year of his rule Ashoka declared war on the Kalingas. The Kalingas fought bravely but Ashoka defeated them. The victory, however, made Ashoka a very changed man. He felt sad and depressed on seeing thousands of corpses strewn on the battlefield. The great bloodbath and sufferings of the people made Ashoka hang down his head in shame and sorrow. He was moved so much by pity and remorse that he made up his mind never to fight again and to give up all future wars.

Thus the Kalinga war became a turning point in Ashoka's life and in the history of India. At the time of the Kalinga war Ashoka's kingdom included Afghanistan, Baluchistan, Kashmir, Nepal and the southern part of India but not the Tamil Kingdoms. Besides renouncing war, Ashoka embraced Buddhism and made it the state religion and used the huge resources of the Mauryan Empire to spread the Law of Piety. He strictly followed Buddha's principles and set a noble living example to all. He visited Lumbini Garden, the birth place of the Buddha, Bodh Gaya, Sarnath and other places associated with Buddha's life. He sent missionaries to various parts of India to spread Buddhism. Some of them even went to foreign countries like Ceylon, Central Asia, Egypt and Europe. Ashoka had the great principles of Buddhism engraved on pillars, rocks, caves in the various parts of India. He built a large number of monasteries, prayer halls and monuments housing the relics of the Buddha.

Ashoka, who ruled for about thirty-seven years, was the greatest Mauryan emperor, one of the greatest kings of India and one of the greatest rulers in world history. Why do we regard him as such a great king?

Ashoka was not only a royal monk but also a great king discharging his duties efficiently. In him were combined great power and virtue, a great territorial empire and a great spiritual empire. He had great ideals of kingship, and he worked very hard for the happiness and welfare of his subjects. He protected the weak and gave impartial justice. He ordered wells to be dug, rest houses to be built, trees to be planted for the benefit of travellers, and hospitals to be constructed for treating people and animals. He believed that it was his duty to treat his people as a father treats his children.

He sincerely practised what he preached and the people were pleased with him. The edicts that he issued showed his greatness as a man and King. Though he was powerful and could have fought many wars after the Kalinga war, he felt that his duty was not to shed blood but to spread the message of Ahinsa (love) everywhere. He even forbade the serving of any form of meat at the Royal Table and thus set an example to his subjects of love for all living creatures. He made Buddhism a world religion and was also able to give political unity to India.

Independent India has honoured the memory of Ashoka. The Ashokan Lion Capital of the Sarnath Pillar has been made the State emblem of India. The wheel of the Sarnath Pillar finds a place in the middle of India's national flag.

India's Hero of Non-Violence: Mohandas Gandhi

Mohandas Gandhi, the boy who was later to be called Mahatma, the Great Soul, was married when he was only thirteen years old. He and his pretty little girl-wife, Kasturbai, lived in his father's house until they were old enough to have a house of their own. Child marriages were then the custom in Hindu families all over India.

One day Mohandas came home from school and Kasturbai could see that something was troubling him. Presently he told her the whole story.

The day before he had been in a great hurry to get home to the big house under the palms and banana trees because his father was ill.

'Oh, there you are!' his father had said. 'I've been waiting for you to read to me.' He pointed to a big heavy book written thousands of years ago by one of India's great poets. Mohandas had opened the book and begun to read aloud.

'I was supposed to go back to gymnasium in a little while,' Mohandas explained to Kasturbai, 'but I couldn't stop reading until my father told me to.'

'You couldn't disobey your father, of course,' agreed Kasturbai. Obedience to parents was considered the most important duty of a Hindu boy or girl. 'Was your teacher very angry with you for missing the class?'

'He did not believe me,' said Mohandas, miserably. 'He knew I didn't like gymnasium and he thought I was lying.'

The girl was almost in tears. 'You! You, who hate lies so much! How shameful of him! But do not grieve, Mohandas. The truth always wins in the end.' And the truth did win, for a day or two later the teacher told Mohandas, 'You are a truthful boy. I was too hasty in accusing you. I believe now that you would not have made up such a story.'

Young Mohandas was brought up strictly, but he was a happy child. He liked to play games like all boys of his age, and he had faults like all boys and girls too. He and his cousin once ate meat to see what it tasted like, even though they knew meat was forbidden to Hindus. Afterwards Mohandas told his cousin he would never again eat meat, and he never did.

Before Mohandas graduated from high school he learned what it was to be unhappy when his beloved father died. His father had been Prime Minister to the Rajah of the Province in which the Gandhis lived. His friends were all learned men, and when they came to see him young Mohandas sat quietly in a corner and listened to what they were saying. He was especially impressed by one thing he learned from these wise men: that there is good in all religions and that the faiths of other people must always be respected.

When the boy left school, his mother sent him to England to study law. This was a great adventure for a Hindu boy. He had to learn to live as the English lived. He had to give up the white knee-length trousers and tunic of the young Hindu and wear European clothes. He had to speak the English language. But he remained firm in his resolve not to eat meat or drink wine.

For four years Mohandas studied hard. He wanted to become a good lawyer. But that wasn't enough. Even then Mohandas Gandhi felt that some day he was going to help his own people and that he must prepare himself for that great work.

At last the day came for Mohandas to return to India. Kasturbai and their son, born just before he went away, were waiting for him.

Kasturbai's big brown eyes brimmed with happy tears. 'Never leave us again,' she begged him.

'Not if I can help it,' he promised. 'I must begin to earn some money, though, to support you and our son.'

That was not easy in a country so full of poor people, and soon the little family had to be parted again. A rich merchant asked Gandhi to go to Pretoria, the capital city of South Africa, to settle a lawsuit for him, and there was nothing for the young man to do but go.

'It's only for a few months,' he called out to Kasturbai who, with her little boy, stood on the pier waving goodbye.

The lawsuit was easily settled, for Gandhi was a good lawyer. And he was a good man. He knew that the man who had lost the case was poor, so he said to the merchant, 'Let me beg of you not to press this poor man now for all the money he owes you. He can pay you a little at a time. I will see that he does so.'

But something far more important than this lawsuit came of Gandhi's visit to South Africa. Travelling from place to place to see his Hindu friends, he found that many of the laws passed by the British, who ruled the country at that time, were unjust to his fellow-countrymen. Hindus had to ride in separate, uncomfortable cars on trains and in the back seats of street-cars. They were not allowed in hotels. They were paid next to nothing for the first five years they worked in the gold-mines, and they had to live outside the town in miserable hovels.

One new law was especially hard on the Hindus. Their taxes were heavy, and the law said that all Hindus who did not pay these taxes by a certain date would be shipped back to their own country. As these Hindus had left their homeland because it was already terribly overcrowded, going back there would mean that they and their families would starve.

Gandhi made up his mind he would persuade the British to get rid of this bad law. He began by uniting the Hindus and getting as many as he could to join in the struggle. Then he explained to them how he thought they should behave towards the Government if they wanted to win.

'Conquer the heart of the enemy with truth and love, not by violence,' he said.

This idea, which came to be known as passive or peaceful resistance, was not new. The founders of India's great religions had taught men thousands of years ago that violent methods harmed those who used them. But unfortunately, people had grown accustomed to the violence of warfare. They said, 'If you believe in something you must fight for it.' And Gandhi said, 'Yes. But not with brute force. You will harm yourselves more than your enemy by being violent.' And they came to see that there was something wonderful in this new old idea, and something wonderful too about the man who believed in it and based his life upon it. They began calling him Gandhiji. Adding ji to the end of a man's name is a Hindu way of showing great respect for him.

Gandhi saw that the work he had set himself to do was going to take a long time, so he went back to India to get his family and take them back with him to South Africa.

On his return he decided that the best way to tell the people of South Africa the truth about the unjust laws would be to write about them in the newspapers. But no South African newspapers would print what he wanted to write, so he started one of his own.

'We will live on a farm,' he said to his followers. 'We will call it Tolstoy Farm after the great Russian writer who taught men to live happily with few possessions. We will publish our newspaper at Tolstoy Farm. We will grow our own food there and spin and weave the cloth for our clothes. And we shall do no harm to our friends or our enemies.'

When a good many people live together there is bound to be some quarrelling, and in the early days at Tolstoy Farm two Hindus began disputing the ownership of some little trifle and the dispute became violent. This grieved Gandhi and he thought of a way to make them sorry they had behaved badly.

'It is my fault if you do wrong,' he told them, 'because I am your leader. So I will take the blame on myself.'

And his way of taking the blame on himself was to go without food for several weeks. When the offenders saw him grow weak with fasting, they were ashamed and tried not to give him any more cause to take the blame for them.

During these years of struggle to help the oppressed Hindus in South Africa, Gandhi had to work hard and face many hardships. But he continued to preach 'No violence!' until the idea no longer seemed strange to his friends. They saw that his way of resisting injustice had a great force behind it, though that force never became violent. And in the end they had a very practical reason for believing in his methods, because before he left them the Government did wipe out the cruel tax law and they knew they had won their victory by Gandhi's kind of passive resistance.

When Gandhi and his family went back to India at last, they spent some time looking for a place where they could build a settlement in the simple Tolstoy Farm style. Gandhi had decided to devote his life to his poor countrymen at home, to live among them, and to teach them to resist evil and oppression by peaceful methods, as he had taught his compatriots in South Africa.

The site he chose for his farm-settlement was outside the city of Ahmadabad, near the West Coast. He called it Ashram, or Place of Rest. He built a school where, besides the usual subjects, boys were taught carpentry and farming and girls were taught how to spin and weave cloth.

Gandhi himself did not stay at Ashram all the time. He travelled, sometimes on foot and sometimes by train in third class cars with hard board seats, so crowded that passengers were always hanging on outside the doors and windows. His work was to be among the poor, and he felt he could understand them better if he lived as one of them. He never seemed to think there was anything especially good or unselfish about this way of living. And everyone who met him talked of his gaiety and enjoyment of life. More and more, as people worked with him, though, they saw him as a Great Soul, a Mahatma.

The first big resistance movement Gandhi started in India was directed against one of his country's most ancient customs.

'What is the use of my teaching that all men are equal,' He asked Kasturbai one day, 'when all over the land millions of our people are considered 'Untouchables'?

The Untouchables were Hindu families who lived by doing the necessary but dirty work of the world. Gandhi called them 'the people of God'. He said, 'Their life is one of service, love and sacrifice, because they keep the cities and villages clean.' He shocked a great many Hindus, including many of his friends, by taking an Untouchable, a girl named Lakshmi, into his home. It was not long, though, before these same people began to follow his example.

Another injustice Gandhi resisted was the 'purdah' custom. By purdah Hindus mean the custom of keeping women shut up at home and preventing them from being educated.

'Why should our women not walk into the fresh air?' he asked. 'What we are doing to our women and to the Untouchables is making us weak and helpless. Let us get rid of these foolish customs with one mighty effort.'

On the flag Gandhi designed for India he drew a picture of a spinning-wheel. Many people wondered why he thought a

spinning-wheel so important, so he explained what it stood for:

'The spinning-wheel is on our flag because it is all the machinery India needs. Our country is different from Europe and America. There machines are all right. But here our people are dying of hunger. They must work to buy food now! They cannot wait for the wonderful machines of the modern world.'

India won her freedom from British rule during Gandhi's lifetime, but he was not happy about the way things turned out. Pakistan (meaning the Land of the Pure) in the North was made into a Muslim state, and the rest of India remained Hindu. So Gandhi's beloved India was now truly divided. All he would say about this separation was: 'I have nothing to do with it.' But he went from town to town and village to village to wherever he heard of violent outbreaks between Hindus and Muslims; and when he appeared men stopped fighting to listen to him.

'Wherever Gandhi is,' said a foreign friend of India, 'that becomes the capital of India.'

Children were Gandhi's constant companions. They vied with each other in being his 'walking-stick', because he liked to walk with a hand on the shoulder of some little boy or girl. His young grandson used to take hold of the end of the old man's cane and pull him along with it. People would laugh and say, 'The leader is being led.'

Mohandas Gandhi, the Mahatma, was mourned all over the world when he died. One winter evening in 1948 the news was broadcast that a Hindu enemy had shot and killed the great man.

4

A. Why is it futile to fight for part of the earth?
B. How can thoughts be destructive?
C. How can thoughts be constructive?
D. Is there a difference between peace in the world and peace within ourselves?

Prayer

1

'In any way that men love me in that same way they find my love
. . .'[1] *Gita*

'The laudable prayers praise we, the creations of the first [spiritual]
world. Whilst we recite them from memory, act thereafter, learn
them, teach them, keep them in memory, desire to remind
ourselves of them.'[2] *Yaçna*

'He, verily, loveth the one that turneth towards Him.'[3] *Bahá'u'lláh*

'. . . strive that your actions day by day may be beautiful
prayers.'[4] *'Abdu'l-Bahá*

2

'Intone, O My servant, the verses of God that have been received by
thee, as intoned by them who have drawn nigh unto Him, that the
sweetness of thy melody may kindle thine own soul, and attract the
hearts of all men. Whoso reciteth, in the privacy of his chamber, the
verses revealed by God, the scattering angels of the Almighty shall
scatter abroad the fragrance of the words uttered by his mouth, and
shall cause the heart of every righteous man to throb. Though he
may, at first, remain unaware of its effect, yet the virtue of the grace
vouchsafed unto him must needs sooner or later exercise its
influence upon his soul. Thus have the mysteries of the Revelation
of God been decreed by virtue of the Will of Him Who is the Source
of power and wisdom.'[5] *Bahá'u'lláh*

3

The Bejewelled Sword

There was once a little child in Persia during the days of Persia's
ancient glory. It was custom in those days that whenever there was
an important feast the people would share gifts with their friends

and loved ones. So this little child prayed very hard and loudly for a bejewelled sword to be his gift.

At the time of the feast, this little boy was waiting eagerly to receive the sword he had prayed so hard for. However, the time passed and the feast was almost over and yet the child did not receive any sword as a gift. He was quite sad and disappointed.

His father, who never believed in God or in any kind of prayers, saw his son's disappointment and said, 'My son, can't you see, your prayers were not answered?'

The son looked at his father and replied, 'Oh yes father, my prayers were answered.'

'How can that be?' asked the father in surprise. 'You did not receive the bejewelled sword that you desired so much.'

'But father, don't you understand?' said the child. 'The answer is "no". God said "no".'   *A Persian Folk Tale*

When 'Abdu'l-Bahá was in New York, He called to Him an ardent Bahá'í and said, 'If you will come to Me at dawn tomorrow, I will teach you to pray.'

Delighted, Mr M arose at four and crossed the city, arriving for his lesson at six. With what exultant expectation he must have greeted this opportunity! He found 'Abdu'l-Bahá already at prayer, kneeling by the side of the bed. Mr M followed suit, taking care to place himself directly across.

Seeing that 'Abdu'l-Bahá was quite lost in His Own reverie, Mr M began to pray silently for his friends, his family and finally for the crowned heads of Europe. No word was uttered by the quiet Man before him. He went over all the prayers he knew then, and repeated them twice, three times – still no sound broke the expectant hush.

Mr M surreptitiously rubbed one knee and wondered vaguely about his back. He began again, hearing as he did so, the birds heralding the dawn outside the window. An hour passed, and finally two. Mr M was quite numb now. His eyes, roving along the wall, caught sight of a large crack. He dallied with a touch of indignation but let his gaze pass again to the still figure across the bed.

The ecstasy that he saw arrested him and he drank deeply of the sight. Suddenly he wanted to pray like that. Selfish desires were forgotten. Sorrow, conflict, and even his immediate surroundings were as if they had never been. He was conscious of only one thing, a passionate desire to draw near to God.

Closing his eyes again he set the world firmly aside, and amazingly his heart teemed with prayer, eager, joyous, tumultuous prayer. He felt cleansed by humility and lifted by a new peace. 'Abdu'l-Bahá had taught him to pray!

The 'Master of 'Akká' immediately arose and came to him. His eyes rested smilingly upon the newly humbled Mr M. 'When you pray,' He said, 'you must not think of your aching body, nor of the birds outside the window, nor of the cracks in the wall!'

He became very serious then, and added, 'When you wish to pray you must first know that you are standing in the presence of the Almighty!'[6]   *Honnold*

4

A. What is prayer? 'Service is prayer.'[8]   *'Abdu'l-Bahá*
B. Why should we pray?

'To prayer we submit ourselves, on prayer we call to protect property and body, to shelter . . .'[9]   *Yaçna*

'Bring thyself to account each day ere thou art summoned to a reckoning . . .'[10]   *Bahá'u'lláh*

C. When should we pray?

'My voice shalt thou hear in the morning, O Lord; in the morning will I direct my prayer unto thee, and will look up.'[11]

Old Testament

'Perform the prayer at the sinking of the sun to the darkening of the night and the recital of dawn . . .'[12]   *Muḥammad*

'. . . supplicate unto Him and beseech in the middle of the night and at early morn, just as the needy and captive one beseeches.'[13]   *'Abdu'l-Bahá*

D. How should we pray?

'. . . the reciting, uttering, singing, and praising the praiseworthy prayers.'[14]   *Yaçna*

E. Will our prayers always be answered?

'God is merciful. In His mercy He answers the prayers of all His servants when according to His supreme wisdom it is necessary.'[15]   *'Abdu'l-Bahá*

For younger children

F. Are prayers only those words spoken with our eyes shut and our arms folded?

G. What actions have you done today that you think are worthy of being called prayers?

H. Why do you think it is important to learn prayers by heart?

Purity

1

'We verily behold your actions. If We perceive from them the sweet smelling savour of purity and holiness, We will most certainly bless you.'[1] *Bahá'u'lláh*

'The pure heart is one that is entirely cut away from self.'[2]

'Abdu'l-Bahá

'. . . And God loves those who cleanse themselves.'[3] *Muḥammad*

'. . . if one speaks or acts with pure mind, because of that, happiness follows him, even as the shadow that never leaves.'[4] *Dhammapada*

'God loveth those who are pure. Naught in the Bayán and in the sight of God is more loved than purity and immaculate cleanliness.'[5] *The Báb*

'Unto the pure all things are pure.'[6] *New Testament*

'May he not perish who leads a pure life . . .'[7] *Yaçna*

'Remembrance of Me cleanseth all things from defilement, could ye but perceive it.'[8] *Bahá'u'lláh*

'Purity and impurity depend on oneself. No one purifies another.'[9] *Dhammapada*

2

'O My Brother! A pure heart is as a mirror; cleanse it with the burnish of love and reverence from all save God, that the true sun may shine within it and the eternal morning dawn.'[10] *Bahá'u'lláh*

'Purity is the best good. Happiness, happiness is to him: Namely, to the best pure in purity.'[11] *Khordah-Avesta*

3

The Sunshade

Agatha was the daughter of a rich goldsmith and lived in a grand house which had a great many rooms and a sweeping staircase and a fine, large garden. Her father gave her as many gold rings and bracelets as she wanted, and her wardrobe was full to overflowing with beautiful dresses of silk and bright satin. But she took no joy in all these things, for she was very ugly. All day she would wander about the house or pick flowers in the garden, not daring to go out into the streets until the dusk was falling.

One day the housekeeper who looked after the goldsmith's house fell ill and Agatha had to go to the market in broad daylight in order to buy meat and vegetables. She pulled her bonnet frills over her forehead so that no one should see her ugly face, but the women in the market-place all recognised her and whispered to each other, 'Look, there goes the goldsmith's daughter. It's true she really is as ugly as they say!'

Agatha passed quickly between the stalls. She hated to hear people making fun of her, and wished she were safe at home.

Suddenly she heard an old woman calling after her. 'Where are you going in such a hurry, Agatha? Come and see my wares.'

The voice sounded kind enough, so Agatha paused and looked round.

'That's better,' said the old woman. 'Come here, my child. I have something to show you.'

She rummaged in an old hamper, pulled out a sunshade and opened it up. It was of delicate, pale-blue silk embroidered with tiny white pearls. 'Do you like it?' she asked.

'Oh yes,' replied Agatha. 'But I spend most of my time indoors, so I have no use for a sunshade.'

The old woman smiled. 'One moment,' she said. 'Hold the sunshade over your head and take a look at yourself!' A mirror gleamed in the old woman's wrinkled hand, and Agatha saw reflected in it the face of a beautiful stranger.

'There you are!' said the old woman. 'As long as you hold the sunshade over your head nothing but the beauty of your kind heart will be seen, and no one will dream of laughing at you.'

'If it were only mine,' the girl sighed, stroking the blue silk.

'It's yours, my child,' said the old woman. 'I have given it to you. Go now, and be happy.'

Agatha could see that the old woman was poor, and could ill afford to give presents, so she took a gold bracelet from her arm and handed it to her saying, 'May I give you something too, to bring you happiness?'

So she went on her way. As she passed shyly through the market-place she felt the admiring glances of the passers-by, and she smiled happily under the blue dome of the sunshade.

As she entered the house she closed the sunshade, and once again she saw her ugly features looking back at her from the hall mirror. 'I will not tell Father anything about it,' she thought. 'How sad he would be to see me beautiful one moment and ugly the next.' So she hid the old woman's gift in a cupboard, and carried on with her work as though nothing had happened.

Before dusk fell Agatha put on a pretty silk dress and left the house. She did not care if people thought it strange for her to be carrying a sunshade when the sun had already set; she wanted to be beautiful! But everyone was so charmed by her loveliness that the sunshade went unnoticed. Long after she had passed by, people were still talking about the beautiful stranger.

There was a big park in the city where a band played every evening beneath bright coloured lights. Agatha had always longed to join in the dancing there, but she had never dared. Now she felt no fear, and danced merrily beneath the fragrant acacia blossoms, gaily whirling the blue sunshade over her head.

All the young men of the city who had previously avoided Agatha now crowded round to talk with her, eager to know whether she were on a short visit to the city, or whether she meant to stay. She wandered happily past the fountains and through the rose-gardens with her admirers, talking and joking with sparkling eyes, until she heard a sudden burst of coarse, cruel laughter.

She stopped in dismay. Had the sunshade lost its magic power? Was she ugly again, and were the people laughing at her? Surely not – all her companions were as attentive as ever. A moment later she saw that a crowd had gathered round a poor hunchback. People were tugging at his clothes and yelling, 'Go away! You're spoiling our fun, you ugly creature!'

'We must help him,' said Agatha. 'What harm has he done?' She forced a way between the dancers and said, 'Leave the poor fellow alone! Have you no thought for other people's feelings?'

'But just look how ugly he is,' shrieked a girl. 'The horrid dwarf!'

Agatha stood silent for a moment, and then she handed the old hunchback her magic sunshade. His features at once became youthful and bright, his back straightened, and he stood noble and tall. His persecutors stepped back in amazement. Agatha hung her head, thinking that all their scorn would now descend on her; but no one seemed to notice her, so astonished were they at the miraculous transformation of the ugly hunchback.

The man still held the sunshade over his head, unable to understand what had happened to him. Agatha held out her hand to take it back, but felt all at once that she no longer wanted it. Without a word she turned and walked away through the park. One by one the bright lights went out, but there was a full moon to light the paths, and the surface of the pond glittered between the silent banks. But was this her true reflection? A beautiful face, radiant with goodness, looked up at her from the deep mirror of the pond. It was even more beautiful than it had been under the sunshade. The stars twinkled in the water, and the breeze carried them on the waves like thousands of little diamonds, to where Agatha knelt on the bank.

A Folk Tale

4

A. How can God help us to become pure?
B. How can we purify ourselves?
C. What do you think pure actions are?

D. What has cleanliness to do with purity?

'By degrees a wise man, little by little, should remove his own impurities, as a smith removes the dross of silver.'[12]   *Dhammapada*

For younger children
E. What is another word for pure? (clean)
F. How do we keep our bodies clean?
G. How can we keep our minds pure?

Take two glasses of clean water, to represent our pure thoughts. Put some mud into one glass.

H. Which glass of water would you like to drink?
I.   Which glass would you offer to a friend?
J.   If our thoughts are muddy, not pure, are they attractive? Are they wholesome?
K. How can we make our thoughts and actions better every day?
L. Who will help us to do this?

Respect for Others

1

'Let truthfulness and courtesy be your adorning.'[1]   *Bahá'u'lláh*

'For one who frequently honours and respects elders, four things increase: age, beauty, bliss, and strength.'[2]   *Dhammapada*

'O believers, obey God, and obey the Messenger and those in authority among you.'[3]   *Muḥammad*

'Wherever you find the attributes of God love that person, whether he be of your family or of another.'[4]   *'Abdu'l-Bahá*

2

'Be generous in prosperity, and thankful in adversity. Be worthy of the trust of thy neighbour, and look upon him with a bright and friendly face. Be a treasure to the poor, an admonisher to the rich, an answerer of the cry of the needy, a preserver of the sanctity of thy pledge . . . Be unjust to no man, and show all meekness to all men. Be as a lamp unto them that walk in darkness, a joy to the sorrowful, a sea for the thirsty, a haven for the distressed, an upholder and defender of the victim of oppression . . . Be a home for the stranger, a balm to the suffering, a tower of strength for the fugitive. Be eyes to the blind, and a guiding light unto the feet of the erring . . .'[5]
Bahá'u'lláh

'He who reverences those worthy of reverence . . . those who have overcome passions and have got rid of grief and lamentation; the merit of him who reverences such peaceful and fearless Ones cannot be measured by anyone as such and such.'[6]   *Dhammapada*

3

Roy Wilhelm, an early pilgrim to the Master in 'Akká, observed the esteem 'Abdu'l-Bahá had won from even those who were not Bahá'ís: 'Our room fronted upon a little garden in which was a fountain, and near by a tent in which 'Abdu'l-Bahá receives many of those who come to see Him. So intense are the hatreds between the followers of the different religious systems that it is unusual for a man to be well spoken of outside his own system, but 'Abdu'l-Bahá is regarded by all classes as a man of such wisdom and justice that it is to Him that they come for explanation of their religious Books, for the adjustment of their business quarrels, and even for the settlement of family difficulties. The inquirer will be told that 'Abbás Effendi ['Abdu'l-Bahá] makes no distinction; that He helps Jew, Muḥammadan, and Christian alike.' So fair was He in His dealings that a just Governor of 'Akká, Aḥmad Big Tawfíq, 'used to send his son to 'Abdu'l-Bahá for instruction, and in the exercise of justice and sound government turned to 'Abdu'l-Bahá for counsel.'[7]   *Honnold*

4

A. What sort of personal qualities and ideals do you feel to be good and worthy of respect?
B. How can we learn to respect what is decent and admirable?
C. Should we only respect the aged?
D. What has 'respect' got to do with being 'respectable' and being respected?
E. Is it easy to obey those whom we respect?

Righteousness

1

'Clothe thyself with the essence of righteousness, and let thine heart be afraid of none except God.'[1] *Bahá'u'lláh*

'Blessed are they which do hunger and thirst after righteousness: for they shall be filled.'[2] *New Testament*

'For I am the abode of Brahman, the never-failing fountain of everlasting life. The law of righteousness is my law; and my joy is infinite joy.'[3] *Gita*

'Easy to do are things that are bad and not beneficial to oneself, but very very difficult indeed to do is that which is beneficial and good.'[4] *Dhammapada*

2

'Cleave unto righteousness, O people of Bahá! This, verily, is the commandment which this wronged One hath given unto you, and the first choice of His unrestrained Will for every one of you.'[5]

Bahá'u'lláh

'One righteous act is endowed with a potency that can so elevate the dust as to cause it to pass beyond the heaven of heavens. It can tear every bond asunder, and hath the power to restore the force that hath spent itself and vanished.'[6] *Bahá'u'lláh*

'When righteousness is weak and faints and unrighteousness exults in pride, then my Spirit arises on earth.

'For the Salvation of those who are good, for the destruction of evil in men, for the fulfilment of the kingdom of righteousness, I come to this world in the ages that pass.'[7] *Gita*

3

The Thief of Cathay

Once an honoured man was having a birthday celebration. His sons and servants were busy receiving guests and messengers bearing gifts and congratulations. A thief, knowing that there would be valuable items among the gifts, slipped into the house and hid himself by lying face down on a beam in the roof of the hall where a great banquet was to be held in honour of the man. From this vantage point the thief could look down over the guests and see all the parcels of silks and jade and jewels that were being offered. He made a note of where these were put and planned to steal them after the guests had departed and the family gone to sleep.

Later that evening, the host lingered over his presents. He was very happy. As he leaned over them to take a final look, he turned his back to the thief hiding on the beam. The thief took a chance to look at the layout of the room so that he would be able to find his way once the lights were put out. As he hung his head over the beam he cast a shadow on the floor.

The host betrayed no sign of having seen the shadow, but he called for his servant and asked him to lay a table for one guest. Then he brought the best food and drink in the house. Turning towards the beam on which the thief lay, and bowing low, he said, 'Will the gentleman who is on the roof-beam now come down and partake of refreshments?'

There was nothing the thief could do but comply. He was led to the table and his host fed him well. When he had eaten his fill, his host gave him a bag of silver coins and begged him to make good use of them. Then the host saw the thief out courteously.

Ten years passed, and again the honoured man held a big birthday celebration. Many visitors came to wish him well and to bring him presents. The man was very old by now and could not greet everyone who called. His grandson met the visitors at the door and invited them to dine with his grandfather in the evening. He then took the gifts in for the old man to see.

Towards the end of the day a stranger came, bearing handsome gifts of gold and jewels. He would not give his name, but insisted that he see the honoured man.

The stranger was admitted to the old man's room, where he was overjoyed to see his host looking so well. The host did not recognise his guest, and, excusing himself by a plea of failing eyesight, inquired his name.

The stranger smiled and said, 'I am an honest man. I have learned to live a righteous life. But it was not always so. Do you not recall how you once asked me to come down from the roof-beam and partake of refreshment?'

The host was astonished, but he grew even more so when he heard how his own kindness to the thief had changed the thief's life to one of righteousness and honour. The coins he had given the thief had been used to begin a small business which had prospered and given work to many.

The guest was invited to stay for the banquet, and this time he did not eat alone. *A Chinese Folk Tale*

4

A. Why is righteousness such an important quality for us to possess?

B. What power does one righteous act possess?

C. What is a righteous act?

D. What righteous acts can you perform? Think both about your daily actions and your life plan.

E. Why is it easy to do bad things?

F. Why is it sometimes hard to do good things?

G. Can you think of a situation where you had to decide to do either right or wrong? What decision did you make? How did you feel about it afterwards?

H. How can we acquire a standard that will help us decide what is right and what is wrong?

Sacrifice

1

'The [person] restrained everywhere is freed from all sorrows.'[1]

Dhammapada

'Do thou sacrifice the thing which thou lovest most in the path of God . . .'[2] *Bahá'u'lláh*

'. . . Prayer and fasting is the cause of awakening and mindfulness and conducive to protection and preservation from tests.'[3]

'Abdu'l-Bahá

2

'O Son of Man! Ponder and reflect. Is it thy wish to die upon thy bed, or to shed thy life-blood on the dust, a martyr in My path, and so become the manifestation of My command and the revealer of My light in the highest paradise? Judge thou aright, O servant!'[4]

Bahá'u'lláh

'. . . nearness to God necessitates sacrifice of self, severance and the giving up of all to Him. Nearness is likeness.'[5] *'Abdu'l-Bahá*

'The sincere lover is a sacrifice to the loved one . . . He must wholly forget himself . . . He must seek the good pleasure of the True One; desire the face of the True One; and walk in the Path of the True One . . . This is the first station of sacrifice.

'The second station of sacrifice is as follows: Man must become like unto the iron thrown within the furnace of fire. The qualities of iron, such as blackness, coldness and solidity, which belong to the earth, disappear and vanish, while the characteristics of fire, such as hardness, glowing and heat, which belong to the Kingdom, become apparent and visible. Therefore iron hath sacrificed its qualities and grades to the fire, acquiring the virtues of that element.'[6]

'Abdu'l-Bahá

'. . . look at Me, follow Me, be as I am; take no thought for yourselves or your lives, whether ye eat or whether ye sleep, whether ye are comfortable, whether ye are well or ill, whether ye are with friends or foes, whether ye receive praise or blame; for all of these things ye must care not at all. Look at Me and be as I am; ye must die to yourselves and to the world, so shall ye be born again and enter the Kingdom of Heaven. Behold a candle how it gives its light. It weeps its life away drop by drop in order to give forth its flame of light.'[7]   'Abdu'l-Bahá

'. . . the moth is a sacrifice to the candle. The spring is a sacrifice to the thirsty one. The sincere lover is a sacrifice to the loved one and the longing one is a sacrifice to the beloved.'[8]   'Abdu'l-Bahá

3

Horatius at the Bridge

Once, long ago, there was a war between the people of Rome and the Etruscans who lived in the towns on the other side of the Tiber River. This river ran through the great city of Rome.

Lars Porsena, the tyrant King of the Etruscans, had gathered a huge army and was marching towards Rome. His soldiers, sure that they would conquer Rome, thought of all the wealth and treasure in the city that they could take away and of the people they could carry off to be their slaves. So they marched along confidently. Rome had never been in such great danger.

The Romans did not have very many fighting men at that time, and they knew they were not strong enough to meet the Etruscans in open battle. Therefore they kept within their city walls and set guards to watch the roads.

One morning the army of Lars Porsena, thousands strong, was seen sweeping over the hills near Janiculum, a town to the north, in a surprise advance. There were horsemen and footmen armed with spears and javelins, and all the people in the country through which they marched were fleeing before them into the city of Rome.

The Roman soldiers stationed on that side of the Tiber herded the frightened people on towards the city before Porsena and his men could overtake them.

The invading soldiers were coming closer. They were marching straight towards the wooden bridge that spanned the Tiber River at Rome.

The white-haired Senators of Rome, the men who ruled that city, did not know what to do. Their army was not strong enough to hold the land on the far side of the river.

But there was the crowded bridge. 'Once Porsena's men gain the bridge we cannot stop them from crossing over,' said the Senators. 'And what hope will there be for Rome then?' They shook their heads mournfully.

They thought of cruel Lars Porsena and the sorrow and ruin his conquering army would bring to their people and their beloved land. Already they could see, looking towards Janiculum, the smoke of the fires that rose from burning homes and villages. The invaders left not a house or a barn untouched.

Still the crowds of women and children, old people and farmers from the plains around, pushing their flocks and herds of sheep and cattle before them, kept coming on over the bridge.

Not far behind them came the soldiers of the Roman garrison running hard to get to the bridge, while Lars Porsena's men raced quickly to cross with them and capture Rome.

Now among the guards at the bridge there was a brave man named Horatius. He was on the farther side of the river and could see in the bright noonday sun, through the rolling clouds of dust, the gleaming helmets and spears of the approaching army.

He could hear the trampling of thousands of feet and the blare of trumpets proclaiming the victory the Etruscan invaders saw ahead of them.

There was only one thing to do. Horatius turned towards the Romans who were behind him. In a loud voice he called, 'Hew down the bridge with all the speed you can! I, with two men to stand by me, will hold the enemy at bay!'

Two brave Romans stepped beside him. Then, with their shields before them, their long spears in their hands, the three men stood at the head of the bridge and kept back the first horsemen Porsena had sent forward to take it.

On the bridge the Romans hewed away at its beams and posts. Axes rang and the chips flew loosening the props that held the bridge in place.

The Senators and the people watched as Horatius and his two companions silently prepared for the next attack. The enemy hordes came rolling forward with banners flying and trumpets sounding. The sun flashed and glittered on helmets, spears and swords.

When the foremost ranks saw the three Romans standing at the head of the bridge, a great shout of laughter went up among them. Three Etruscan horsemen sprang from their horses, drew their swords, and with shields raised high, rushed forward to attack the Romans who barred their way.

But it was they who fell, not the three Romans. And the same fate met others of the enemy who came forward. The enemy army watched in grim amazement. The Etruscans could not advance while the three Romans held the head of the bridge for only three had room to battle in that narrow passageway. On the city side the citizens of Rome were working desperately to destroy the bridge.

A mighty roar of anger rose from the invaders and the crowd of soldiers seethed with rage. Horatius was wounded by a spear thrust but the three men fought on. At last the trumpet's blare died down and the enemy army began to shrink back.

Now the bridge was tottering, ready to fall. 'Come back! Come back and save your lives!' the people shouted to Horatius and the two men with him.

But just then some of Porsena's horsemen dashed towards them again.

'Run for your lives!' cried Horatius to his friends. 'I'll keep guard. No one shall go through!'

The two darted across the bridge. They had hardly reached the other side when there was a great crashing of beams and timber. The bridge toppled over to one side and fell with a great splash into the Tiber.

When Horatius heard the crash of the bridge, he knew his city was safe. A shout of triumph rose from the opposite bank.

With his face still towards the enemy Horatius moved slowly backward till he stood on the river's bank. A dart thrown by one of Porsena's men put out his left eye but Horatius did not stop. He hurled his spear at an oncoming horseman and then turned quickly around. He saw the white porch of his own home among the trees on the other side of the stream.

Horatius sheathed his sword and plunged into the deep swift stream. He was still wearing his heavy armour when he sank out of sight and not a Roman or an Etruscan thought he would ever be seen again.

The wounded weary man fought hard to keep afloat in the swirling yellow waters. But Horatius was a strong man and the best swimmer in Rome. Soon his crest and helmet appeared above the waves and a great cheering rang out from the Roman side. He was half-way across the river and safe from the spears and darts which Porsena's soldiers had hurled after him.

As Horatius reached the side friendly hands stretched out to bring him to shore. Joyful shouts burst from every Roman throat as he stumbled upon the bank. Then even Porsena's men shouted, for they had never seen a man so brave and strong as he. He had kept them out of Rome but in so doing he had performed a deed they could not help but praise.

As for the Romans, Senators and citizens thronged about him to press his hands and thank him. The young men took him up and put him on their shoulders. Then they carried him through the roaring crowds to his home.

Horatius had given no thought to his own safety. He had thought only of his city and how it could be saved.

> With weeping and with laughter,
> Still was the story told,
> How well Horatius kept the bridge
> In the brave days of old.
>
> *Adapted from Macaulay*

The Banyan Deer

There was once a Deer the colour of gold. His eyes were like round jewels, his horns were white as silver, his mouth was red like a flower, his hoofs were bright and hard. He had a large body and a fine tail.

He lived in a forest and was king of a herd of five hundred Banyan Deer. Near by lived another herd of Deer, called the Monkey Deer. They, too, had a king.

The Maharaja of that country was fond of hunting the deer and eating deer meat. He did not like to go alone, so he called the people of his town to go with him, day after day.

The townspeople did not like this for while they were gone no one did their work. So they decided to make a park and drive the deer into it. Then the Maharaja could go into the park and hunt and they could go on with their daily work.

They made a park, planted grass in it and provided water for the deer, built a fence all around it and drove the deer into it.

Then they shut the gate and went to the Maharaja to tell him that in the park near by he could find all the deer he wanted.

The Maharaja went at once to look at the deer. First he saw there the two deer kings, and granted them their lives. Then he looked at their great herds.

Some days the Maharaja would go to hunt the deer, sometimes his cook would go. As soon as any of the deer saw them they would shake with fear and run. But when they had been hit once or twice they would drop down dead.

The king of the Banyan Deer sent for the king of the Monkey Deer and said, 'Friend, many of the deer are being killed. Many are wounded besides those who are killed. After this, suppose one from my herd goes up to be killed one day, and the next day one from your herd goes. Fewer deer will be lost this way.'

The Monkey Deer agreed. Each day the deer whose turn it was would go and lie down, placing its head on the block. The cook would come and carry off the one he found lying there.

One day the lot fell to a mother deer who had a young baby. She went to her king and said, 'O King of the Monkey Deer, let the turn pass me by until my baby is old enough to get along without me. Then I will go and put my head on the block.'

But the king did not help her. He told her that if the lot had fallen to her she must die.

Then she went to the king of the Banyan Deer and asked him to save her.

'Go back to your herd. I will go in your place,' said he.

The next day the cook found the king of the Banyan Deer lying with his head on the block. The cook went to the Maharaja who came himself to find out about this.

'King of the Banyan Deer! Did I not grant you your life? Why are you lying here?'

'O great Maharaja,' said the king of the Banyan Deer, 'a mother came with her young baby and told me that the lot had fallen to her. I could not ask anyone else to take her place, so I came myself.'

'King of the Banyan Deer! I never saw such kindness and mercy. Rise up. I grant your life and hers. Nor will I hunt anymore the deer in either park or forest.' *A Story from Indonesia*

A messenger brought news to Bahá'u'lláh while he was in Baghdád that a certain Mírzá Muḥíṭ-i-Kirmání wished to meet Him. Mírzá Muḥíṭ had rejected the claim of the Báb in Medina. 'He requested that his proposed interview be regarded as strictly confidential. "Tell him," was Bahá'u'lláh's reply, "that in the days of My retirement in the mountains of Sulaymáníyyih, I, in a certain ode which I composed, set forth the essential requirements from every wayfarer who treads the path of search in his quest of Truth. Share with him this verse from that ode: If thine aim be to cherish thy life, approach not our court; but if sacrifice be thy heart's desire, come and let others come with thee. For such is the way of Faith, if in thy heart thou seekest reunion with Bahá; shouldst thou refuse to tread this path, why trouble us? Begone!"' [9] *Nabíl*

4

A. What does sacrifice mean?

'This plane of sacrifice is the realm of dying to the self, that the radiance of the living God may then shine forth.' [10] *'Abdu'l-Bahá*

B. How can giving up something very precious to us be beneficial to us or to others?

C. How do the Manifestations of God teach us the meaning of sacrifice?

D. What stories can you think of where one person has sacrificed himself for another?

E. When we observe the Fast are we making any sacrifices? What is the purpose of this sacrifice?

F.   Fred was asked to sacrifice his pocket money to help build a
     village school. He said, 'All right, if I have to give, I will, but I
     don't really see why I should.' Do you think his sacrifice will be
     acceptable?

G.   Can you think of some of the sacrifices your parents made for
     you?

H.   Do you think that love is proved in sacrifice?

Self-Knowledge and Self-Respect

1

'He hath known God who hath known himself.'[1] *Bahá'u'lláh*

'. . . God loveth the Highest Perfection.'[2] *Bahá'u'lláh*

'In the unreal they imagine the real, in the real they see the unreal; they who feed on wrong thoughts never achieve the real.'[3]
Dhammapada

'As a solid rock is not shaken by the wind, even so the wise are not ruffled by praise or blame.'[4] *Dhammapada*

'Remembrance of Me cleanseth all things from defilement . . .'[5]
Bahá'u'lláh

2

'Far, far from Thy glory be what mortal man can affirm of Thee, or attribute unto Thee, or the praise with which he can glorify Thee!

'Whatever duty Thou hast prescribed unto Thy servants of extolling to the utmost Thy majesty and glory is but a token of Thy grace unto them, that they may be enabled to ascend unto the station conferred upon their own inmost being, the station of the knowledge of their own selves.'[6] *Bahá'u'lláh*

3

Coyote and Woodpecker

Coyote and his family lived near a forest. In the forest was a great old hollow tree, and Woodpecker and his family lived there. One day, as Coyote was walking, he met Woodpecker.

'How are you today, my friend?' said Coyote.

'Very well, thank you,' replied Woodpecker. 'And how are you?'

They talked together for a while. Then Coyote said, 'Friend Woodpecker, bring your wife and children tonight and join my family for supper.'

'Thank you, friend Coyote,' said Woodpecker. 'We will gladly come.'

That evening, Woodpecker and his family went to the coyotes' home. They fluttered to the ground and then, as they always do after flying, the woodpeckers stretched themselves. As they lifted their wings, the coyotes could see their pretty red and yellow feathers underneath. And as the woodpeckers ate supper, whenever they raised their wings, their bright feathers could be seen.

After the woodpeckers had eaten, they thanked their host politely. 'Please come to our house tomorrow for supper, friend Coyote,' said Woodpecker. And Coyote said yes, he and his family certainly would.

After the woodpeckers left, Coyote turned to his family and said, 'Did you see how those woodpeckers showed off their bright red and yellow feathers? No doubt they think they are more beautiful than we are, and they want to be sure we know it. Well, we will show them that coyotes are just as beautiful as woodpeckers.'

The next day, Coyote made all his family work hard gathering many loads of fire wood. When evening came, he built a big fire and called his family there. He tied a burning stick to each of them, under their arms, so that the burning end pointed forward. Then he did the same to himself. 'Now we coyotes will show those woodpeckers who has beautiful colours!' he told his family. 'And don't you forget to raise your arms often, to be sure they see we are just as good as they are!' Then the coyotes went to the woodpeckers' house.

When they came to the hollow tree, Woodpecker welcomed them

and invited them in very politely. Together, the woodpecker family and the coyote family sat down to supper. As they ate, the coyotes kept raising their arms to show the bright fire underneath. But suddenly one of Coyote's sons yelled, 'Ayee! My fire is burning me, papa!'

'Hush!' said Coyote. 'Don't give us away.'

'Ah!' sighed one of Coyote's daughters. 'My fire is out!' This was too much for Coyote, and he scolded her.

Then Woodpecker spoke. 'Tell me, Friend Coyote,' he said, 'why is it that your colours are bright red and yellow at first but later become ash grey?'

'Oh, that,' said Coyote, smiling pleasantly although he was very angry inside. 'That is the best thing about our colours, for they do not stay the same – as other people's do – but turn many shades.'

Coyote made an excuse so that he and his family could leave, for they were all smarting from their burns.

After they left, Woodpecker gathered his family around and said, 'Now, my children, you have seen what Coyote has tried to do. Never pretend to be what you are not. Always be just what you really are, and you will never need to put on false colours.'

Wendy Heller

4

A. Can you be friends with a person you do not respect?

B. What is self–respect?

C. How does knowledge of our own selves help us to gain self–respect? Why should we know our own selves?

    '. . . man should know his own self and recognise that which leadeth unto loftiness or lowliness, glory or abasement, wealth or poverty.'[7] *Bahá'u'lláh*

D. How can we learn to respect ourselves?

    'Indulge not in heedlessness . . .'[8] *Dhammapada*

    'He [the true seeker] should not wish for others that which he doth not wish for himself, nor promise that which he doth not fulfil.'[9] *Bahá'u'lláh*

E. Is self–respect the same thing as self–love?

Service

1

'That one indeed is a man who, today, dedicateth himself to the service of the entire human race.'[1]   *Bahá'u'lláh*

'Service is prayer.'[2]   *'Abdu'l-Bahá*

'I know thy works, and charity, and service, and faith, and thy patience and thy works; and the last is to be more than the first.'[3]

New Testament

'This wronged servant has spent His days and nights . . . urging the peoples to service.'[4]   *'Abdu'l-Bahá*

2

'There is no greater result than bonds of service in the Divine kingdom and attainment to the good-pleasure of the Lord. Therefore I desire that your hearts may be directed to the kingdom of God, that your intentions may be pure and sincere, your purposes turned towards altruistic accomplishment unmindful of your own welfare; nay, rather, may all your intentions centre in the welfare of humanity, and may you seek to sacrifice yourselves in the pathway of devotion to mankind.'[5]   *'Abdu'l-Bahá*

3

When a Turkish man, living in Haifa, lost his position, he, his wife and children were in a desperate need. They went to 'Abdu'l-Bahá for help and were naturally greatly aided. When the poor man became ill, again the Master stood ready to help. He provided a doctor, medicine and provisions to make him comfortable. When this man felt he was to die, he asked for 'Abdu'l-Bahá and called his children to him. 'Here', he told the children, 'is your father, who will take care of you when I am gone.'

One morning four small children arrived at the home of 'Abdu'l-

Bahá and announced, 'We want our father.' The Master, hearing their voices, knew who they were. They shared their sorrow with Him – their own father had died.

'Abdu'l-Bahá brought them in and gave them drink, sweets and cakes. He then went with them to their home. Their announcement had been premature – their father had merely fainted, but the next day he passed away.

The Master arranged for the funeral and provided food, clothing and travel-tickets for the family to go to Turkey. His sympathetic heart was as wide as the universe.[6]   *Honnold*

'Abdu'l-Bahá sorrowed with the sorrowful and the stricken and the afflicted, in deep compassion. He rejoiced with the truly joyous.

Thousands thronged to His door to seek relief . . . To them all, 'Abdu'l-Bahá gave freely and abundantly. No one found His door shut . . . He did not merely wait for the oppressed and the bewildered and the fallen to come to Him. He went out to find them and to serve them.[7]   *Balyuzi*

Howard Colby Ives recalled one meal at which 'Abdu'l-Bahá 'served me with His own hands most bountifully, urging me to eat, eat, be happy. He Himself did not eat but paced regally around the table, talking, smiling, serving.' Later he wrote that 'He has been known to go into the kitchen and prepare a meal for His guests. He never failed in such small attentions as seeing that the room where His visitors were entertained contained every possible comfort, though He paid no attention to His own comfort.' His response when He was at one time asked to act as honorary chairman of a Bahá'í Assembly was simply, "'Abdu'l-Bahá is a servant."[8]

Honnold

4

A. Why should we forfeit our own interests for the sake of others?
B. Can we willingly serve other people without genuinely loving them? ˙
C. How can we show love for humanity?
D. What sort of helpful service can you contribute at home, at school, in the community?

Sharing

1

'Verily, the misers go not to celestial realms. Fools do not indeed praise liberality; the wise man rejoices in giving and thereby becomes happy thereafter.'[1]   *Dhammapada*

'O Ye Rich Ones on Earth! The poor in your midst are My trust; guard ye My trust, and be not intent only on your own ease.'[2]
Bahá'u'lláh

'Give to him that asketh thee, and from him that would borrow of thee turn not thou away.'[3]   *New Testament*

2

'Charity is pleasing and praiseworthy in the sight of God and is regarded as a prince among goodly deeds. Consider ye and call to mind that which the All-Merciful hath revealed in the Qur'án: "They prefer them before themselves, though poverty be their own lot. And with such as are preserved from their own covetousness shall it be well." (Qur'án 59:9) . . . Blessed is he who preferreth his brother before himself.'[4]   *Bahá'u'lláh*

3

St Martin

When St Martin was a very young boy, he was made a knight so that he could serve in the army of the Emperor of France in place of his father who was old and ill.

Martin was sent to a place called Amiens. One morning he saddled his beautiful white horse and went riding among the hills outside the town. As he was enjoying the cool morning air he met a very poor man. The man was so very poor that he didn't have any clothes. Martin's heart was full of pity. Having nothing else to give, he cut his cloak in two with his sword and gave one half to the beggar.

On the following night Martin had a dream. Jesus Christ appeared to him wearing the half of the cloak he had given to the poor man the previous day. In giving to the poor man St Martin was giving to Jesus Himself.

Stories of 'Abdu'l-Bahá and the Poor of 'Akká

This scene you may see almost every day of the year in the streets of 'Akká. There are other scenes like it, which come only at the beginning of the winter season. In the cold weather which is approaching, the poor will suffer for, as in all cities, they are thinly clad. Some day at this season . . . you may see the poor of 'Akká gathered at one of the shops where clothes are sold, receiving cloaks from the Master. Upon many, especially the most infirm or crippled, he himself places the garment, adjusts it with his own hands, and strokes it approvingly, as if to say, 'There! Now you will do well.' There are five or six hundred poor in 'Akká, to all of whom he gives a warm garment each year.

On feast days he visits the poor at their homes. He chats with them, inquires into their health and comfort and leaves gifts for all . . . Those respectable poor who cannot beg must suffer in silence – those whose daily labour will not support their families – to these he sends bread secretly. 'His left hand knoweth not what his right hand doeth.'[5]   *Phelps*

Mary Lucas, a pilgrim to 'Akká in 1905, found that the Master usually ate but one simple meal a day. In eight days He was present at most meals, often coming just to add joy to the occasion, though He was not hungry. If He knew of someone who had had no meal during a day, the family supper was gladly packed up and sent to the needy.[6]   *Honnold*

'Abdu'l-Bahá's family was taught to dress in such a way that they would be 'an example to the rich and an encouragement to the poor'. Available money was stretched to cover far more than the Master's family needs. One of His daughters wore no bridal gown when she married – a clean dress sufficed. The Master was queried why He had not provided bridal clothes. With candour He replied simply, 'My daughter is warmly clad and has all that she needs for her comfort. The poor have not. What my daughter does not need I will give to the poor rather than to her.'[7]   *Honnold*

In 'Akká the Master's room often contained not even a bed as He was continually giving His own to those more needy than He. Wrapped in a blanket, He would lie on the floor or even on the roof of His home. It was not possible to buy a bed in the town of 'Akká; a bed ordered from Haifa took at least thirty-six hours to arrive. Inevitably, when the Master went on His morning round of visitations and found a feverish individual tossing on bare ground, He sent him His bed. Only after His own situation was inadvertently discovered did He receive another bed, thanks to some kind friend.[8] *Honnold*

The Wonderful Peartree

Long, long ago on a summer afternoon when the sun shone brightly, a stingy fruit pedlar halted his wheelbarrow at the side of the road along which many people were always going and coming. He had tied an umbrella to the top of a pole so that it shaded his baskets of luscious brown pears. 'The day is hot. It is dusty,' he said to himself. 'Travellers will be thirsty. I shall sell every one of my ripe juicy pears.'

All sorts of men passed the wheelbarrow of this fruit pedlar. Some had money to buy pears, and they went on their way licking their lips. Others could not spare even a few pennies. They could only look thirstily at the baskets on the wheelbarrow under the umbrella.

In the midst of the afternoon there came along an old man dressed like a farmer. He wore a blue jacket and blue trousers which were dusty and dirty, as though he had just finished his work. Over one shoulder he carried a hoe, and he looked very tired. He had not shaved for many days, and his untidy queue grew out of a little forest of bristles. He looked as though he had allowed the rains to wash his face and the winds to comb his hair for him.

But if you had examined him closely, you would have seen that there was something strange about this old man. His eyes were brighter and his face was finer than those of the other farmers who passed along the crowded road. But the fruit pedlar saw only that he was shabby and that he was too poor to buy his wares.

'O worthy fruit pedlar,' the old man said as he paused before the wheelbarrow, 'I am thirsty. I have no money to buy your pears, but I feel sure that you will be glad to spare one for a man of such great age as mine.'

'Depart, worthless beggar,' the stingy fruit pedlar cried. 'My pears are for sale. I do not give them away to every rascal who stops at my wheelbarrow.'

'I am old. My tongue is aching with thirst,' the aged farmer insisted. 'I do not ask for a fine pear. Give me the poorest, the smallest one in your baskets, and I will call down blessings upon you.'

'Why should I need your blessings, old wretch? Get you gone before I beat you!' The fruit seller shouted so loud that the noise drew a crowd about his wheelbarrow.

'For shame, fruit pedlar,' said a bystander. 'This farmer is old and weary. He is thirsty and poor. Give him a pear! One small pear will bring you but little money, and it will give him refreshment. You will be repaid by the satisfaction your kind action will give you.' The other bystanders echoed his plea, for they too felt pity for the tired dusty old man.

'You are generous with my property,' the stingy fruit pedlar cried angrily. 'I give no pears away. I should not gain satisfaction by such a foolish action. If you care so much for this old fool, why do you not give yourselves that satisfaction you speak of by buying a pear for him with your own money?'

The same bystander who had spoken first laid down a few copper coins and selected a large pear from the fruit pedlar's basket. He put it into the hands of the thirsty old farmer, who received it with a bow and with polite words of thankfulness.

So unusual was the appearance of the old farmer that the crowd lingered while he ate the ripe juicy pear down to the core. Then to their surprise, he picked out all the seeds and turned them over and over in the palm of his hand. One of them he selected, and the others he threw away.

'You have been so kind to me, honourable gentlemen,' he said to the crowd, 'that I shall now show you something which you have perhaps never seen and which may amuse you.'

Taking up his hoe, the old man dug a hole in the earth. In this he placed the seed which he had chosen with such care. He scattered earth over it and pressed it down with his foot.

'For my little play I have need of a pot of hot water. Does anyone here know where I might find such a thing?' he asked of the crowd, which by this time was much interested in his curious actions. One young man who was fond of a joke and who lived near by brought him a kettle from his own kitchen. The old farmer sprinkled the ground with the hot water, and, in less time than it takes to tell it, a tiny green shoot appeared in the earth where the seed had been planted.

A few moments more and it was a peartree almost a foot high. And as the crowd stood by, dumbfounded, it grew and it grew until it was very tall. Before their very eyes buds appeared, the tree burst into bloom, the blossoms fell off and the fruit formed. The little pears swelled and swelled. They grew brown and soft, and lo, they were ripe!

By this time the crowd was so great that it blocked the highway. More and more people gathered as the news of the strange happening spread through the neighbourhood.

'You young lads whose legs are more nimble than mine, climb up the tree,' the old farmer said. 'Pick the ripe fruit and hand it down to us thirsty ones.' The young men stripped the branches. Everyone in the crowd was given a pear. Even the stingy fruit pedlar, who had left his wheelbarrow to watch, ate of the fruit from the wonderful peartree.

When the fruit had been eaten the old farmer raised his hoe and with two or three blows he cut down the peartree. It fell to the ground, and as the crowd watched, its leaves seemed to shrivel and its branches to grow smaller. At last the only part left was the slender tree trunk. The old farmer picked this up and, using it as a staff upon which to lean, he went on his way with a low bow to the crowd, who stood speechless with wonder. So quickly was it over that they would scarcely have believed it had happened if there had not remained in their hands the cores of the pears they had eaten.

But hardly had the old farmer gone out of sight than there came a sharp scream from the stingy fruit pedlar. 'My pears! My pears!' he cried. 'They have all disappeared. All my money spent for those pears and now they are gone! It was that wretch of a farmer. He must have been a wizard. Ai, ai, it was my pears he used to deck his wonderful tree.'

'If that is true,' said a bystander, 'the old man rewarded you well. You deserved nothing less for your treatment of him.' But the stingy fruit pedlar did not hear. He was already running as hard as he could, in search of the old farmer.

But he never did catch up with him. The only thing he found was the old farmer's staff, the trunk of the peartree. And that staff was really the pole to which the fruit seller had tied his umbrella in order to shelter his fruit.

The old man was certainly a wizard who had taken the form of a farmer. Perhaps he had been sent just to give the stingy pedlar a lesson in his duty to his fellows. It is indeed true that those who do not pity the poor and who do not have respect for the aged should receive punishment of one sort or another.   *A Story from China*

4

A. What are the rewards for those who give generously?
B. If we share with others, who benefits?
C. Is it just money that we can share?
D. How do you feel when you have shared your possessions with another?

Silence

1

'Observe silence and refrain from idle talk.'[1] *Bahá'u'lláh*

'. . . one should be restrained in speech . . .'[2] *Dhammapada*

'In silent wonder the wise see [God] as the life flaming in all creation.'[3] *Mundaka Upanishad*

'Meditation is in truth higher than thought. The earth seems to rest in silent meditation . . .'[4] *Chandogya Upanishad*

'The tongue is a wild beast: loose it – it bites.'[5] *'Alí*

2

'. . . the tongue is a smouldering fire, and excess of speech a deadly poison. Material fire consumeth the body, whereas the fire of the tongue devoureth both heart and soul. The force of the former lasteth but for a time, whilst the effects of the latter endureth a century.'[6] *Bahá'u'lláh*

'Through the faculty of meditation man attains to eternal life, through it he receives the breath of the Holy Spirit – the bestowals of the Spirit are given during reflection and meditation.'[7]

'Abdu'l-Bahá

3

The Dumb Prisoner

'A Bábí was brought in chains from Yazd today!' whispered one man to another in Iṣfáhán, and the rumour soon began to spread. The Bahá'ís, who were always eager for news of their fellow believers, were among the first to hear the rumour. They immediately tried to find out more about the new arrival, but no one could give them the slightest information about their fellow believer's identity. They did not know who he was, or to which part of the prison he had been taken.

In the end, Síná, who had himself been released from the prison of Iṣfáhán only two days before, offered to go and find out from the jailer, who had become his friend.

Slowly and carefully he picked his way back through the narrow lanes to the dismal prison . . .

Those who passed Síná on the way must have been impressed by his radiant, kindly face, and the neat green turban and sash which were the signs of his holy lineage. If any had recognised him as the Bahá'í who had just been released from prison, they could never have believed he was on his way to visit his jailer now.

The jailer was prepared to help Síná. 'I can take you to the Bábí you want to see,' he said, 'but let me tell you that it is no use trying to talk to him. The man is deaf and dumb.' 'Deaf and dumb!' thought Síná as he followed the jailer. 'I wonder who he can be.'

They passed into the dirtiest section of the prison which was reserved for the worst types of criminals. Here, in a cell packed with people, Síná caught sight of Varqá in chains and stocks. The two poets were old friends and, of course, had much to tell each other. The astonished jailer and prisoners standing around could not believe their eyes! They stared with wonder at this holy Siyyid who had graced their cell with his presence and worked a miracle in front of their very eyes. 'The dumb man speaks!' they said to each other excitedly. 'The Siyyid has given him the power of speech and hearing!'

No one, however, was as puzzled as Síná who was supposed to have performed the miracle. 'You see,' Varqá told him by way of explanation, 'they spoke to me in such insulting language on the way from Yazd that I pretended not to hear them. It was quite convenient to be deaf and dumb before you arrived!' *Gloria Faizi*

Pino and Paint

Pino was much like all the other Indian boys of the Southwest. Like them, he lived in a house of sun-dried brick, called adobe; like them he spent much of his time helping his father and mother make pottery painted with bright designs he was learning to copy. When he was not busy working with the fine red clay, he played and ate and slept and grew, just like all the other boys.

Pino was like them in every way but one. He could not talk.

'Do not worry,' Pino's father said often to his wife. 'Some day our son will talk. And meanwhile, see how fast he learns.'

It was true; there was not a boy around the settlement whose eyes were brighter, whose ears were keener, whose feet would run more swiftly or whose hands were more deft and sure.

There were many things Pino liked to do, but best of all he liked to go to the Indian agency with his father when he went to sell the pottery and to buy supplies.

Pino liked everything about those days. He liked the trip over the twisting trail to the settlement. He liked the wide empty stretches of desert on all sides. Better still, he liked scrambling up behind his father and jogging along with the solid feeling of a horse below him.

How Pino wished that he might some day have a horse of his own! But when they reached the agency, there were other things to think of and wish for.

All the men lounging in the scant shade in front of the building called, 'Hello there, Ata,' to Pino's father and 'Hello, Pino!' to Pino himself.

Pino's father called back, 'Hello there!' and Pino smiled and waved his hand. All the men knew that this was Pino's way of saying hello.

Then they unloaded the pottery and carried it inside and, while Ata bargained, Pino rambled around the dim, fragrant room, soberly eyeing the bolts of calico, the piles of moccasins, the shelves of bright-labelled tins, the knives and tools and sacks and cartons and boxes of goods. But in all the store nothing brought a gleam to Pino's eyes today. There was nothing he wanted but a horse.

His father put a firm hand on his shoulder.

'This has been a good day,' his father said, and Pino could see that he looked happy. 'We have sold all but that cracked pitcher.'

Pino smiled his approval and took the cracked pitcher from his father's hands as they walked out together.

Now there was time to visit with the men. They used few words but there was friendliness in their voices. A good trading day, all agreed. Good weather. Everything felt fine.

As they waited quietly between speeches, up came Tall Hat, the horse trader.

'How went everything with you, Tall Hat?' Pino's father said to his friend, while Pino stood by listening.

'Pretty good, thanks,' Tall Hat replied, 'except for that pinto pony.'

He paused to light a cigar.

'That horse is crazy. He lets no one ride him. I guess he is good for nothing. Every time I am left with him on my hands.' He sighed as he looked towards the pony, standing alone in the corral. 'I'd trade him for that cracked water pitcher, I'm that tired of him.'

As he finished, all the men chuckled at Tall Hat's joke. But Pino did not know that it was a joke. He wanted that pony very much. So he silently held up the cracked water pitcher to Tall Hat.

Again everyone laughed, except Tall Hat. Without a word he took the pitcher and stood looking down at Pino. Then he turned to the boy's father and said, 'The pony is traded to Pino.'

Pino was not half a step behind as Tall Hat strode over to the corral. He was hanging over the topmost rail as Tall Hat swung a loop and lassoed the pinto pony. Then Tall Hat put a halter on the pinto and led him over to the boy. Putting the lead rope into Pino's hand, he said, 'Now he is yours, my friend.'

Pino beamed his thanks, and when he and his father rode out of the settlement on their way home, the lead rope was still in Pino's hand and the pony was following behind.

Pino was very happy. He kept looking back at his pony and thinking what a handsome animal he was and how splendidly he held his head. 'I shall call him Paint to myself,' Pino thought happily, 'for he is a paint pony, and such a fine one, too. I wonder why Tall Hat thought he was crazy.'

As they drew near Pino's home, he found out. The pony suddenly decided to stop. Pino's father's horse, of course, kept right on going. Pino, with the lead rope looped snugly around his waist, sailed through the air and landed right in the dusty road.

Pino picked himself up and sat there in the dust looking sadly at the horse.

'Now why did you do that, Paint?' he wondered silently.

At that the pony pricked up his ears and stared at Pino. 'Why,' the pony thought in surprise, 'you can talk!'

Then they both stared at each other, for without either of them uttering a sound, they both could understand every word the other thought!

'Imagine a horse being able to talk,' thought Pino.

'Well,' thought the pony, 'imagine a boy talking like a horse!'

At that moment Pino's father, who by now had reached home and dismounted, came out to the road and called back, 'Come on, Pino!'

'Get on my back,' said the pony, 'for if anyone is to ride me it shall be you.'

So to the amazement of his father and mother, Pino rode into the yard sitting easily on the back of the 'crazy' pony.

'You see,' said his father to his mother, 'although the boy cannot speak, he is a natural horseman.'

'Your father is right,' said the pony, when Pino repeated his father's words to Paint, 'for what horseman can talk to his horse as you can?'

From that day on Pino and Paint were great friends, and always together.

Of course Pino still had work to do. But every afternoon when he had finished helping his mother with pottery, he could hear Paint calling to him.

'Come on, Pino, let's go! I'm tired of standing in the corral all day. Let's go for a ride,' Paint would say, though Pino's mother never heard a word.

Then Pino would take a running jump onto his friend's back and away they would go. Sometimes they explored the Painted Mountain country with its vast stretches of bright-coloured rocks and its great bowl of bright blue sky overhead.

They visited with prairie dogs on guard at the doorways to their underground cities; they drank together from small, clear hidden springs. They told each other their thoughts as they jogged homeward in the gold and purple twilight. And always they were not just horse and rider, but good friends who spoke the same silent language.

On market days they rode into the settlement, where all the men marvelled at the way Pino had tamed Tall Hat's crazy pony.

When Rodeo Day came and his father and mother rumbled off in the wagon, Pino, mounted proudly on Paint, went trotting along behind them.

Pino and Paint saw everything there was to see that wonderful day, and when the big event, the pony race, came along, they were beside the track, watching.

'What is this?' Paint asked as the horses formed up at the starting line.

'It's the big pony race,' Pino told him.

'Why aren't we in it then?' asked Paint. 'Why aren't we racing? Hey, move over there!' Paint whinnied to the other ponies. 'Make room for us.'

To the amazement of everyone, especially the riders, all the horses moved over and made room for Pino and Paint.

When Pino and Paint had joined them, the gun barked and off they all went!

Down the track they pelted, with dust clouds flying. Pino and Paint were far in the rear, but Paint was getting the feel of the track.

What a thunder of hoofs as the dust clouds swirled! And through it all Pino and Paint edged forward past more and more of the flying feet.

Coming around the last turn, Paint put on a desperate burst of speed. With Pino, breathless from excitement, crouching close to his neck, Paint thundered past the lead horses and up the home stretch.

One last frenzied effort, and Paint had crossed the finish line – Pino and his pony had won the race!

'Paint! We've won!' Pino cried out loud as Paint slowed down to walk, his sides heaving. 'We've won!' Pino screamed, beside himself with joy. But Paint said nothing.

'Paint!' cried Pino again. 'Can't you hear me?'

Now his father came running up, open-mouthed with surprise, for he had heard Pino's shouts.

'My son!' he cried. 'You can speak!'

Pino, too, was surprised. 'Yes,' he said after he had tried again, 'I can speak.'

But Paint said not a word. He could no longer understand what Pino was saying, now that he talked like other boys. Or perhaps the trouble was that Pino could not understand Paint any more.

At first, when he realised this, Pino felt very sad. But he could see how good it would be to talk to the other boys and to the men at the agency house.

'And we shall always be friends,' Pino whispered to Paint in boy talk as he led the pony back to the judge's stand.

And they are friends to this day, for there is one thing they both still understand – that they like each other.

Adapted from Dan Noonan

The Talkative Tortoise

A talking tortoise lived high up the slopes of the Himalaya Mountains. Two wild geese occasionally came to his part of the forest and they became friends. Once when the geese came to visit the tortoise, they spoke about a beautiful place, a golden cave, where everyone lived happily together.

'It sounds a wonderful place,' sighed the tortoise. 'I should love to visit. I'm afraid everyone here is tired of my chatter. I'd like to meet some more people and see the golden cave. How can I go there? Can I walk?'

The geese laughed. 'Of course not. You can only fly there, and you don't have wings!'

The tortoise looked so sad that the two geese felt sorry for him. 'All right,' they said, 'we'll take you. Bite hold of this stick and we'll hold it in our beaks and fly you to the golden cave – but whatever you do, don't open your mouth!

Off they flew with the tortoise hanging onto the stick. As they flew over a village, some men called out, 'Look at that silly tortoise!'

The tortoise wanted to say 'What's so silly?' but he remembered the golden cave and he remained silent. However, when some children laughed rudely and pointed at him, the tortoise became very angry. He opened his mouth to say, 'What's so funny' and . . . fell splash into a lake below. So he never saw the golden cave, nor got to talk to any more friends.   *The Panchatantra*

4

A. Does silence only mean not talking?
B. When should we observe silence?
   Only at times of prayer and meditation?
   Only when we are studying?
   Only when we are told to 'Be quiet'?
C. What is the difference between observing silence and just not talking?
D. Can you think of a time when we should not be silent?

Sincerity

1

'He [the true seeker] should not wish for others that which he doth not wish for himself, nor promise that which he doth not fulfil.'[1]

Bahá'u'lláh

'And when you speak, be just . . .'[2] *Muḥammad*

'Better than a thousand utterances with useless words is one single beneficial word, by hearing which one is pacified.'[3] *Dhammapada*

'When man speaks words of truth he speaks words of greatness . . .'[4] *Chandogya Upanishad*

2

'By My Self! Whoso hath in bygone ages asked Us to produce the signs of God, hath, no sooner We revealed them to him, repudiated God's truth. The people, however, have, for the most part, remained heedless. They whose eyes are illumined with the light of understanding will perceive the sweet savours of the All-Merciful, and will embrace His truth. These are they who are truly sincere.'[5]

Bahá'u'lláh

'Sincerity is the foundation-stone of faith. That is, a religious individual must disregard his personal desires and seek in whatever way he can wholeheartedly to serve the public interest; and it is impossible for a human being to turn aside from his own selfish advantages and sacrifice his own good for the good of the community except through true religious faith.'[6] *'Abdu'l-Bahá*

3

The Master once told a pilgrim the following story. He was concluding an interview by telling of the time when He was travelling with a party which included a merchant. When the caravan halted in a certain village, quite a few people gathered around to meet 'Abdu'l-Bahá. The travellers later continued their journey and when they stopped in another town the same thing happened, and then it happened again. The merchant noticed this very obvious love and respect, which were showered on the Master. He then took Him aside and told Him he wished to become a Bahá'í.

When the Master asked him why he desired this, he replied, without apparent shame, 'You are a Bahá'í, and wherever you go, great crowds of people flock out to meet you, while no one comes to meet me; so I wish to become a Bahá'í.' 'Abdu'l-Bahá probed deeper. He asked him if that was the real reason. Whereupon the merchant replied with candour, 'I also think it will help my business, as I will have all these people come to meet me.'

It was then that he was told very frankly, 'Do not become a Bahá'í. It is better for you to remain as you are.'[7]   *Honnold*

Wolf in Sheep's Clothing

A wolf, once upon a time, found it so hard to get close enough to attack a flock of sheep that he often went hungry. For a long time the shepherd had guarded his lambs and sheep so carefully that the wolf was becoming desperate.

One night the wolf found a sheepskin that had been thrown away and forgotten. The wolf resolved to disguise himself and so gain an easy living. Quickly he slipped the sheepskin over his own hide and next morning strolled into the pasture with the grazing sheep as if he were one of them.

Soon the lamb that had belonged to the sheep whose skin the wolf was wearing began to follow the wolf. Leading her a little distance apart from the rest of the flock, the wolf in sheep's clothing made a good meal of her. For a while he succeeded in deceiving the other sheep and enjoying hearty meals.

Even the shepherd was fooled by the wolf in disguise, for when evening came, the wolf in sheep's clothing was shut up with the sheep in their fold.

But it happened that the shepherd had a longing for mutton broth for his supper that night. Picking up a knife, he went to the fold, and reaching in, seized the first animal he came to. Mistaking the wolf for a sheep, the shepherd killed him on the spot.   *Aesop*

The Sweet Jar

Nikoo and Jimmy were brothers. Their mother left them at home one day whilst she went to visit her sick aunty. Before she left she asked her children not to touch the jar or special sweets which she had placed in the cupboard and was saving for Diwali. All morning the children kept watching the cupboard. After lunch Nikoo went to sleep. Jimmy felt that it was time to explore – can you guess the first place he wished to investigate?

Yes, the sweet jar. He took a chair, and climbed up, opened the cupboard door and carefully took a lovely yellow sweet.

Unfortunately as he was climbing down his elbow knocked one of his mother's best glasses and it smashed into many pieces.

The noise woke up Nikoo, who felt very sad that his brother had disobeyed their mother. He tried to think of something to do that would make her happy when she returned from aunty's. Nikoo decided to wash up the dishes.

When he had finished he carried a tray with the dishes to the cupboard but, oh dear! He tripped over the cat and all the dishes were smashed.

Just then mother entered the house only to meet the scene of disaster. What do you think she felt about 1) Jimmy breaking one glass? 2) Nikoo breaking all the dishes?

What has this story to teach us about sincere intentions?

4

A. What is sincerity?
B. Discuss the qualities of a sincere person. What should we strive for in ourselves? What should we look for in others? (honesty,

genuineness of intention, freedom from hypocrisy, freedom
from falseness)

C. Why should a true friend be a sincere friend?

Sometimes it is difficult for us to judge whether a person is sincere or
not. However, the following teaching of Bahá'u'lláh gives us a
guideline: 'Expect not that they who violate the ordinances of God
will be trustworthy or sincere in the faith they profess. Avoid them,
and preserve strict guard over thyself, lest their devices and mischief
hurt thee.'[8]   *Bahá'u'lláh*

Sorrow

1

'Be not the cause of grief, much less of discord and strife.'[1]
Bahá'u'lláh

'Be as a lamp unto them that walk in darkness, a joy to the sorrowful
. . . a haven for the distressed . . . '[2]   *Bahá'u'lláh*

'Here he laments, hereafter he laments; in both states the evil-doer
laments . . . Here he is happy, hereafter he is happy; in both states
the well-doer is happy.'[3]   *Dhammapada*

'A merry heart maketh a cheerful countenance; but by sorrow of the
heart the spirit is broken.'[4]   *Old Testament*

2

'O ye beloved of God! When the winds blow severely, rains fall
fiercely, the lightning flashes, the thunder roars, the bolt descends
and storms of trial become severe, grieve not; for after this storm,
verily, the divine spring will arrive, the hills and fields will become
verdant, the expanses of grain will joyfully wave, the earth will
become covered with blossoms, the trees will be clothed with green
garments and adorned with blossoms and fruits. Thus blessings
become manifest in all countries. These favours are results of those
storms and hurricanes.

'The discerning man rejoiceth at the day of trials, his breast
becometh dilated at the time of severe storms, his eyes become
brightened when seeing the showers of rain and gusts of wind,
whereby trees are uprooted; because he forseeth the result and the
end, the leaves, blossoms and fruits; while the ignorant person
becometh troubled when he seeth a storm, is saddened when it
raineth severely, is terrified by the thunder and trembleth at the
surging of the waves which storm the shores.

'As ye have heard of the former times, when Christ – glory be to
Him! – appeared, a storm of trials arose, afflictions appeared, the

winds of tests blew, the thunder of temptation descended and hosts
of people surrounded the houses of the friends; then the weak ones
were shaken and were misled after once being guided; but the
disciples withstood the hardships and endured the storms of ordeals,
remaining firm in the Religion of God. Then observe that which
occurred after the storm and what appeared subsequent to that
severity, whereby the members trembled.

'God changed the sorrow to joy, the destructive darkness of
calamity into the shining light from the Supreme Concourse. The
people at the beginning persecuted and reviled the believers in God
and said of them: "These are the people of aberration." Then, when
their light appeared, their stars shone and their lamps illuminated,
the people returned into love and affinity; they prayed to them,
offered words of glory night and day and remembered them in
eulogy, reverence, honour and majesty.

'Therefore, O ye beloved of God, be not grieved when people
stand against you, persecute you, afflict and trouble you and say all
manner of evil against you. The darkness will pass away and the
light of the manifest signs will appear, the veil will be withdrawn
and the Light of Reality will shine forth from the unseen Kingdom
of El-Abhá. This we inform you before it occurs, so that when the
hosts of people arise against you for my love, be not disturbed or
troubled; nay, rather, be firm as a mountain, for this persecution and
reviling of the people upon you is a pre-ordained matter. Blessed is
the soul who is firm in the path!'[5]   'Abdu'l-Bahá

'O My servants! Sorrow not if, in these days and on this earthly
plane, things contrary to your wishes have been ordained and
manifested by God, for days of blissful joy, of heavenly delight, are
assuredly in store for you. Worlds, holy and spiritually glorious,
will be unveiled to your eyes. You are destined by Him, in this
world and hereafter, to partake of their benefits, to share in their
joys, and to obtain a portion of their sustaining grace. To each and
every one of them you will, no doubt, attain.'[6]   Bahá'u'lláh

3

Sadfish-Gladfish

Once upon a time, the Lord Mayor of London went for a walk and
noticed that all the people looked sad. Presently a mounted police

sergeant came along. Both he and his horse looked sad.

'Sergeant,' asked the Mayor, 'why do you look so sad?'

'Well, Lord Mayor,' said the Sergeant, saluting, 'everywhere I go the people look sad. It's the way they are made, I suppose. And it makes me feel sad, too. Even my horse feels sad.'

As he spoke his horse burst into tears.

'Oh,' said the people who were passing. 'That poor horse is crying!' and they began to cry too. Then other people passing saw them crying, and they began to cry. Very soon everyone was crying – bus drivers and taxi drivers and postmen and policemen and doctors and nurses and mothers and fathers and babies and dogs and cats and pigeons and sparrows. What a lot of tears there were! They cried so much that the streets were flooded and the water in the river Thames rose higher and higher.

Next morning, when the Lord Mayor got up, he went to collect his letters and morning paper from the front hall. But he could not do it because the hall was flooded with water. He went through to the kitchen and found his letters and paper there on the floor. Beside them was a little fish.

'The river must have overflowed in the night!' he said to his wife, and he picked up the fish and put it tail downwards into a jug of water that was on the table.

'What a sad-looking fish!' said his wife.

The fish flicked its tail, turned its head downwards and immediately looked a happy fish. They were surprised.

'I know what it is!' said the Lord Mayor. 'It's a sadfish–gladfish. I've heard of them. One way up they look happy and the other way up they look sad.'

They sat down to breakfast and the Lord Mayor opened his letters. 'I say, my dear,' he said, reading the first one. 'Just listen to this: "Dear Lord Mayor of London, All the people here look so sad that when they catch sight of each other they burst into tears. It is very wet here. Oh dear, what shall we do? Yours sincerely, The Mayor of Sydney, Australia."

As he finished reading, the fish turned upwards again and immediately looked sad.

'I've got it!' shouted the Lord Mayor. 'Watch this!' He stood on his head.

'How do I look?'

'You look happy to me now,' said the wife.

The Lord Mayor stood up.

'Now you look sad!' she said. Then she stood on her head.

'You look happy!' cried the Lord Mayor.

She stood up.

'Now, you look sad. That's it, then!'

The Lord Mayor sent for the chief policeman in all London.

'Tell everyone to stand on their heads!' he said.

Presently he went for a walk. All the people and the cats and the dogs and the pigeons and sparrows were standing on their heads. They all looked happy. No one was crying and the streets weren't flooded any more.

The Chief of Police saluted. 'It is very difficult saluting standing on my head, Lord Mayor,' he said. 'In fact, it is very difficult to do anything. Especially for the mounted policemen whose horses are all standing on their heads too.'

'Well, I don't want everybody crying!' said the Lord Mayor. 'But we can't stand on our heads forever. Oh, look at those bus drivers driving upside-down. That is dangerous!'

Just then he remembered the letter he had got from the Mayor of Sydney, that morning.

'I know what I'll do!' he thought. 'The people in Australia are upside-down to us and we're upside-down to them. If they came here and we went there, we'd all be upside-down without standing on our heads, and we'd all look happy too because we'd be the other way up.'

He telephoned the Mayor of Sydney in Australia.

'This is the Lord Mayor of London speaking,' he said. 'I'll tell you what we'll do. We'll swop over people and horses and dogs and cats and pigeons and sparrows and then everyone will look happy again.'

'That is a good idea!' said the Mayor of Sydney.

So that is what they did.

This took place long ago and the people have got mixed up since then. Some look sad and some look happy.

But in the middle of the pond, in Regent's Park in London, you will find a statue of a sadfish-gladfish to remind us of what happened. He looks a sad fish. Yet stand on your head and look at him and you will see he looks very happy.

Adapted from Donald Bissett

4

A. What can we do to help someone who is sad?

B. Can we prevent others from becoming sad?

'Ye know full well how hard it is for this Youth to allow, though it be for one night, the heart of any one of the beloved of God to be saddened by Him.'[7]   *Bahá'u'lláh*

C. Why is it better to be 'a joy to the sorrowful' rather than a 'cause of sorrow'?

D. To what extent are we responsible for our own sorrows?

For younger children

E. Discuss the meaning of 'Do not be a cause of sorrow'.

F. What sorts of things do we do that make our friends sad?

G. Why should we try not to do such things?

H. If someone is feeling sad, what should we do to try to cheer them up?

I. If we are always looking sad, are we going to cause others to feel happy?

Thoughts

1

'Mind foreruns [all] good conditions, mind is chief, mind-made they are; if one speaks or acts with pure mind, because of that, happiness follows him . . .'[1]   *Dhammapada*

'When a man has faith then he thinks.'[2]   *Chandogya Upanishad*

'Centre your thoughts in the Well-Beloved, rather than in your own selves.'[3]   *Bahá'u'lláh*

'Of the good thoughts, words, and works, which have been done, or will yet be done, the praisers and propagators are we, that we may belong to the good.'[4]   *Yaçna*

2

'When a man thinks then he can know. He who does not think does not know: know the nature of thought.

'When a man has faith then he thinks. He who has not faith does not think: know the nature of faith.'[5]   *Chandogya Upanishad*

'Hatreds can never cease by hatred in this world; by love alone they cease. This is an ancient law. The others know not that in this quarrel we perish; those of them who realise it have their quarrels calmed thereby . . . In the unreal they imagine the real, in the real they see the unreal; they who feed on wrong thoughts never achieve the real . . . Here he rejoices, hereafter he rejoices; in both states the well-doer rejoices, he rejoices, exceedingly rejoices, seeing the purity of his own deeds.'[6]   *Dhammapada*

'I charge you all that each one of you concentrate all the thoughts of your heart on love and unity. When a thought of war comes oppose it by a stronger thought of peace. A thought of hatred must be destroyed by a more powerful thought of love. Thoughts of war bring destruction to all harmony, well-being, restfulness and content . . . Thoughts of love are constructive of brotherhood, peace, friendship, and happiness.'[7]   *'Abdu'l-Bahá*

'In man five outer powers exist, which are the agents of perception, that is to say, through these five powers man perceives material beings. These are sight, which perceives visible forms; hearing, which perceives audible sounds; smell, which perceives odours; taste, which perceives foods; and feeling, which is in all parts of the body, and perceives tangible things. These five powers perceive outward existences.

'Man has also spiritual powers: imagination, which conceives things; thought, which reflects upon realities; comprehension, which comprehends realities; memory, which retains whatever man imagines, thinks, and comprehends. The intermediary between the five outward powers and the inward powers, is the sense which they possess in common, that is to say, the sense which acts between the outer and inner powers, conveys to the inward powers whatever the outer powers discern. It is termed the common faculty, because it communicates between the outward and inward powers, and thus is common to the outward and inward powers.

'For instance, sight is one of the outer powers; it sees and perceives this flower, and conveys this perception to the inner power – the common faculty – which transmits this perception to the power of imagination, which in its turn conceives and forms this image and transmits it to the power of thought; the power of thought reflects, and having grasped the reality, conveys it to the power of comprehension; the comprehension, when it has comprehended it, delivers the image of the object perceived to the memory, and the memory keeps it in its repository.

'The outward powers are five: the power of sight, of hearing, ᐤf taste, of smell, and of feeling.

'The inner powers are also five: the common faculty, and the powers of imagination, thought, comprehension, and memory.'[8]

'Abdu'l-Baha

3

Sea Memories

Often I think of the beautiful town
　　That is seated by the sea;
Often in thought go up and down

The pleasant streets of that dear old town,
  And my youth comes back to me.
    And a verse of a Lapland song
    Is haunting my memory still:
    'A boy's will is the wind's will,
And the thoughts of youth are long, long thoughts.'

I can see the shadowy lines of its trees,
  And catch, in sudden gleams,
The sheen of the far-surrounding seas,
And islands that were the Hesperides
  Of all my boyish dreams.
    And the burden of that old song,
    It murmurs and whispers still:
    'A boy's will is the wind's will,
And the thoughts of youth are long, long thoughts.'

I remember the black wharves and the ships,
  And the sea tides tossing free;
And the Spanish sailors with bearded lips,
And the beauty and mystery of the ships,
  And the magic of the sea.
    And the voice of that wayward song
    Is singing and saying still:
    'A boy's will is the wind's will,
And the thoughts of youth are long, long thoughts.'
Henry Wadsworth Longfellow

4

A. Discuss the differences between human beings and animals, remembering 'Abdu'l-Bahá's statement regarding the inner powers.
B. Why has the human race been given these powers and not animals?
C. How should we use these wonderful gifts?
D. Is thought powerful? Can we change things, or make things happen, by thinking about them?
E. Does it matter if we think good thoughts or bad?

Time

1

'. . . dedicate the precious days of your lives to the betterment of the world . . .'[1] *Bahá'u'lláh*

'Waste not your time in idleness and sloth. Occupy yourselves with that which profiteth yourselves and others.'[2] *Bahá'u'lláh*

'Though month after month with a thousand, one should make an offering for a hundred years, yet, if only for a moment, one should honour one whose self has been well trained, that honour is, indeed, better than a century of sacrifice.'[3] *Dhammapada*

'There is a bridge between time and Eternity; and this bridge is . . . the Spirit of Man. Neither day nor night cross that bridge, no old age, nor death nor sorrow.'[4] *Chandogya Upanishad*

2

'In the world of God there is no past, no future, and no present; all are one . . . in the world of God there is no time. Time has sway over creatures, but not over God . . . Morning, noon, and evening are related to this earth, but in the sun there is neither morning, noon, nor evening.'[5] *'Abdu'l-Bahá*

3

The Grasshopper and the Ants

This is a very well-known story by Aesop that teaches us a lot about using our time wisely:

The merry notes of the violin which the grasshopper was playing floated on the air and reached the place where the ants were busy collecting food.

'It's the grasshopper again!' they said. 'He's always playing that violin of his. He never seems to do any work.'

Just then the grasshopper danced by. He stopped when he saw the ants. 'Why are you working on such a beautiful day?' he asked. 'Don't you feel the gaiety of spring? Why aren't you dancing and singing?'

'We must collect our food now,' said the Queen of the ants. 'If we don't, what will we do when the winter comes?'

'Oh, winter's a long way off,' said the grasshopper. 'You take life much too seriously.'

'But you must work today if you want to eat tomorrow,' said another ant. 'You can play your violin when you have finished,' said another as the little ants scurried busily about.

The grasshopper didn't wish to heed their advice. 'Go on with your work, my little friends,' he said. 'I'm going to dance in the meadow in the sun.' And so the grasshopper left the busy ants and went on his way, singing.

The spring soon passed and the warm days of summer came. All day long the grasshopper played his violin in the shade of the bright summer flowers, or lazily sat in the sun, or slept on a blade of grass.

But the summer was soon over, the days began to get colder and the leaves turned from green to brown and fell from the trees. Many of the animals began their winter sleep.

One morning the grasshopper woke up and was surprised to see that snow had fallen during the night. He shivered and looked for a green leaf for food. But although he searched and searched he could

not find a thing. The land was covered with a thick carpet of snow and the ground underneath was as hard as iron. The long winter had come. 'Oh dear, oh dear! What shall I do!' cried the grasshopper. 'I shall die of hunger, I shall freeze to death!' The grasshopper wandered around looking for a place to keep warm but there was no such place. 'How silly I was not to listen to the ants. While I am dying of cold and hunger they are sitting in their warm house with plenty to eat.'

And sobbing loudly the grasshopper sat down in the snow. The ants heard his sad cry and as they were really kind creatures they came hurrying to help him. By this time the poor grasshopper was frozen stiff. The ants picked him up and carried him back to their nest. The ants cared for the grasshopper until he felt better and the spring had returned again. Never did the grasshopper forget the lesson he had been taught.

Do you know what the lesson is?

4

There are three aspects of time to consider: the relativity of time, using time wisely, and punctuality. The relativity of time is difficult for children to grasp. Using time wisely and punctuality, however, are concepts that can easily be discussed.

A. Sunita is never late for any appointment. What other virtue is she displaying as well as punctuality?

B. Govind arrives late for school every day. In what way does this action inconvenience others?

C. Monica can't get up early in the morning. How can she try to discipline herself to become an early riser?

D. Can a person who is always late for appointments and meetings ever be considered wholly reliable?

E. How much of your free time is well spent and how much frittered away?

F. What are some good things to do with our time?

Tranquillity

1

'Create in me a pure heart, O my God, and renew a tranquil conscience within me, O my Hope!'[1]   *Bahá'u'lláh*

'My object is none other than the betterment of the world and the tranquillity of its peoples.'[2]   *Bahá'u'lláh*

'Peace is health and construction . . .'[3]   *'Abdu'l-Bahá*

'For the man who forsakes all desires and abandons all pride of possession and of self reaches the goal of peace supreme.'[4]   *Gita*

'Just as a lake, deep, clear, and still, even so on hearing the teachings the wise become exceedingly peaceful.'[5]   *Dhammapada*

'Calm is the mind, calm is the speech, and action and right knowledge of him who is wholly freed, perfectly peaceful, and who is such a stable one.'[6]   *Dhammapada*

'The day is approaching when thy agitation will have been transmuted into peace and quiet calm. Thus hath it been decreed in the wondrous Book.'[7]   *Bahá'u'lláh*

2

'The greatest bestowal in the world of existence is a tranquil heart, and it is impossible for man to obtain a tranquil heart save through the good pleasure of the Lord. That is, a man may so adorn the temple of his being with lofty attributes and philanthropic deeds as to be pleasing at the Threshold of the Almighty. This is the only Path and there is no other Path. My point is this: Let all your thoughts, your ideals, your aims and purposes revolve day and night around one common object – that is to live in accord with the good pleasure of the Lord. Then all the doors of felicity will be opened before your faces, you will become successful in all your undertakings, and you will be confirmed in all your accomplishments. The basic principle is the good pleasure of the Lord: and the good pleasure of God is obtained through a tranquil heart, and the tranquillity of the heart is only gained by living in accord with the Divine Teachings and Exhortations. When a person attains to this station he is contented and peaceful. Then he will become prosperous in all affairs and enter into Paradise.'[8]   *'Abdu'l-Bahá*

3

The Selfish Giant

Every afternoon, as they were coming from school, the children used to go and play in the Giant's garden.

It was a large, lovely garden, with soft green grass. Here and there over the grass stood beautiful flower-like stars; and there were twelve peach-trees that in the springtime broke out into delicate blossoms of pink and pearl, and in the autumn bore rich fruit. The birds sat on the trees and sang so sweetly that the children used to stop their games in order to listen to them. 'How happy we are here!' they cried to each other.

One day the Giant came back. He had been to visit his friend the Cornish Ogre and had stayed with him for seven years. After the seven years were over he had said all he had to say, and he determined to return to his own castle. When he arrived, he saw the children playing in the garden.

'What are you doing there?' he cried gruffly, and the children ran away.

'My own garden is my own garden,' said the Giant. 'I will allow nobody to play in it but myself.' So he built a high wall all around it, and put up a notice:

TRESPASSERS WILL BE PROSECUTED

He was a very selfish Giant.

The poor children now had nowhere to play. They tried the road, but the road was dusty and full of stones. They used to wander round the high wall when their lessons were over, and talk about the beautiful garden inside. 'How happy we were there,' they said to one another.

Then the spring came, and all over the country there were little blossoms and little birds. Only in the garden of the selfish Giant it was still winter. The birds did not care to sing in it, as there were no children; and the trees forgot to blossom. Once a beautiful flower put its head out from the grass, but when it saw the notice board it was so sorry for the children that it slipped back into the ground again and went off to sleep. 'Spring has forgotten this garden,' cried the snow and the frost, 'so we will live here all year.'

The snow covered up the grass with her great white cloak, and the frost painted all the trees silver. Then they invited the North Wind to stay with them, and he came. He was wrapped in furs, and he roared all day about the garden, and blew the chimney-pots down.

'This is a delightful spot,' the North Wind said, 'we must ask the hail on a visit.'

So the hail came. Every day for three hours he rattled on the roof of the castle till he broke most of the slates, and then he ran round the garden as fast as he could go. He was dressed in grey, and his breath was like ice.

'I cannot understand why the spring is so late in coming,' said the selfish Giant, as he sat at the window and looked out at his cold white garden. 'I hope there will be a change in the weather.'

But the spring never came, nor the summer. The autumn gave golden fruit to every garden, but to the Giant's garden she gave none. So it was always winter there, and the North Wind, and the hail, and the frost, and the snow danced about through the trees.

One morning the Giant was lying awake in bed when he heard some lovely music. It sounded so sweet to his ears that he thought it must be the King's musicians passing by. It was really only a little linnet singing outside his window, but it was so long since he had heard a bird sing in his garden that it seemed to him to be the most beautiful music in the world. Then the hail stopped dancing over his head, and the North Wind ceased roaring, and a delicious perfume came to him through the open casement.

'I believe the spring has come at last,' said the Giant, and he jumped out of bed and looked out.

He saw a most wonderful sight. Through a little hole in the wall the children had crept in and they were sitting in the branches of trees. And the trees were so glad to have the children back again that they had covered themselves with blossoms and were waving their arms gently above the children's heads. The birds were flying about and twittering with delight, and the flowers, were looking up through the grass and laughing.

It was a lovely scene; only in one corner it was still winter. It was the farthest corner of the garden, and in it was standing a little boy. He was so small that he could not reach up to the branches of the tree, and he was wandering all around it, crying bitterly. The poor tree was still quite covered with frost and snow, and the North Wind was blowing and roaring above it. 'Climb up, little boy,' said the tree, and it bent its branches down as low as it could; but the boy was too tiny.

The Giant's heart melted as he looked out. 'How selfish I have been!' he said. 'Now I know why the spring would not come here. I will put that poor little boy on the top of the tree, and then I will knock down the wall, and my garden shall be the children's play-ground for ever and ever.' He was really very sorry for what he had done.

So he crept downstairs and opened the front door quite softly, and went out into the garden. But when the children saw him they all ran away. Only the little boy did not run, for his eyes were so full of tears that he did not see the Giant coming. And the Giant stole up behind him and took him gently in his hand, and put him up into the tree. And the tree broke at once into blossom, and the birds came and sang on it, and the little boy stretched out his two arms and flung them round the Giant's neck, and kissed him.

The other children, when they saw that the Giant was not wicked any longer, came running back, and with them came the spring.

'It is your garden now, little children,' said the Giant, and he took a great axe and knocked down the wall. And when the people went to market at twelve o'clock they found the Giant playing with the children in the most beautiful garden they had ever seen.

All day long they played, and in the evening they came to the Giant to bid him goodbye.

'But where is your little companion,' he said, 'the boy I put into the tree?' The Giant loved him the best because he had kissed him.

'We don't know,' answered the children. 'He has gone away.'

'You must tell him to be sure and come here tomorrow,' said the Giant. But the children said they did not know where he lived and had never seen him before; and the Giant felt very sad.

Every afternoon, when school was over, the children came and played with the Giant. But the little boy whom the Giant loved stayed away. The Giant was very kind to all the children, yet he longed for his first little friend, and often spoke of him.

Years went by, and the Giant grew very old and feeble. He could not play about any more, so he sat in a huge armchair and watched the children at their games, and admired his garden. 'I have many beautiful flowers,' he said, 'but the children are the most beautiful of all.'

One winter morning he looked out of his window as he was dressing. He did not hate the winter now, for he knew that it was merely the spring asleep, and that the pretty flowers were resting.

Suddenly he rubbed his eyes in wonder, and looked and looked. It certainly was a marvellous sight. In the farthest corner of the garden was a tree covered with lovely white blossoms. Its branches were all golden, and silver fruit hung from them, and underneath it stood the little boy he had loved.

Downstairs ran the Giant in great joy, and out into the garden. He hastened across the grass, and near to the child. And when he came quite close his face grew red with anger, and he said: 'Who has dared to wound you?' For on the palms of the child's hands were the prints of two nails, and the prints of two nails were on the little feet.

'Who?' cried the Giant. 'Tell me that I may take my sword and slay him.'

'Nay!' answered the child. 'These are the wounds of love.'

'Who are you?' said the Giant, and a strange awe fell on him, and he knelt before the little child.

And the child smiled on the Giant, and said to him:

'You let me play once in your garden. Today you shall come with me to my garden which is Paradise.'

And when the children ran in that afternoon, they found the Giant lying dead under the tree, all covered with white blossoms.

Oscar Wilde

4

A. What is tranquillity?
B. Is it easy to be tranquil?
C. Is the world today tranquil?

'The world is in great turmoil, and the minds of its people are in a state of utter confusion.'[9]   *Bahá'u'lláh*

'The evidences of discord and malice are apparent everywhere, though all were made for harmony and union.'[10]

Bahá'u'lláh

D. How can the world become tranquil?

'The well-being of mankind, its peace and security, are unattainable unless and until its unity is firmly established.'[11]

Bahá'u'lláh

'If the learned and worldly-wise men of this age were to allow mankind to inhale the fragrance of fellowship and love, every understanding heart would apprehend the meaning of true liberty, and discover the secret of undisturbed peace and absolute composure.'[12]   *Bahá'u'lláh*

E. Can world peace be established without establishing inner peace?

Troubles and Tests

1

'Be not troubled in poverty nor confident in riches, for poverty is
followed by riches, and riches are followed by poverty.'[1]

Bahá'u'lláh

'He whose mind is untroubled by sorrows . . . he is the sage of
unwavering mind.'[2] *Gita*

'When the wise rests his mind in contemplation on our God beyond
time . . . then he rises above pleasures and sorrow.'[3]

Katha Upanishad

'. . . whether affected by happiness or by pain, the wise show
neither elation nor depression.'[4] *Dhammapada*

2

'The necessity and particularity of the assured and believing ones is
to be firm in the Cause of God and withstand the hidden and evident
tests. Thanks be to God that you are distinguished and made
eminent by this blessing. Anybody can be happy in the state of
comfort, ease, health, success, pleasure and joy; but if one will be
happy and contented in the time of trouble, hardships and prevailing
disease, it is the proof of nobility. Thanks be to God that the dear
servant of God is extremely patient under the disastrous
circumstances, and in the place of complaining gives thanks.'[5]

'Abdu'l-Bahá

'To the loyal soul, a test is but God's grace and favour; for the valiant
doth joyously press forward to furious battle on the field of anguish,
when the coward, whimpering with fright, will tremble and shake.
So too, the proficient student, who hath with great competence
mastered his subjects and committed them to memory, will happily
exhibit his skills before his examiners on the day of his tests. So too
will solid gold wondrously gleam and shine out in the assayer's
fire.'[6] *'Abdu'l-Bahá*

3

The Story of Job

Job was a man who lived in the land of Uz. He was a very good, upright man who loved God and obeyed His laws. He had ten children, seven sons and three daughters. He was also a very rich man – the Bible says he had 7,000 sheep, 3,000 camels, 500 pairs of oxen, 500 she asses and a very fine and beautiful house.

Then some terrible calamities occurred. He lost all his wealth and his children died. However, even though Job was very sad, he continued to pray to God and worship Him saying that 'God has given everything to me and so He can take it if he wants.'

Poor Job. Troubles still followed him. He came out in boils from the soles of his feet to the top of his head and he sat down in ashes from the fire. All his old friends spoke unkindly to him and left him, including his wife, but he never ceased from praising God and he prayed for all those who had deserted him.

God saw that throughout these terrible troubles Job still loved Him and so He blessed him, restoring his household. He became so prosperous that the Bible tells us he was twice as rich as he was before, had seven more sons and three more daughters, and he lived for 140 years!

The Little Match-Girl

It was snowing and the wind blew cold as darkness fell over the city. It was New Year's Eve. In the gathering gloom a little girl with bare feet padded through the streets. She had been wearing her mother's slippers when she left home, but they were far too big, and she had lost them while hurrying across a busy road. One of them was nowhere to be found and a little boy had run off with the other. So now her bare feet were mottled blue and red with the bitter cold.

In her old apron the little girl carried bundles of matches which her father had sent her out to sell, but all day long nobody had bought a single match from her. Cold and hungry, she made her weary way through the city. Brilliant lights streamed from the windows of big houses, where blazing fires crackled merrily in the hearth, and the smell of roast goose hung on the air, for it was New Year's Eve.

The little girl crouched down in a corner between two houses. She drew her knees up to her chest, but this seemed to make her even colder. She was afraid to go home, for she had sold nothing the whole day! Not a penny had she earned, and her father would surely be angry with her. But it was just as cold at home, for the wind whistled through the cracks in the walls and floorboards.

How wonderful it would be to light a match! All she had to do was to take one out of its bundle, strike it on the wall, and warm her fingers at the flame. She drew out a match and struck it. How it sparkled and gleamed! How the flames leapt and the shadows danced! It seemed to the little girl as if she were sitting by an enormous iron stove with brass ornaments on it. She stretched out her frozen feet to warm them – and the flame went out. Gone was the burnt-out match smoking between her fingers.

She struck another. The match flared up, making a new circle of brightness. The light fell on the stone wall, which immediately became as transparent as gauze. She found herself looking into a cosy room, where a table stood spread with a white linen tablecloth and set with silver, while in the middle steamed an enormous roast goose. The goose leapt out of the dish and began to waddle towards her – and the match went out. She saw nothing but the cold, grey wall before her.

Once again she struck a match, and found herself sitting at the foot of a magnificent Christmas tree. Thousands of tiny candles twinkled on the tips of the green branches, and brilliant paper streamers and tinsel hung down to the floor. The little girl stretched

both her hands towards it – and the match went out. The candles seemed to climb higher and higher, until she saw that they were the cold, bright stars above her. One of them fell across the wintry sky, drawing a long fiery tail behind it. Someone must be dying, she thought, for her old grandmother, who had always been so kind to her, had said, 'Whenever you see a falling star, you will know that a soul is on its way to God!'

She struck another match. It threw a warm circle of light all round her, and within the bright circle stood her grandmother, smiling gently down at her.

'Oh, Grandmother,' cried the poor girl, 'take me with you, please! I know I shall never see you again once the match burns out. You will vanish just as the warm stove, the roast goose, and the beautiful Christmas tree did!' Quickly she struck the remaining matches, one after the other, for she did not want her grandmother to disappear.

Never had her grandmother looked so kind. She gathered the little girl into her arms and swept her up to heaven. How bright everything was! Here she felt neither cold, nor hunger, nor fear – for they were with God.

Early next day the people found the little match-girl huddled against the wall, the spent matches scattered about her. She was dead – but there was a smile of happines on her lips.

'Poor soul, she was trying to warm herself,' the people said; but no one guessed what beautiful things the little match-girl had seen by the light of her matches, nor how happy she was with her grandmother that glorious New Year's morning.

Adapted from Hans Christian Andersen

4

A. What human quality must we acquire in order to help us overcome tests? (patience)
B. If others become a test for us, what qualities do we need to overcome our feelings? (love, forbearance)
C. Why are we tested and afflicted with troubles?
D. What are the benefits of preparing for tests?
E. Can we pray for preservation from tests?

> '. . . prayer and fasting is the cause of awakening and mindfulness and conducive to protection and preservation from tests.'[7]

'Abdu'l-Bahá

Trust in God

1

'And if thou art overtaken by affliction in My path, or degradation for My sake, be not thou troubled thereby. Rely upon God, thy God and the Lord of thy fathers.'[1] *Bahá'u'lláh*

'God is sufficient unto me, He verily is the All-Sufficing! In Him let the trusting trust.'[2] *Bahá'u'lláh*

'True reliance is for the servant to pursue his profession and calling in this world, to hold fast unto the Lord, to seek naught but His grace . . .'[3] *Bahá'u'lláh*

'That seeker must, at all times, put his trust in God . . . and cleave unto Him . . .'[4] *Bahá'u'lláh*

'It is better to trust in the Lord than to put confidence in man.'[5]

Old Testament

2

'The day is approaching when God will have exalted His Cause and magnified His testimony in the eyes of all who are in the heavens and all who are on the earth. Place, in all circumstances, Thy whole trust in Thy Lord, and fix Thy gaze upon Him, and turn away from all them that repudiate His truth. Let God, Thy Lord, be Thy sufficing succorer and helper.'[6] *Bahá'u'lláh*

3

I now proceed to relate what befell the remaining companions of the Báb, those who had been privileged to share the horrors of the confinement with Bahá'u'lláh. From His own lips I have often heard the following account: 'All those who were struck down by the storm that raged during that memorable year in Ṭihrán were Our fellow-prisoners in the Síyáh-Chál, where we were confined. We were all huddled together in one cell, our feet in stocks, and around our necks fastened the most galling of chains. The air we breathed was laden with the foulest impurities, while the floor on which we sat was covered with filth and infested with vermin. No ray of light was allowed to penetrate that pestilential dungeon or to warm its icy coldness. We were placed in two rows, each facing the other. We had taught them to repeat certain verses which, every night, they chanted with extreme fervour. "God is sufficient unto me; He verily is the All-Sufficing!" one would now intone, while the other would reply: "In Him let the trusting trust." The chorus of these gladsome voices would continue to peal out until the early hours of the morning. Their reverberation would fill the dungeon, and, piercing its massive walls, would reach the ears of Náṣiri'd-Dín Sháh, whose palace was not far distant from the place where we were imprisoned. "What means this sound?" he was reported to have exclaimed. "It is the anthem the Bábís are intoning in their prison," they replied. The Sháh made no further remarks, nor did he attempt to restrain the enthusiasm his prisoners, despite the horrors of their confinement, continued to display.'[7]   *Nabíl*

My Aunty Claire

Not many years ago, people in Africa had not heard about the one true God and His Messengers, especially Bahá'u'lláh, God's Teacher for today. It was very important that someone should go to tell the people about Bahá'u'lláh.

At that time I was a very small girl living in a city called Cardiff in Britain. I had a very nice lady looking after me and my sister. Her name was Claire Gung, but I called her Aunty Claire. She said, 'If someone is needed to go to Africa, I will go.' We were all sad to say goodbye to her. We thought she was very brave to go to such a far-off country all alone.

Aunty Claire travelled all the way from England to Africa by ship. She didn't have a lot of luggage, only a few clothes and her sewing machine so that she could start work as soon as she arrived. Aunty Claire was really quite scared as she travelled on that boat. She did not know what Africa was going to be like, so she prayed and asked God for His help. She knew that the only way she could get along in Africa was to depend on God all the time. And she did.

She arrived safely and began her life in Africa. At first she made clothes for other people and then she decided to open a little school for small children. She rented an old building, got some paint and tools and began fixing it up and decorating it. She worked so hard that some people could not understand how she did it. But she knew. Every night she prayed to God and always asked Him to help her accomplish her work.

She finally opened her school, calling it 'Aunty Claire's Kindergarten'. The children loved her. Not only African children attended, but Indian, Chinese and English children also. She even had a little prince in her school. His father was the King whose palace walls were very close to the school. So close, in fact, that often during splendid occasions Aunty Claire could hear the loud beat of the drums from the palace.

It was a lovely school where the children learned to love one another and to love God as well as to read and write, sing and paint. Aunty Claire was happy because she knew she was doing what God wanted her to do.

Aunty Claire knew that children liked pretty things so she painted the school many different bright colours: the front door of the school was bright red.

Aunty Claire always prayed and asked God to protect her children and her school. And He did. One day some soldiers attacked the palace and tried to kill the King. They burned the palace to the ground and broke into all the nearby buildings, breaking some things and stealing others. But there was one building with a red door very close by that was not even touched. Can you guess what that building was? Of course, it was Aunty Claire's school. Many people wondered why, but Aunty Claire knew. Do you know? Aunty Claire trusted in God and He helped her.

'Trust in God but Tie your Camel'

Once there was a man who had a servant called Kafool. The man decided to make a journey. He bought a camel and a horse and set off across the desert. After travelling all day they reached a deserted caravanserai and, realising how tired they were, decided to stay the night there.

As the locality was infested with robbers the master decided that Kafool should keep guard over the horse and camel while he slept for the first half of the night, and the master would keep watch for the other half.

After their supper the master slept, but after an hour he woke up and asked his servant what he was doing as he seemed to be asleep. The servant replied, 'I'm trusting in God.'

'Very good,' said the master and went back to sleep.

After a few more hours the master woke up and saw Kafool looking very sad.

'What are you doing now?' he asked.

'I'm trusting in God to tell me where the robbers have taken our camel,' the servant sighed.   *A Folk Tale*

4

A. What does it mean to trust in God?
B. Discuss the meaning of 'In Him let the trusting trust'.
C. What is true reliance?
D. How is loving one another connected with having trust in God?

Trustworthiness

1

'Be worthy of the trust of thy neighbour . . .'[1]   *Bahá'u'lláh*

'. . . [friends] are the best in whom to trust . . .'[2]   *Dhammapada*

'Be ye trustworthy on earth, and withhold not from the poor the things given unto you by God through His grace.'[3]   *Bahá'u'lláh*

'. . . keep that which is committed to thy trust . . .'[4]
New Testament

2

'Know thou for a certainty that whoso disbelieveth in God is neither trustworthy nor truthful. This, indeed, is the truth, the undoubted truth. He that acteth treacherously towards God will, also, act treacherously towards his king. Nothing whatever can deter such a man from evil, nothing can hinder him from betraying his neighbour, nothing can induce him to walk uprightly.'[5]
Bahá'u'lláh

'The fourth Ṭaráz concerneth trustworthiness. Verily, it is the door of security for all that dwell on earth and a token of glory on the part of the All-Merciful. He who partaketh thereof hath indeed partaken of the treasures of wealth and prosperity. Trustworthiness is the greatest portal leading unto the tranquillity and security of the people. In truth the stability of every affair hath depended and doth depend upon it. All the domains of power, of grandeur and of wealth are illumined by its light.'[6]   *Bahá'u'lláh*

3

The Captain's Box

It was a misty grey morning. A brother and sister lay asleep on their beds. Mary and Sammy lived at the very top of an old house. Their bedroom had a low sloping roof and their window looked over the wide, murky river that ran through the city, then out to the open sea.

Their father was a sea captain. It was time for him to go away on his big ship on a long journey. Father crept into their bedroom and kissed the sleeping children. Mary, who was nine years old, woke up but her four-year-old brother was sound asleep.

'My darling Mary,' her father said, 'I am leaving now to go on a long journey. You are my big girl. I want you to be very brave while I am away and look after your mother and brother. I want you to look after this key. It is the key to my wooden chest which is under your bed. You mustn't open the chest until I tell you to. Do you understand?' Mary nodded. She loved her father very much and was so sad that he was going away that she couldn't speak. She took the key and put it in a safe place.

So the captain left on his long voyage. After he had been away for eight months a very sad thing happened. The mother of Mary and Sammy died leaving the children all alone. There was no one now to look after them. Mary worked very hard. She ran messages for people, did their washing – anything to earn enough money to look after her brother and herself. Every day she went to the Post Office to see if there was a letter from her father but each time the postmaster would say, 'Sorry little one, there's nothing today.'

Sammy would cry – he was so cold, tired and hungry. Mary would comfort him and sing him to sleep. Kind neighbours would help as much as they could but even so the children became very short of money. Mary sold as much of the furniture as she could until there was nothing left to sell.

'Why don't we open father's box?' asked Sammy. 'There may be something inside.'

'No,' replied his sister firmly. 'Father said we shouldn't open it until he says.'

'But when will he come?' cried Sammy. 'He never writes and he has left us all alone.'

'I'm sure he'll come soon,' his sister comforted him. But father did not come – one year, two years passed and the children became even more in need. But still Mary would not open the box, though many times she took the key and looked longingly at it. Then she would remember the words of her father and put it back in its place.

After two and a half years of hard work Mary became sick. She couldn't work any longer to look after herself and Sammy. Weak with hunger the two children huddled together in bed when a knock came on the door. Mary hardly had the strength to say 'Come in'. In the dim evening light Mary couldn't see who it was but she soon recognised the voice.

'My dearest children,' replied the sea captain, 'why should I find you like this?' All three hugged each other and laughed and cried all at once. Father explained that his ship had been wrecked at sea and it had taken all this time for him to come home. 'But why are you so poor? Why didn't you open the box? I wrote you a letter telling you to.'

'I didn't get your letter,' replied Mary, 'and you told me not to.'

'Then let's open the box now,' said the captain. 'Come, give me the key.' The key slowly turned in the rusty lock and the lid creaked open. When the children saw the contents they gasped. They were so astonished they couldn't speak. They saw the box was full of gold coins.

'My dear children,' their father said, 'this money was for you. I thought that if you were in need you would open it. How I regret you didn't receive my letter. However, I am here now and I will not leave you again. We will leave this house and find a beautiful place to live where you will become strong and well and we will live in happiness and comfort together.'

And so they did.   *Adapted by Irene Taafaki*

4

A. What sort of friend do you prize: one on whom you can always depend, or one who is unreliable?

B. Is it easy to win the confidence of others if you are unreliable?

C. What qualities do we need to cultivate in ourselves so that people will consider us trustworthy?

D. How is it that trustworthiness is the 'greatest door to the security and tranquillity of mankind'?

E. Can you explain why someone who is trustworthy attains the 'treasuries of wealth and affluence'?

Truthfulness

1

'One should utter the truth . . .'[1]   *Dhammapada*

'The earth is propped up by truth . . .'[2]   *Rig Veda*

'Truthfulness is the foundation of all the virtues of the world of humanity.'[3]   *'Abdu'l-Bahá*

'If ye continue in my word . . . ye shall know the truth and the truth shall make you free.'[4]   *New Testament*

'The gift of Truth excels all gifts;
The flavour of Truth excels all flavours;
the pleasure in truth excels all pleasures . . .'[5]   *Dhammapada*

'There is no evil that cannot be done by a lying person who has trangressed the one law [of truthfulness] and who is indifferent to a world beyond.'[6]   *Dhammapada*

'When a man speaks words of truth he speaks words of greatness: know the nature of truth.'[7]   *Chandogya Upanishad*

2

'Truthfulness is the foundation of all the virtues of the world of humanity. Without truthfulness, progress and success in all of the worlds of God are impossible for a soul. When this holy attribute is established in man, all the divine qualities will also become realised.'[8]   *'Abdu'l-Bahá*

3

The Boy Who Cried Wolf

A young boy was taking care of a flock of sheep in a mountain village. He had taken the sheep to graze on a nearby hillside. The sheep grazed and the boy watched. He was very bored.

Then he had an idea. It would be more exciting if he could trick the villagers into thinking that a wolf was attacking the flock. It would be fun to see them come running, and then to see the expression on their faces when he told them the joke. They would look so foolish.

So the boy ran to the edge of the field and looked down into the village. 'Wolf! Wolf!' he cried as loudly as he could.

Immediately the villagers heard the cry they came running up the hillside. They panted and puffed, but they ran as hard as they could to protect their sheep from the wolf. The boy watched them as they ran. He laughed to see their red faces.

When the villagers reached the top of the hill, the boy said, 'Ha! Ha! I fooled you! There is no wolf. My, you looked funny running up that hill.'

But the villagers were not at all amused. They were very angry that the boy had played such a trick on them. They went home, grumbling and complaining.

A month passed. Again the young shepherd was on the top of the hill with the sheep. Once again he became bored watching the sheep grazing. He remembered how funny the men had looked running and puffing up the hill. He remembered how much he had laughed. And he thought that he would like to play this trick again.

So the boy went a second time to the edge of the field and called down to the village below, 'Wolf! Wolf!'

Once again the villagers came running when they heard the call. They huffed and puffed up the hill and got very red in the face. The boy just stood and laughed as he watched them. Once again he told them that there was no wolf. He laughed harder than before as he saw their faces change from concern for their sheep to anger at him. He did not realise they were angry at him. He thought they were simply annoyed at being seen to be so foolish.

Another month passed. Once again the young shepherd was watching his flocks on the hillside, and once again he became bored. He remembered his earlier pranks and how much fun he had had, so he decided to play his trick one more time. He went to the edge of the field and called down into the village, 'Wolf! Wolf!'

This time the villagers waited a bit before they ran up the hill. They looked at each other and scratched their heads. They wondered aloud whether the shepherd was playing another of his tricks. But they decided not to risk it and eventually they ran up the hill to the field to chase away the wolf.

Again the shepherd watched them running and getting very red in the face, and again he laughed at their predicament. When they arrived in the field he told them there was no wolf. He laughed harder than ever, but not one villager so much as smiled. They did not think it was funny at all.

'You have tricked us for the last time,' they said angrily, and the boy had to wipe away the tears of laughter from his face as he watched them depart.

Another month passed. The summer was at its height and the shepherd was watching his flocks on the same hillside. It was very hot. The shepherd was very bored. Then, out of the corner of his eye he saw a flash of black and he realised that a wolf had come upon the flock. Here was excitement indeed! But the shepherd knew he could not protect the flock by himself. He would need help. He rushed to the side of the field and called down into the village, 'Wolf! Wolf!' and waited for the villagers to come running to help him save the sheep.

But down in the village the villagers went about their business in the usual way. They heard the boy call 'Wolf!' but they just shook their heads and said to one another, 'Pay no attention. He is up to his tricks again. This time we will not be so foolish. We will ignore him.'

Up on the hillside the wolf had managed to carry away one sheep already. The shepherd boy tried to chase the wolf away, but the wolf snarled at him so fiercely that the boy ran away in terror. He tried to call down to the village again.

'Wolf! Wolf!' he cried.

The villagers heard his call, but they shook their heads again and said to each other, 'He must think we are fools. We will not go up the hill this time, no matter how often he calls.'

The young shepherd was in despair. The villagers would not come, no matter how often he called. In the end the wolf ate all the sheep, while the boy could do nothing but look on helplessly. Now he was not laughing at all.   *Folk Tale*

The Illiterate Teacher and his Learned Pupil

A group of learned divines stopped at the shop of a poor, illiterate man to nail the shoe of one of the donkeys on which they rode. These dignitaries of Islam were on their way to visit a sacred shrine which lay beyond the gates of Ṭihrán, and which they were in the habit of visiting on Fridays.

But this Friday was to be different from other days, for among those who entered the blacksmith's shop was Abu'l-Faḍl, who was to become one of the greatest scholars of the Bahá'í world, and the man who attended to the donkey's shoe was the one who was destined to rend asunder the veils of tradition which so enveloped the mind of Abu'l-Faḍl as to prevent him from investigating the new Cause.

'Is it true, O learned divine,' asked the blacksmith of Abu'l-Faḍl as he worked on the donkey's shoe, 'that it is recorded in our traditions that every raindrop is brought down to earth by an angel from the sky?' 'Yes,' replied Abu'l-Faḍl. 'It is true.'

The blacksmith went on with his work. He picked up a nail and hammered it into place. Then he said, 'I have heard that, according to our traditions, no angel ever enters a house where there is a dog. Is there indeed such a tradition?' 'There is,' replied Abu'l-Faḍl. The blacksmith hammered in the last nail and said, 'I presume that no raindrops ever fall in a place where there is a dog.'

Abu'l-Faḍl felt hot with shame and embarrassment as he realised that an illiterate man had had to point out to him the obvious conclusion to be derived from the two well-known traditions. As he left the shop and joined his learned companions, one of them said, 'The man you were talking to is a Bábí.'

That same evening Abu'l-Faḍl began investigating the new Faith.

Why Jimmy Skunk Wears Stripes

Jimmy Skunk, as everybody knows, wears a striped suit, a suit of black and white. There was a time, long, long ago, when all the Skunk family wore black. Very handsome their coats were, too, a beautiful glossy black. They were very, very proud of them, and took the greatest care of them, brushing them carefully ever so many times a day.

There was a Jimmy Skunk then, just as there is now, and he was head of all the Skunk family. Now, this Jimmy Skunk was very proud, and thought himself very much of a gentleman. He was very independent, and cared for no one. Like a great many other independent people, he did not always consider the rights of others. Indeed, it was hinted in the wood and on the Green Meadows that not all of Jimmy Skunk's doings would bear the light of day. It was openly said that he was altogether too fond of prowling about at night, but no one could prove that he was responsible for mischief done in the night, for no one saw him. You see, his coat was so black that in the darkness of the night it was not visible at all.

Now, about this time of which I am telling you, Mrs Ruffed Grouse made a nest at the foot of the Great Pine, and in it she laid fifteen beautiful buff eggs. Mrs Grouse was very happy, very happy indeed, and all the little meadow folks who knew of her happiness were happy too, for they all loved shy, demure, little Mrs Grouse. Every morning when Peter Rabbit trotted down the Lone Little Path through the wood past the Great Pine he would stop for a few minutes to chat with Mrs Grouse. Happy Jack Squirrel would bring her the news every afternoon. The Merry Little Breezes of Old Mother West Wind would run up a dozen times a day to see how she was getting along.

One morning Peter Rabbit, coming down the Lone Little Path for his usual morning call, found a terrible state of affairs. Poor little Mrs Grouse was heart-broken. All about the foot of the Great Pine lay the empty shells of her beautiful eggs. They had been broken and scattered this way and that.

'How did it happen?' asked Peter Rabbit.

'I don't know,' sobbed poor little Mrs Grouse. 'In the night when I was fast asleep something pounced upon me. I managed to get away and fly up in the top of the Great Pine. In the morning I found all my eggs broken, just as you see them here.'

Peter Rabbit looked the ground over very carefully. He hunted around behind the Great Pine, he looked under the bushes, he studied the ground with a very wise air. Then he hopped off down the Lone Little Path to the Green Meadows. He stopped at the house of Johnny Chuck.

'What makes your eyes so big and round?' asked Johnny Chuck. Peter Rabbit came very close so as to whisper in Johnny Chuck's ear, and told him all that he had seen. Together they went to Jimmy Skunk's house. Jimmy Skunk was in bed. He was very sleepy and very cross when he came to the door. Peter Rabbit told him what he had seen.

'Too bad!' said Jimmy Skunk, and yawned sleepily.

'Won't you join us in trying to find out who did it?' asked Johnny Chuck.

Jimmy Skunk said he would be delighted to come, but that he had some other business that morning and he would join them in the afternoon. Peter Rabbit and Johnny Chuck went on. Pretty soon they met the Merry Little Breezes and told them the dreadful story.

'What shall we do?' asked Johnny Chuck.

'We'll hurry over and tell Old Dame Nature,' cried the Merry Little Breezes, 'and ask her what to do.'

So away flew the Merry Little Breezes to Old Dame Nature and told her all the dreadful story. Old Dame Nature listened very attentively. Then she sent the Merry Little Breezes to all the little meadow folks to tell everyone to be at the Great Pine that afternoon. Now, whatever Old Dame Nature commanded, all the little meadow folks were obliged to do. They did not dare to disobey her.

Promptly at four o'clock that afternoon all the little meadow folks were gathered around the foot of the Great Pine. Broken-hearted little Mrs Ruffed Grouse sat beside her empty nest, with all the broken shells about her.

Reddy Fox, Peter Rabbit, Johnny Chuck, Billy Mink, Little Joe Otter, Jerry Muskrat, Hooty the Owl, Bobby Coon, Sammy Jay, Blacky the Crow, Grandfather Frog, Mr Toad, Spotty the Turtle, and the Merry Little Breezes all were there. Last of all came Jimmy Skunk. Very handsome he looked in his shining black coat, and very sorry he appeared that such a dreadful thing should have happened. He told Mrs Grouse how badly he felt, and he loudly demanded that the culprit should be run down without delay and severely punished.

Old Dame Nature has the most smiling face in the world, but this time it was very, very grave indeed. First she asked little Mrs Grouse to tell her story all over again that all might hear. Then each in turn was asked to tell where he had been the night before. Johnny Chuck, Happy Jack Squirrel, Striped Chipmunk, Sammy Jay, and Blacky the Crow had gone to bed when Mr Sun went down behind the Purple Hills. Jerry Muskrat, Billy Mink, Little Joe Otter, Grandfather Frog, and Spotty the Turtle had been down in Farmer Brown's cornfield. Hooty the Owl had been hunting in the lower end of the Green Meadows. Peter Rabbit had been down in the Berry Patch. Mr Toad had been under the big piece of bark which he called a house. Old Dame Nature called on Jimmy Skunk last of all. Jimmy protested that he had been very, very tired and had gone to bed very early indeed, and had slept the whole night through.

Then Old Dame Nature asked Peter Rabbit what he had found among the shells that morning.

Peter Rabbit hopped out and laid three long black hairs before Old Dame Nature.

'These,' said Peter Rabbit, 'are what I found among the egg shells.'

Then Old Dame Nature called Johnny Chuck. 'Tell us, Johnny Chuck,' said she, 'what you saw when you called at Jimmy Skunk's house this morning.'

'I saw Jimmy Skunk,' said Johnny Chuck, 'and Jimmy seemed very, very sleepy. It seemed to me that his whiskers were yellow.'

'That will do,' said Old Dame Nature, and she called Old Mother West Wind.

'What time did you come down on the Green Meadows this morning?' asked Old Dame Nature.

'Just at the break of day,' said Old Mother West Wind, 'as Mr Sun was coming up from behind the Purple Hills.'

'And who did you see so early in the morning?' asked Old Dame Nature.

'I saw Bobby Coon going home from old Farmer Brown's cornfield,' said Old Mother West Wind. 'I saw Hooty the Owl coming back from the lower end of the Green Meadows. I saw Peter Rabbit down in the Berry Patch. Last of all, I saw something like a black shadow coming down the Lone Little Path towards the house of Jimmy Skunk.'

Everyone was looking very hard at Jimmy Skunk. Jimmy began to look very unhappy and very uneasy.

'Who wears a black coat?' asked Dame Nature.

'Jimmy Skunk!' shouted all the little meadow folks.

'What might make whiskers yellow?' asked Old Dame Nature.

No one seemed to know at first. Then Peter Rabbit spoke up. 'It might be the yolk of an egg,' said Peter Rabbit.

'Who are likely to be sleepy on a bright sunny morning?' asked Old Dame Nature.

'People who have been out all night,' said Johnny Chuck, who himself always goes to bed with the sun.

'Jimmy Skunk,' said Old Dame Nature, and her voice was very stern, very stern indeed, and her face was very grave. 'Jimmy Skunk, I accuse you of having broken and eaten the eggs of Mrs Grouse. What have you to say for yourself?'

Jimmy Skunk hung his head. He hadn't a word to say. He just wanted to sneak away by himself.

'Jimmy Skunk,' said Old Dame Nature, 'because your handsome black coat, of which you are so proud, has made it possible for you to move about in the night without being seen, and because we can no longer trust you upon your honour, henceforth you and your descendants shall wear a striped coat which is the sign that you cannot be trusted. Your coat hereafter shall be black and white, that will always be visible.'

And this is why to this day Jimmy Skunk wears a striped suit of black and white.   *Adapted by Irene Taafaki*

4

A. Why is truthfulness basic to good human relationships?
B. Should we ever try to hide a bitter truth with a sweet lie?
C. Which person would you like for a friend, the one who always tells you the truth or the one you can never quite be sure is telling the truth?
D. Can you think of any circumstances when it is better not to tell the truth?

Unity

1

'Unity of heart, and unity of mind . . . do and procure for you.'[1]
Atharva Veda

'So powerful is the light of unity that it can illuminate the whole earth.'[2] *Bahá'u'lláh*

'Be ye as the fingers of one hand, the members of one body.'[3]
Bahá'u'lláh

'Easily seen are others' faults, hard indeed to see one's own . . .'[4]
Dhammapada

2

'What is real unity? When we observe the human world we find various collective expressions of unity therein. For instance, man is distinguished from the animal by his degree or kingdom. This comprehensive distinction includes all the posterity of Adam and constitutes one great household or human family which may be considered the fundamental or physical unity of mankind . . . The unity which is productive of unlimited results is first a unity of mankind which recognises that all are sheltered beneath the overshadowing glory of the All-Glorious, that all are servants of one God; for all breathe the same atmosphere, live upon the same earth, move beneath the same heavens, receive effulgence from the same sun and are under the protection of one God. This is the most great unity, and its results are lasting if humanity adheres to it . . .'[5] *'Abdu'l-Bahá*

3

The Bundle of Sticks

There was once a farmer with several sons who could never agree among themselves. He had often told them how foolish they were to be always quarrelling, but they kept on and paid no attention to his advice.

One day the father called his sons before him and showed them a bundle of sticks tied tightly together. 'See which one of you can break this bundle in two,' he commanded.

Each son in turn took the bundle in his hands and tried his best to break it. They all tried, but in vain, for the bundle was so strong that not one of them could even bend it. At last they gave it back to their father saying, 'We cannot break it.'

Then the father untied the bundle and gave a single stick to each of his sons. 'Now see what you can do,' he said. Each one broke his stick with the greatest of ease.

'My sons,' said the wise father, 'you, like these sticks, will be strong if you stand together; but once you quarrel and become separated, then you are destroyed.'

4

A. Why should we be united?
B. What strength is there in unity?
C. How can we become united?
D. How can unity 'illuminate the whole earth'?

Wisdom

1

'He who holds fast to wisdom asks after the heavenly abode.'[1]

Yaçna

'Mind foreruns [all] good conditions, mind is chief . . .'[2]

Dhammapada

'If any of you lack wisdom, let him ask of God, that giveth to all men liberally . . . and it shall be given him.'[3]   *New Testament*

'The sword of wisdom is hotter than summer heat, and sharper than blades of steel, if ye do but understand.'[4]   *Bahá'u'lláh*

'Just as a lake, deep, clear, and still, even so on hearing the teachings the wise become exceedingly peaceful.'[5]   *Dhammapada*

'As a solid rock is not shaken by the wind, even so the wise are not ruffled by praise or blame.'[6]   *Dhammapada*

2

'Above all else, the greatest gift and the most wondrous blessing hath ever been and will continue to be wisdom. It is man's unfailing protector. It aideth him and strengtheneth him. Wisdom is God's emissary and the revealer of His Name the Omniscient. Through it the loftiness of man's station is made manifest and evident. It is all-knowing and the foremost teacher in the school of existence. It is the guide and is invested with high distinction. Thanks to its educating influence earthly beings have become imbued with a gem-like spirit which outshineth the heavens. In the city of justice it is the unrivalled Speaker Who, in the year nine, illumined the world with joyful tidings of this Revelation. And it was this peerless Source of wisdom that at the beginning of the foundation of the world ascended the stair of inner meaning and when enthroned upon the pulpit of utterance, through the operation of divine Will, proclaimed two words. The first heralded the promise or reward, while the second voiced the ominous warning of punishment. The promise gave rise to hope and the warning begat fear. Thus the basis of world order hath been firmly established upon these twin principles. Exalted is the Lord of Wisdom, the Possessor of Great Bounty.'[7] *Bahá'u'lláh*

3

The Wise King and the Little Bee

Many, many years ago there lived in the holy city of Jerusalem a mighty king whose name was Solomon. And his fame was in all the nations round about. For God had given Solomon a wise and understanding heart. He was wiser than any man who lived before him and any man who came after. And all the earth sought the presence of Solomon to hear his wisdom, and he always judged wisely and well.

Now, suppose I were to tell you that a little bee, a little, tiny insignificant bee, once proved itself to be wiser than this wisest of men? You would probably not believe it. Yet it is true. There is an old, old story to prove it, and because Solomon was as humble as he was wise, the story has a happy ending. And here it is:

It happened that among the countries which rang with the fame of Solomon's wisdom and riches was the country over which ruled the proud and beautiful Queen of Sheba. She longed to prove to everyone that Solomon was not the wisest man in the world. She would have liked to set him some difficult task which he could not perform, or better still, ask him a simple question which he would not be able to answer. She thought and she thought and at last an idea came to her.

She called together all the most skilled craftsmen in the land, and she commanded them to fashion for her a bouquet of flowers. It was to be of roses of Sharon and lilies of the valley. And the flowers were to be made so beautifully, so perfectly, that no one standing within a few inches of them would be able to tell if they were real or false. The craftsmen went to work and shortly afterwards brought the bouquet to the queen. The little bells of the lilies of the valley and the purple blossoms of the roses of Sharon were so perfect that the queen could not believe they were not real. And her skilled workmen had laboured long and hard to distil a perfume that matched perfectly the fragrance of the real flowers.

The queen was more than pleased. 'Now we shall see,' said she, 'how wise Solomon truly is.'

So she announced that she would pay him a visit; to do him honour, she said. And she came to Jerusalem with a very great train, with camels that bore spices and much gold, and with boxes full of precious stones.

Solomon received her graciously. The best rooms in the palace were offered to her and her companions. The finest musicians and dancers entertained her. And a lavish banquet was planned for her. On the evening of the banquet, the queen sent her most trusted servant to procure a bouquet of real roses of Sharon and lilies of the valley. When the merry-making and feasting were in full swing, the queen entered with the two bouquets. Everyone gasped. Never had they seen such beautiful bouquets, such perfect flowers and one the exact copy of the other.

'O, great and mighty king,' said the Queen of Sheba, standing at a little distance from Solomon and holding out the two bouquets, 'the whole world rings with stories of your wisdom. Tell me, you who can always see the truth, which of these bouquets is made up of real flowers and which of false?'

There was a deep silence in the vast hall. Not one person there could see any difference between the two bouquets. The little white bells of the lilies of the valley swayed gently in each and the lovely purple blossoms of the roses of Sharon sent out a faint perfume from each.

The deep silence was broken by a whispering and murmuring which started in one corner, travelled to another and soon filled the vast hall. Solomon leaned forward and wrinkled his brow. He heard the excited and anxious mutterings of his people, but both bouquets looked exactly alike. Perhaps they were both real? Or, perhaps they were both false? Suddenly, above the hum in the hall, Solomon's sharp ear caught another sound. It was made by a little bee buzzing against a window. Solomon smiled. He was wise enough to know that all wisdom comes from God and that God has given to each of His creatures a special wisdom of its own. So he motioned to one of his servants to open the window. No sooner was this done than the bee flew into the room. The king's eyes followed it. Straight and sure it flew to one of the bouquets and was soon lost to sight deep within the blossoms. So engrossed in watching the queen or in whispering to each other were the people that no one noticed what had happened.

The king sat up very straight and met the queen's mocking eyes.

'My gracious and honoured guest,' he said, 'the true flowers are those,' and he pointed to the bouquet chosen by the little bee.

The queen was astonished.

'It was a true report that I heard in my own land of your arts and of your wisdom,' she said. 'But I did not believe the words until I came and have myself seen it. You have wisdom beyond the fame of which I have heard. Happy are your men, happy are your servants, happy are all those who stand before you always and hear your wisdom.'

Then a great shout and roar of praise rang out from all the people. But the king himself was silent. In his heart he was giving thanks for the little bee that had come to help him.   *Folk Tale*

The Lion-Makers

In a certain town were four Brahmins. Three were famous scholars, but they had no common sense. The fourth had never been able to learn anything at all. He had nothing but common sense.

One day the four friends met to talk things over.

'What is the use of knowing a lot,' said they, 'and being very clever if one does not travel, win the favour of kings and make a lot of money? Whatever we do, let us all travel.'

So they set out. But when they had gone a little way, the eldest of them said, 'One of us, the fourth, is a stupid fellow. He has nothing but sense. Now nobody gains the favourable attention of kings just by having common sense. One must be a scholar too. Therefore, I don't think we ought to share our earnings with him. Let him turn back and go home.'

Then the second Brahmin turned to the man of sense and said, 'You know this is true. Please go home.'

But the third said, 'No, no. This is no way to behave, for we have been friends and played together since we were little boys. Come along, my good friend. You shall have a share of the money we earn.'

To this the others at last agreed and they continued on their journey. Soon they came to a forest and there in front of them lay the bones of a dead lion.

Then one of the educated men said, 'Here is a good chance to show how much we know. Here lies some kind of creature, dead. Let us bring it to life by means of all we have learned.'

The first Brahmin said, 'I know how to put together the skeleton.'

The second said, 'I can give it skin, flesh and blood.'

The third said, 'I can give it life.'

So the first put together all the bones. The second gave it skin, flesh and blood. But while the third was busy breathing life into it, the fourth, the man of common sense, spoke up.

'My worthy and learned friends,' he said, 'common sense would tell us that this creature is a lion. I would not advise you to bring it to life. If you do, he will surely eat every one of us.'

The Brahmins were very angry. 'You simpleton!' they said. 'Are you trying to tell us that you know more than we do?'

'I only know what my common sense tells me,' said the fourth Brahmin. 'However, if you insist on going ahead, just wait until I climb this convenient tree.'

After the fourth Brahmin climbed up the tree, the lion was brought to life. He rose up, opened wide his jaws, and ate up all three scholars.

But the man of sense, after the lion had gone off, climbed down from the tree and went home.   *Adapted from the Panchatantra*

The Lion and the Goat

A greedy lion had been eating up the animals of a certain country as fast as he could catch them.

The goat, who was the chief of the animals, decided one day that this must stop. 'I shall have to find a way of sending that lion out of the country,' he said to himself. Crawling into a large cave opening onto the roadside, the goat lay in wait, hoping the lion would soon come by.

Sure enough, on his way to the village not long afterwards, the lion passed the cave and saw the goat with his flowing beard and curved horns.

'What are you doing there?' asked the lion.

'Oh,' replied the goat, 'I have been waiting for you. You see, I have eaten up a hundred elephants, a hundred tigers, and a hundred wolves, but only ninety-nine lions. I need just one more lion to make it a hundred.' The goat again said, 'The gods are good to me to

have sent you here.' And the goat shook his horns and stroked his beard before making a leap as though to spring upon the lion.

Hastily the lion retreated. 'This creature looks like a goat,' he said to himself, 'but he does not talk like one. He is probably some wicked spirit in the form of a goat. Caution is often the better part of valour. I think I shall not proceed to the village but return to my home in the woods – fast.'

'I am sorry you are in such a hurry,' said the goat from his cave. 'Will you be back tomorrow?' the goat asked.

'I will not,' replied the lion, running faster.

'Then I shall have to come looking for you in the wood,' said the goat. But as he disappeared, the lion called back, 'You won't find me in the wood, or here, or anywhere else in this country, ever again.'

Adapted from the Panchatantra

4

A. Does having wise thoughts help us to make wise decisions?
B. How can we develop in ourselves the ability to make wise decisions?
C. How do we acquire wise thoughts?
D. What are 'noble' thoughts? How can we acquire these?
E. Do you think that happiness and success may depend upon the wisdom of our thoughts?

Work is Worship

1

'A man attains perfection when his work is worship of God . . .'[1]
Gita

'In liberty from the bonds of attachment, do thou therefore the work to be done: for the man whose work is pure attains indeed the Supreme.'[2] *Gita*

'Also unto thee, O Lord, belongeth mercy: for thou renderest to every man according to his work.'[3] *Old Testament*

'Commit thy works unto the Lord, and thy thoughts shall be established.'[4] *Old Testament*

'It is enjoined upon every one of you to engage in some form of occupation, such as crafts, trades, and the like. We have graciously exalted your engagement in such work to the rank of worship unto God, the True One.'[5] *Bahá'u'lláh*

'I, the Creator, have created thee for the industrious and the active.'[6] *Yaçna*

2

'O My Servants! Ye are the trees of My garden; ye must give forth goodly and wondrous fruits, that ye yourselves and others may profit therefrom. Thus it is incumbent on every one to engage in crafts and professions, for therein lies the secret of wealth, O men of understanding! For results depend upon means, and the grace of God shall be all-sufficient unto you. Trees that yield no fruit have been and will ever be for the fire.'[7] *Bahá'u'lláh*

'Briefly, all effort and exertion put forth by man from the fullness of his heart is worship, if it is prompted by the highest motives and the will to do service to humanity. This is worship: to serve mankind and to minister to the needs of the people. Service is prayer.'[8]
'Abdu'l-Bahá

3

Dr Grenfell

Dr Grenfell was an English doctor and life-long friend to the fishermen and their families off the ice-bound coast of Labrador. It was a job full of adventure and it suited his personality perfectly. When he first arrived there, he found that the sufferings of the fishermen in those frozen seas were far worse than anyone could have believed, but the young doctor was not discouraged.

His fee was sometimes nothing more than a little butter or a few potatoes but this never worried the doctor who was happy knowing that he was serving humanity.

During his sixteen years of hard but happy service the fishermen's beloved doctor built them four hospitals and equipped a floating hospital.

A nearly fatal accident happened when he was determined to save a little boy's life. A boy who lived across the ice on the far side of the harbour had hurt himself badly – he was in danger of losing his leg. Dr Grenfell loaded his dog-sledge with blankets, medicines, food and firewood and set out on the long trip. 'Come on, Jack, Nrin, Hoody, Jerry, Sue, Watch, Spy!' he called to his seven dogs.

It was a sunny morning when they set off. They travelled until evening, rested at a cottage and then proceeded early the next morning.

Dr Grenfell decided to try and shorten his journey to the sick boy by taking his sledge across the ice-bound harbour instead of going all the way around it. He travelled half-way across the frozen sea and reached an island in the middle in safety and then proceeded across the remaining short distance. However, suddenly the ice began to crack and the dogs and sledge were marooned on an ice-pan surrounded by gaps of icy black water.

The ice-pan began to sink. Slowly the doctor and dogs swam to a larger block of ice. The doctor was frozen with the terrible cold. His loving dogs nestled close to him. They at least had warm coats, unlike he. He wondered whether it was more painful to freeze to death than to die of slow starvation. They would all die anyway.

Then he made a very difficult decision. He killed three of his dogs, as painlessly as possible, wrapped himself in their skins and, surrounded by his four remaining dogs, he dozed asleep wondering if they would ever survive the night.

The next morning when he awoke he managed to make a signal and was seen and rescued by some fishermen who were out looking for their beloved doctor. Grenfell couldn't rejoice completely in his rescue. He kept thinking of the dogs he had had to sacrifice. When he recovered from the long illness that followed his exposure he erected a memorial in their memory inscribed:

> To the memory of three Noble Dogs, Hoody, Watch, Spy whose lives were given for me on the Ice. April 21, 1908.

Adapted by Irene Taafaki

The Old Man and his Wife

There was an old man who lived in a wood,
As you may plainly see,
He said he could do as much work in a day,
As his wife could do in three.
'With all my heart,' the old woman said,
'If that you will allow,
To-morrow you'll stay at home in my stead,
And I'll go drive the plough.

'But you must go milk Tidy the cow,
For fear that she go dry;
And you must feed the little pigs
That are within the sty.
And you must mind the speckled hen,
For fear she lay away;

And you must reel the spool of yarn
That I spun yesterday.'

The old woman took a staff in her hand,
And went to drive the plough;
The old man took a pail in his hand,
And went to milk the cow.
But Tidy hinched, and Tidy flinched,
And Tidy broke his nose,
And Tidy gave him such a blow,
That the blood ran down to his toes.

'High, Tidy! ho, Tidy! high, Tidy!
Tidy! stand thou still;
If ever I milk you, Tidy, again,
'Twill be sore against my will.'
He went to feed the little pigs
That ran within the sty;
He hit his head against the beam,
And he made the blood to fly.

He went to mind the speckled hen,
For fear she'd lay astray;
And he forgot the spool of yarn
His wife spun yesterday.
So he vowed by the sun, the moon, and the star,
And the green leaves on the tree;
'If my wife do not a day's work in her life,
She shall ne'er be blamed by me!'

Anon

The Brownie of Blednock

Did you ever hear how a Brownie came to the village of Blednock
and was frightened away again?

It was one November evening, just when the milking was done
and before the children were put to bed. The people of the village
were standing by their doorsteps talking about their bad harvest and
the turnips, and what chances there were of a good price for their
cattle at the coming fair.

All at once the queerest humming noise seemed to come up from
the riverside. It came nearer and nearer, and all the good people
stopped talking and began to look down the road. And, indeed, it

was no wonder that they stared, for there, coming up the middle of the highway, was the strangest little creature that human eyes had ever seen.

He looked like a wee, wee man. He had a long blue beard which almost touched the ground. His legs were twisted, his knees knocked together as he walked, and his arms were so long that his hands trailed in the mud as he came along. He seemed to be humming something over and over. As he came nearer, the good people of the village could make out the words:

'Have ye work for Aiken-Drum?
Any work for Aiken-Drum?'

Oh, how frightened the people were! The children screamed and hid their faces in their mothers' gowns and the milkmaids threw down the pails of milk they were carrying. Even the dogs crept in behind the doors, whining and hiding their tails between their legs. Some of the men who were not too frightened to look the wee man in the face laughed and hooted at him.

'Did you ever see such eyes?' cried one.

'His mouth is so big he could swallow the moon and never even notice it,' said the other.

'Look at his long blue beard!' said a third.

And still the poor little man came slowly up the road, crying:

'Have ye work for Aiken-Drum?
Any work for Aiken-Drum?'

Good Grannie Duncan, the kindest old woman in the village, called out at last: 'He's just a Brownie, a simple, kindly Brownie. I've heard tell of Brownies before. Many a long day's work will they do for the people who treat them well.'

Gathering courage from her words, all the village folk crowded around the little man. When they were close to him, they saw that his face was kind and gentle and that his tiny eyes had a merry twinkle in them.

'Strange little creature,' said an old man, 'tell us what you want and where you came from.'

'I cannot well tell thee whence I came,' said the wee man. 'My country is a nameless land and is very different from this land of yours. For there we all learn to serve, while here everyone wishes to be served. When there is no work for us to do at home, we sometimes set out to visit thy land to see if there is any work we can do there. If thou wilt, I will stay here awhile. I do not wish anyone to wait on me, and I want no wages, nor clothes, nor bedding. All I ask for is a corner of the barn to sleep in, and a bowl of broth set down on the floor at bedtime. If no one meddles with me, I shall be ready to help anyone who needs me. I'll gather your sheep on the hill. I'll take in the harvest by moonlight. I'll sing your bairns to sleep in their cradles. You'll find that the bairns all love Aiken-Drum. And, good housewives, I'll churn for you and bake your bread on a busy day. The menfolk, too, may find me useful when there is corn to thrash, or untamed colts in the stables, or when the waters are out in flood.'

No one knew quite what to say in answer to the little creature's strange request. It was an unheard-of thing for anyone to come and offer his services for nothing. Some thought it could not be true; others said it were better to have nothing to do with the little creature.

Then up spoke good Grannie Duncan again:

'He's but a Brownie, I tell you, a harmless Brownie. Many a story I've heard in my young days about the work that a Brownie can do, if he be treated well and let alone. Have we not all been complaining about bad times, small wages, and the hard work we all have to do? And now, when a workman comes ready to your hand, you will have nothing to do with him just because he is strange looking. And I've heard that a Brownie can stalk a whole ten-acre field in a single night! Shame on you, say I!'

'A ten-acre field in a single night!' cried out all the men of the village at once. 'A ten-acre field!' repeated one. 'And in a single night!' added another. That settled the matter. The miller at once offered the Brownie a corner of his barn to sleep in, and good Grannie Duncan promised to make him some broth at bedtime and to send her grandchild, wee Janie, down to the barn with it every evening. Then all the people of the village said, 'Goodnight,' and went to their homes. But they were careful to look over their shoulders once in a while, for fear that the strange little man was following them.

But if they were afraid of him that night, they had a very different story to tell about him before a week had passed. Whatever he was or wherever he came from, he was the most wonderful little worker that these people had ever known. And the strange thing was that he did most of the work at night. Village folk came from all parts of the countryside to catch a glimpse of this queer little worker, but they were never successful, for he was never to be seen when one looked for him. They might have gone to the miller's barn twenty times a day, and twenty times a day they would have found nothing but a heap of straw and an empty broth bowl.

But whenever there was work to be done, whether it was a tired child to be sung to, or a house to be made tidy, or a batch of bread to be worked up, or a flock of sheep to be gathered together on a stormy night, Aiken-Drum always knew of it and appeared ready to help just at the right time.

Many a time some poor mother who had been up all night with a crying child would sit down with it on her lap in front of the fire in the morning and fall asleep. When she awoke she would find that Aiken-Drum had made a visit to her house; for the floor would be scrubbed and the dishes washed, the fire made up and the kettle put on to boil. But the little Brownie would have slipped away as if he were afraid of being thanked.

The little children were the only ones who ever saw him when he was not working, and, oh, how they loved him! When school was out you could see them away down by the stream crowding around the little dark brown figure, and you could hear the sound of low, sweet singing; for Aiken Drum knew all the songs that children love well.

By and by the name of Aiken-Drum came to be a household word among the good people of the village, for, although they seldom saw him near at hand, they loved him like one of their own people.

And he would never have gone away if everyone in the village had remembered what good Grannie Duncan told them about Brownies. 'A Brownie works for love,' she had said to them over and over again. 'He will not work for pay. If anyone tries to pay him, the wee creature's feelings will be hurt, and he will vanish in the night.'

But a good man of the village and his wife forgot all that had been said, and one day they planned to make something for Aiken-Drum.

'He should not work for nothing,' said the good man.

'He has already worn out his coat and trousers slaving for us,' said his wife.

So one day they made him a little pair of green trousers and a little brown coat. That night the two good people laid a parcel by the side of the bowl of broth in the miller's barn.

In the middle of the night someone heard the Brownie saying to himself, 'A nice pair of green trousers and a little brown coat for me. I can come here no more till one of the children of this village travels the world over and finds me first.'

So this strange little creature had to go away. He vanished in the night as any Brownie is sure to do if someone tries to pay him.

And the good people of Blednock talked of the kind deeds of the little strange man who came one evening into their midst, and they wondered and wondered if he would ever come back to them again.   *Elizabeth Grierson*

4

A. What sorts of work could you do now to be of service to humanity and thus to worship God?
B. Does worshipping God through working mean that we do not have to pray?
C. Are we worshipping God if we do some work but complain the whole time we are doing it?
D. What would the world be like if no one worked?

Sources

'ABDU'L-BAHÁ. *'Abdu'l-Bahá in London*. London: Bahá'í Publishing Trust, 1982.
—— *Memorials of the Faithful*. Translated and annotated by Marzieh Gail. Wilmette, Illinois: Bahá'í Publishing Trust, 1971.
—— *Paris Talks*. London: Bahá'í Publishing Trust, 10th edn 1961.
—— *The Promulgation of Universal Peace*. Compiled by Howard MacNutt. Wilmette, Illinois: Bahá'í Publishing Trust, 2nd edn 1982.
—— *The Secret of Divine Civilization*. Translated by Marzieh Gail. Wilmette, Illinois: Bahá'í Publishing Trust, 1957.
—— *Selections from the Writings of 'Abdu'l-Bahá*. Compiled by the Research Department of the Universal House of Justice and translated by a committee at the Bahá'í World Centre and by Marzieh Gail. Haifa: Bahá'í World Centre, 1978.
—— *Some Answered Questions*. Collected and translated by Laura Clifford Barney. Wilmette, Illinois: Bahá'í Publishing Trust, rev. edn 1981.
—— *Tablets of Abdul-Baha Abbas*. Chicago: Bahá'í Publishing Society, 1915.
—— *Will and Testament of 'Abdu'l-Bahá*. Wilmette, Illinois: Bahá'í Publishing Committee, 1944.
ALI, AMEER, SYED. *The Spirit of Islam*. London: Christophers, rev. edn 1922.
ARBERRY, ARTHUR J. *The Koran Interpreted*. London: George Allen & Unwin Ltd, 1963.
Avesta. Vol. II ('Vispered and Yaçna'). Translated by Arthur Henry Bleek. Hertford: for Muncherjee Hormusjee Cama by Stephen Austin, 1864.
BÁB, THE. *Selections from the Writings of the Báb*. Compiled by the Research Department of the Universal House of Justice and translated by Habib Taherzadeh with the assistance of a committee at the Bahá'í World Centre. Haifa: Bahá'í World Centre, 1976.
Bahá'í Prayers. A selection of prayers revealed by Bahá'u'lláh, The Báb, and 'Abdu'l-Bahá. Wilmette, Illinois: Bahá'í Publishing Trust, 1982.
The Bahá'í Revelation. A selection from the Bahá'í Holy Writings. London: Bahá'í Publishing Trust, 1955.
Bahá'í World Faith. Selected Writings of Bahá'u'lláh and 'Abdu'l-Bahá. Wilmette, Illinois: Bahá'í Publishing Trust, 1971.
BAHÁ'U'LLÁH. *Epistle to the Son of the Wolf*. Translated by Shoghi Effendi. Wilmette, Illinois: Bahá'í Publishing Trust, 1962.
—— *Gleanings from the Writings of Bahá'u'lláh*. Translated by Shoghi Effendi. Wilmette, Illinois: Bahá'í Publishing Trust, rev. edn 1963.
—— *The Hidden Words*. Translated by Shoghi Effendi. Wilmette, Illinois: Bahá'í Publishing Committee, rev. edn 1954.

—— *The Kitáb-i-Íqán*. Translated by Shoghi Effendi. Wilmette, Illinois: Bahá'í Publishing Trust, 1950.

—— *Prayers and Meditations*. Translated by Shoghi Effendi. Wilmette, Illinois: Bahá'í Publishing Trust, 1962.

—— *The Seven Valleys and the Four Valleys*. Translated by Marzieh Gail in consultation with Ali-Kuli Khan. Wilmette, Illinois: Bahá'í Publishing Trust, 3rd rev. edn 1978.

—— *Tablets of Bahá'u'lláh*. Compiled by the Research Department of the Universal House of Justice and translated by Habib Taherzadeh with the assistance of a committee at the Bahá'í World Centre. Haifa: Bahá'í World Centre, 1978.

BALYUZI, H. M. *'Abdu'l-Bahá*. London: George Ronald, 1971.

The Bhagavad Gita. Translated by Juan Mascaró. Harmondsworth, Middlesex: Penguin Books, 1984.

BLOMFIELD, LADY. *The Chosen Highway*. Wilmette, Illinois: Bahá'í Publishing Trust, 1967.

The Dhammapada. Translated with notes by Nárada Thera. London: John Murray, 1954.

The Divine Art of Living. Selections from Writings of Bahá'u'lláh and 'Abdu'l-Bahá. Compiled by Mabel Hyde Paine. Wilmette, Illinois: Bahá'í Publishing Trust, rev. edn 1960.

ESSLEMONT, J. E. *Bahá'u'lláh and the New Era*. London: Bahá'í Publishing Trust, 4th rev. edn 1974.

Excellence in All Things. Compiled by the Research Department of the Universal House of Justice. Oakham: Bahá'í Publishing Trust, 1981.

FATHEA'ZAM, HOOSHMAND. *The New Garden*. New Delhi: Bahá'í Publishing Trust, 2nd edn 1963.

GAIL, MARZIEH. *Dawn over Mount Hira*. Oxford: George Ronald, 1976.

GRUNDY, JULIA M. *Ten Days in the Light of 'Akká*. Wilmette, Illinois: Bahá'í Publishing Trust, 1979.

Holy Bible. Containing the Old and New Testaments. Translated under King James. Cambridge: Cambridge University Press, 1911.

HONNOLD, ANNAMARIE. *Vignettes from the Life of 'Abdu'l-Bahá*. Oxford: George Ronald, 1982.

Hymns of the Atharva-Veda. Translated by Maurice Bloomfield. Oxford: Clarendon Press, 1897.

IVES, HOWARD COLBY. *Portals to Freedom*. London: George Ronald, 1967.

LINDSTROM, JANET. *The Kingdoms of God*. Wilmette, Illinois: Bahá'í Publishing Trust, rev. edn 1974.

Living the Life. London: Bahá'í Publishing Trust, 1974.

Magnified Be Thy Name. Compiled by the Child Education Committee of the National Spiritual Assembly of the Bahá'ís of the British Isles. London: Bahá'í Publishing Trust, 1956.

MAXWELL, MAY. *An Early Pilgrimage*. Oxford: George Ronald, 1953.

NABÍL-I-A'ZAM. *The Dawn-Breakers*. Nabíl's Narrative of the Early Days of the Bahá'í Revelation. Translated by Shoghi Effendi. London: Bahá'í Publishing Trust, 1953.

PHELPS, MYRON H. *Abbas Effendi, His Life and Teachings*. London: The Knickerbocker Press, 1903.

The Rig Veda. Translated by Wendy O'Flaherty. Harmondsworth, Middlesex: Penguin Books, 1984.

SHOGHI EFFENDI. *The Advent of Divine Justice*. Wilmette, Illinois: Bahá'í Publishing Trust, 1963.

—— *Call to the Nations*. Haifa: Bahá'í World Centre, 1977.

Star of the West. The Bahá'í Magazine. Vols. 9 and 16. Chicago: Bahá'í News Service.

The Upanishads. Translated by Juan Mascaró. Harmondsworth, Middlesex: Penguin Books, 1965.

World Order. A Bahá'í Magazine. Vol. 6, No. 1 (Fall 1971). Wilmette, Illinois.

The Yajur Veda. Translated by Devi Chand. Hoshiarpur: All India Dayanand Salvation Mission, 1959.

References

Animals

1. *Kitáb-i-Íqán*, p. 194
2. *Bahá'í Revelation*, p. 303
3. *Yaçna*, LXX, v. 45, p. 139
4. *Yajur Veda*, 36, 18
5. *Dhammapada*, XXVI, v. 405, p. 86
6. *Bahá'í Revelation*, p. 303
7. *Spirit of Islam*, pp. 157–8
8. *An Early Pilgrimage*, pp. 33–4
9. *Gleanings*, CXXV, p. 265

Backbiting

1. *Gleanings*, CXXV, p. 265
2. *Dhammapada*, XXV, v. 361, 363, p. 81
3. *Qur'án*, XLIX, v. 11–12, p. 231
4. Arabic *Hidden Words*, no. 27
5. Psalms 15:3
6. Persian *Hidden Words*, no. 66
7. *Gleanings*, CXXV, p. 264

Cleanliness

1. Quoted in *Bahá'u'lláh and the New Era*, p. 99
2. *Selections from the Writings of 'Abdu'l-Bahá*, pp. 146–7
3. Matt. 5:8
4. *Qur'án*, II, v. 222, p. 59
5. *Selections from the Writings of the Báb*, p. 80
6. *Dhammapada*, XXI, v. 299, p. 72
7. Quoted in *Bahá'u'lláh and the New Era*, p. 99
8. *Selections from the Writings of the Báb*, p. 80
9. Quoted in *The Chosen Highway*, p. 98
10. *The Dawn-Breakers*, p. 273

Compassion

1. *Dhammapada*, XXI, v. 300, p. 72
2. *Gleanings*, CXXX, p. 285
3. *Bhagavad Gita*, 3, v. 20
4. *Promulgation of Universal Peace*, p. 204

5. *Promulgation of Universal Peace*, p. 199
6. *Portals to Freedom*, p. 85

Concern

1. *Gleanings*, CXXX, p. 285
2. *Paris Talks*, p. 16
3. *Bahá'í Revelation*, pp. 301–2
4. *Abbas Effendi, His Life and Teachings*, pp. 2–10
5. *Tablets of Bahá'u'lláh*, p. 129
6. *Gleanings*, CXLVII, p. 316
7. *Gleanings*, CXXV, p. 265
8. Persian *Hidden Words*, no. 44
9. Arabic *Hidden Words*, no. 31
10. *Paris Talks*, p. 15

Contentment

1. Arabic *Hidden Words*, no. 18
2. *Dhammapada*, XV, v. 204
3. Persian *Hidden Words*, no. 39
4. *Qur'án*, IV, v. 36, p. 105
5. Arabic *Hidden Words*, no. 17
6. *Yaçna*, LIX, v. 2, p. 128
7. I Tim. 6:6
8. *Gleanings*, CXXXIV, p. 290
9. *'Abdu'l-Bahá*, p. 9
10. *Ten Days in the Light of 'Akká*, p. 103
11. *Gleanings*, CXXV, p. 265
12. *Dhammapada*, XV, v. 199–200
13. Arabic *Hidden Words*, no. 21

Co-operation

1. *Gleanings*, CXXXII, p. 288
2. *Bahá'í Revelation*, p. 148
3. *Paris Talks*, p. 139
4. *Qur'án*, III, v. 98, p. 87
5. Isaiah 2:4
6. *Divine Art of Living*, pp. 107–8

Courage

1. Arabic *Hidden Words*, no. 48
2. *Bhagavad Gita*, 16, v. 1–3
3. *Rig Veda*, 10:173, v. 1
4. Psalms 27:14
5. *Dhammapada*, III, v. 39

6. *Memorials of the Faithful*, pp. 6–7
7. *World Order* Magazine, Fall 1971, 'Five Books about 'Abdu'l-Bahá' (Kazemzadeh), p. 83
8. *Vignettes from the Life of 'Abdu'l-Bahá*, no. 34, p. 137
9. *Dawn over Mount Hira*, pp. 88–9
10. *Dhammapada*, III, v. 40, p. 23
11. *Bahá'í Revelation*, p. 138

Courtesy

1. *Tablets of Bahá'u'lláh*, p. 88
2. *Epistle to the Son of the Wolf*, p. 50
3. *Gleanings*, CXVIII, p. 279
4. *Dhammapada*, X, v. 132
5. *Qur'án*, IV, v. 88, p. 113
6. *Tablets of Bahá'u'lláh*, p. 88
7. Quoted in *Bahá'u'lláh and the New Era*, p. 78
8. *The Chosen Highway*, pp. 162–3
9. *Epistle to the Son of the Wolf*, p. 50

Criticism

1. *Dhammapada*, IV, v. 50, p. 26
2. *Gleanings*, CXLVI, p. 315
3. Luke 6:41
4. Persian *Hidden Words*, no. 44
5. Arabic *Hidden Words*, no. 26
6. *Ten Days in the Light of 'Akká*, p. 103
7. *Vignettes from the Life of 'Abdu'l-Bahá*, no. 80, p. 12
8. *Gleanings*, CXLVI, p. 315
9. Matt. 7:1, 7:2, 7:3, 7:5
10. *Dhammapada*, XXIII, v. 320, p. 75

Deeds not Words

1. Persian *Hidden Words*, no. 5
2. *Gleanings*, CXXIX, p. 305
3. James 1:22
4. *Bhagavad Gita*, 3, v. 21
5. *Qur'án*, IV, v. 124, p. 119
6. *Tablets of Bahá'u'lláh*, p. 156
7. Matt. 7:16–20
8. *Bhagavad Gita*, 2, v. 47
9. *Dhammapada*, IV, v. 51, p. 27
10. *Bahá'í Revelation*, p. 302
11. *Qur'án*, IV, v. 44
12. *Dhammapada*, IX, v. 122, p. 41

Detachment

1. Persian *Hidden Words*, no. 14
2. Persian *Hidden Words*, no. 40
3. *Gleanings*, CXXVI, p. 272
4. *Epistle to the Son of the Wolf*, p. 54
5. *Bahá'í World Faith*, p. 46
6. *Dhammapada*, XXIV, v. 336, p. 77
7. *Bhagavad Gita*, 6, v. 24
8. *Upanishads* (Isa Upanishad), p. 49
9. *Upanishads* (Katha Upanishad, Part II), p. 58
10. *Tablets of Bahá'u'lláh*, p. 155
11. *Upanishads* (Katha Upanishad, Part II), pp. 57–8
12. *Bahá'í Revelation*, pp. 267–8
13. *Dawn-Breakers*, p. 238
14. *Dawn-Breakers*, pp. 462–3
15. *Vignettes from the Life of 'Abdu'l-Bahá*, no. 14, p. 169
16. *Epistle to the Son of the Wolf*, p. 54
17. *Dhammapada*, VI, v. 81, p. 31
18. *Gleanings*, CXXV, p. 264

Distinction

1. *Promulgation of Universal Peace*, p. 190
2. *Dhammapada*, II, v. 27, p. 20
3. Quoted in *Advent of Divine Justice*, p. 21
4. *Promulgation of Universal Peace*, p. 190
5. *Promulgation of Universal Peace*, p. 190
6. *Selections from the Writings of 'Abdu'l-Bahá*, p. 144
7. *Secret of Divine Civilization*, p. 14
8. *Tablets of Bahá'u'lláh*, p. 138

Education

1. *Gleanings*, V, p. 9
2. *Gleanings*, CXXII, p. 260
3. *Bhagavad Gita*, 18, v. 45
4. *Qur'án*, 39, v. 11, p. 166
5. *Dhammapada*, XVIII, v. 241–3, p. 63
6. *Kingdoms of God*, pp. 19–21
7. *Gleanings*, CXXII, p. 259
8. *Tablets of Bahá'u'lláh*, p. 35
9. *Promulgation of Universal Peace*, p. 133
10. *Promulgation of Universal Peace*, p. 134

Environment

1. *Epistle to the Son of the Wolf*, p. 131

2. *Selections from the Writings of 'Abdu'l-Bahá*, p. 147
3. *Qur'án*, XVI, v. 66, p. 293
4. *Yajur Veda*, 36, 17
5. *Living the Life*, p. 20
6. *Call to the Nations*, pp. 9–10

Faith

1. *Tablets of Bahá'u'lláh*, p. 156
2. *Gleanings*, C, p. 205
3. *Bhagavad Gita*, 4, v. 39
4. James 2:26
5. *Magnified Be Thy Name*, p. 30
6. *Gleanings*, LXXIII, p. 141
7. Matt, 17:20
8. Luke 17:6
9. *Kitáb-i-Íqán*, p. 120

Family

1. *Bahá'í World Faith*, p. 229
2. *Upanishads* (Brihad-Aranyaka Upanishad, 2.4), p. 131
3. *Bhagavad Gita*, 1, v. 44
4. *Qur'án*, XVII, v. 23, p. 304
5. *Promulgation of Universal Peace*, p. 168
6. *Upanishads* (Brihad-Aranyaka Upanishad, 2.4), p. 131

Forbearance

1. *Gleanings*, V, p. 8
2. *Dhammapada*, XIV, v. 184, p. 53
3. *Qur'án*, XVI, v. 128, p. 301
4. Ephesians 4:2
5. *Gleanings*, CIX, p. 215
6. *Epistle to the Son of the Wolf*, p. 58
7. *Gleanings*, CXV, p. 242
8. *Gleanings*, V, p. 8
9. *Gleanings*, CXXXIX, p. 305
10. *Gleanings*, C, p. 204
11. *The Chosen Highway*, pp. 137–9
12. *Gleanings*, CIX, p. 215
13. *Dhammapada*, I, v. 4, p. 5

Forgiveness

1. *Qur'án*, XXIV, v. 22, p. 48
2. *Dhammapada*, XVII, v. 223, p. 60

3. Matt. 6:14
4. *Revelation of Bahá'u'lláh*, p. 298
5. *Prayers and Meditations*, CLXXXIV, p. 339
6. *Vignettes from the Life of 'Abdu'l-Bahá*, no. 9, p. 40
7. Matt. 5:39
8. *Some Answered Questions*, p. 309

Friendliness

1. *Gleanings*, CXLVI, p. 315
2. *Dhammapada*, XV, v. 197, p. 56
3. Proverbs 18:24
4. *Gleanings*, CXXX, p. 285
5. *Gleanings*, CXLVII, pp. 316–17
6. *Gleanings*, CXLVI, p. 315
7. *Will and Testament of 'Abdu'l-Bahá*, p. 13

Friendship

1. *Gleanings*, CXLVI, p. 316
2. *Gleanings*, CXI, p. 217
3. *Dhammapada*, XXIII, v. 328, pp. 75–6
4. *Dhammapada*, VI, v. 78, p. 31
5. *Yaçna*, LVII, v. 20, p. 127
6. John 15:13
7. *Yajur Veda*, 36, 18
8. *Tablets of Bahá'u'lláh*, p. 164
9. Persian *Hidden Words*, no. 3
10. *Gleanings*, CXXX, p. 285
11. *Gleanings*, CXXX, p. 285
12. *Paris Talks*, p. 15
13. *Yajur Veda*, 39, 19
14. *Dhammapada* (Penguin), VI, v. 78, p. 46
15. Persian *Hidden Words*, no. 56
16. *Will and Testament of 'Abdu'l-Bahá*, p. 13

Generosity

1. Persian *Hidden Words*, no. 54
2. Persian *Hidden Words*, no. 49
3. *Dhammapada*, XIII, v. 177, p. 51
4. *Rig Veda*, 10:117, 6
5. *Qur'án*, II, v. 211, p. 57
6. Persian *Hidden Words*, no. 49
7. *Gleanings*, V, p. 7
8. Adapted from *The Chosen Highway*, p. 157

Giving

1. *Tablets of Bahá'u'lláh*, p. 71
2. *Bhagavad Gita*, 3, 20
3. I Cor. 13:13
4. *Qur'án*, II, v. 211, p. 57
5. *Prayers and Meditations*, XXIX, pp. 33–4
6. *Prayers and Meditations*, CLXXXIV, p. 337
7. *Tablets of Bahá'u'lláh*, p. 156
8. *Gleanings*, C, p. 202

Good Conduct

1. *Epistle to the Son of the Wolf*, p. 29
2. *Upanishads* (Katha Upanishads), p. 57
3. *Dhammapada*, VIII, v. 111, p. 38
4. *Yaçna*, XLVII, v. 4, p. 111
5. *Qur'án*, LXI, v. 2, p. 274
6. *Tablets of Bahá'u'lláh*, p. 126
7. *Gleanings*, CXXXI, p. 287
8. *Tablets of Bahá'u'lláh*, p. 156
9. Persian *Hidden Words*, no. 76
10. *Promulgation of Universal Peace*, p. 190

Good Language

1. *Tablets of Bahá'u'lláh*, p. 219
2. *Tablets of Bahá'u'lláh*, p. 27
3. *Dhammapada*, X, v. 133, p. 43
4. *Qur'án*, XLIX, v. 11, p. 231
5. Ephesians 4:31
6. *Tablets of Bahá'u'lláh*, pp. 219–20
7. *Dhammapada*, X, v. 133, p. 43

Gratitude

1. *Bahá'í Prayers*, p. 19
2. *Gleanings*, CXXX, p. 285
3. *Promulgation of Universal Peace*, p. 469
4. Col. 3:15
5. *Qur'án*, II, v. 49, p. 35
6. *Promulgation of Universal Peace*, p. 236

Guidance

1. *Qur'án*, III, v. 44, p. 80
2. Isaiah 58:11
3. John 16:13

4. *Gleanings*, CXXXIX, p. 305
5. *Magnified Be Thy Name*, p. 8
6. *Qur'án*, III, v. 6, p. 74
7. *Dhammapada*, VI, v. 76–7, p. 31
8. *Bhagavad Gita*, 16, v. 23
9. *Qur'án*, III, v. 41, p. 80
10. *Gleanings*, CXXXIX, p. 305

Happiness

1. *Dhammapada*, XV, v. 207, p. 57
2. *Dhammapada*, I, v. 16, p. 17
3. Proverbs 3:13
4. Arabic *Hidden Words*, no. 33
5. Proverbs 14:21
6. Proverbs 16:20
7. Proverbs 29:18
8. *Dhammapada*, XV, v. 197, 199, 200, p. 56
9. *Promulgation of Universal Peace*, p. 218
10. Quoted in *The New Garden*, p. 82

Health and Healing

1. *Bahá'í Prayers*, p. 87
2. *Dhammapada*, XV, v. 204, p. 57
3. *Bahá'í World Faith*, p. 376
4. *Bahá'í World Faith*, p. 376
5. *Memorials of the Faithful*, pp. 157–8
6. *Vignettes from the Life of 'Abdu'l-Bahá*, no. 3, p. 37
7. *Vignettes from the Life of 'Abdu'l-Bahá*, no. 4, pp. 37–8
8. *Vignettes from the Life of 'Abdu'l-Bahá*, no. 5, p. 38
9. *Bahá'u'lláh and the New Era*, p. 97
10. *Selections from the Writings of 'Abdu'l-Bahá*, p. 150
11. *Bahá'í World Faith*, pp. 375–6
12. *'Abdu'l-Bahá*, pp. 12–13

Honesty

1. *Gleanings*, CXXXVI, p. 297
2. *Qur'án*, VI, v. 153, p. 168
3. Luke 8:15
4. *Upanishads* (Mundaka Upanishad, Part III, 1, 6), p. 80
5. *Dhammapada*, XVII, v. 223, p. 60
6. *Dhammapada*, XVII, v. 224, p. 60
7. *Gleanings*, CXXXVII, pp. 298–9
8. *Epistle to the Son of the Wolf*, p. 23
9. *Vignettes from the Life of 'Abdu'l-Bahá*, no. 88, pp. 93–4

Hospitality

1. *Paris Talks*, p. 15
2. *Dhammapada*, XXIII, v. 331, p. 76
3. *Paris Talks*, p. 16
4. *Qur'án*, XXIV, v. 27, p. 49
5. I Peter 4:8–9
6. *Star of the West*, vol. 9, no. 3, p. 40
7. *An Early Pilgrimage*, pp. 23–4
8. *Dawn-Breakers*, pp. 38–43
9. *Paris Talks*, p. 15
10. *Paris Talks*, p. 15
11. *Paris Talks*, p. 15

Humility

1. Arabic *Hidden Words*, no. 24
2. *Qur'án*, II, v. 43, p. 34
3. Matt. 5:5
4. *Dhammapada* XVII, v. 221, p. 60
5. *Gleanings*, CXXX, p. 285
6. *Epistle to the Son of the Wolf*, p. 30
7. *Bahá'í World Faith*, p. 384
8. *The Chosen Highway*, pp. 214–15
9. Arabic *Hidden Words*, no. 68
10. Arabic *Hidden Words*, no. 25

Joy

1. *Gleanings*, CXXXIII, p. 289
2. *Upanishads* (Taittiriya Upanishad 2.7), p. 110
3. *Paris Talks*, p. 109
4. Luke 15:10
5. *Bahá'í Prayers*, p. 143
6. *Promulgation of Universal Peace*, p. 335
7. John 16:22
8. *Bahá'í Prayers*, p. 152
9. *Upanishads* (Taittiriya Upanishad 3.1–6), p. 111

Justice

1. Arabic *Hidden Words*, no. 2
2. Proverbs 4:18
3. *Qur'án*, XVI, v. 92, p. 296
4. *Dhammapada*, XIX, v. 256, p. 65
5. Arabic *Hidden Words*, no. 2

Kindness

1. *Gleanings*, CXXXII, p. 289
2. *Qur'án*, II, v. 265, p. 67
3. *Dhammapada* XVII, v. 223, p. 60
4. *Yajur Veda*, 36, 18
5. II Peter 1:7
6. Isaiah 54:8
7. Isaiah 54:10
8. *Dhammapada*, XXV, v. 376, p. 83
9. *Bahá'í Revelation*, pp. 301–2
10. *Abbas Effendi, His Life and Teachings*, p. 10
11. *Vignettes from the Life of 'Abdu'l-Bahá*, p. 33

Knowledge

1. *Tablets of Bahá'u'lláh*, p. 156
2. *Bahá'í Revelation*, p. 150
3. *Yaçna*, XLVII, v. 4, p. 111
4. *Qur'án*, XXXIX, v. 11, p. 166
5. *Tablets of Bahá'u'lláh*, p. 52
6. *Dhammapada*, XI, v. 152, p. 46
7. *Dhammapada*, XXIII, v. 321–2, p. 75
8. *Gleanings*, LXXXIX, pp. 176–7

Liberty

1. *Gleanings*, CLIX, p. 336
2. *Dhammapada*, XXI, p. 71
3. *Qur'án*, II, v. 6, p. 42
4. Psalms 119:44–5
5. *Gleanings*, CLIX, p. 336
6. *Bahá'í Revelation*, p. 214
7. *Vignettes from the Life of 'Abdu'l-Bahá*, no. 2, pp. 9–10
8. *The Chosen Highway*, pp. 41–2
9. *The Chosen Highway*, pp. 44–5
10. *God Passes By*, p. 185
11. *Abbas Effendi, His Life and Teachings*, pp. 57–63
12. *Qur'án*, III, v. 17, p. 75
13. *Qur'án*, XVI, v. 83, pp. 295–6
14. *Gleanings*, XLV, p. 99

Love

1. Persian *Hidden Words*, no. 3
2. *Paris Talks*, p. 179
3. John 15:12
4. *Bhagavad Gita*, 11, v. 54

5. *Promulgation of Universal Peace*, p. 218
6. *Divine Art of Living*, pp. 108–9
7. *Gleanings*, XLIII, p. 95
8. *Dhammapada*, I, v. 5, p. 15

Obedience

1. *Gleanings*, CII, p. 207
2. *Paris Talks*, p. 132
3. *Qur'án*, IV, v. 17, p. 102
4. Arabic *Hidden Words*, no. 40
5. *Gleanings*, CLV, pp. 332–3

Parents

1. *Selections from the Writings of 'Abdu'l-Bahá*, no. 117, p. 140
2. *Qur'án*, XXXI, v. 13, p. 113
3. Exodus 20:12
4. *Atharva-Veda*, III, 30, v. 2
5. *Bahá'í World*, vol. XII, p. 896
6. *Bahá'í Prayers*, p. 65
7. *Tablets of Abdul-Baha*, pp. 262–3
8. *Selections from the Writings of the Báb*, p. 94

Patience

1. *Gleanings*, LXVI, p. 129
2. Arabic *Hidden Words*, no. 48
3. *Qur'án*, III, v. 200, p. 99
4. *Dhammapada*, CVII, v. 222, p. 60
5. Luke 8:15
6. *Dhammapada*, XIV, v. 184, p. 53
7. *Seven Valleys*, p. 5

Peacefulness

1. *Epistle to the Son of the Wolf*, p. 24
2. *Tablets of Abdul-Baha*, p. 25
3. *Dhammapada*, I, v. 6, p. 16
4. *Dhammapada*, VII, v. 96, p. 35
5. *Bhagavad Gita* 2, v. 55
6. *Upanishads* (The Supreme Teaching), pp. 142–3
7. *Paris Talks*, p. 29
8. *Paris Talks*, p. 28

Prayer

1. *Bhagavad Gita*, 4, v. 11
2. *Yaçna*, LIX, v. 20–21
3. *Gleanings*, CXXXIV, p. 291

4. *Paris Talks*, p. 81
5. *Gleanings*, CXXXVI, p. 295
6. *Vignettes from the Life of 'Abdu'l-Bahá*, no. 27, pp. 131–2
7. Adapted by Gloria Faizi from a story told by 'Abdu'l-Bahá
8. *Paris Talks*, p. 177
9. *Yaçna*, LVII, v. 7–8, p. 126
10. Arabic *Hidden Words*, no. 31
11. Psalms 5:3
12. *Qur'án*, XVII, v. 80, p. 311
13. *Divine Art of Living*, no. 32, p. 33
14. *Yaçna*, LIX, v. 24, p. 121
15. *Promulgation of Universal Peace*, p. 247

Purity

1. *Gleanings*, CXLI, p. 307
2. *'Abdu'l-Bahá in London*, p. 107
3. *Qur'án*, IX, v. 9. p. 208
4. *Dhammapada*, I, v. 2, p. 15
5. *Selections from the Writings of the Báb*, p. 80
6. Titus 1:15
7. *Yaçna*, XXIX, v. 5, p. 83
8. *Gleanings*, CXXXVI, pp. 294–5
9. *Dhammapada*, XII, v. 165, p. 49
10. *Seven Valleys*, p. 21
11. *Avesta* (Khordah-Avesta, I, v. 1–3), p. 3
12. *Dhammapada*, XVIII, v. 239, p. 62

Respect for Others

1. *Gleanings*, CXXXIX, p. 305
2. *Dhammapada*, VIII, v. 109, p. 38
3. *Qur'án*, IV, v. 62, p. 109
4. *Paris Talks*, p. 38
5. *Gleanings*, CXXX, p. 285
6. *Dhammapada*, XIV, v. 195–6, p. 55
7. *Vignettes from the Life of 'Abdu'l-Bahá*, no. 43, p. 30

Righteousness

1. *Gleanings*, CLIII, p. 323
2. Matt. 5:6
3. *Bhagavad Gita*, 14, v. 27
4. *Dhammapada*, XII, v. 163, p. 48
5. *Gleanings*, XLIII, p. 94
6. *Gleanings*, CXXXI, p. 287
7. *Bhagavad Gita*, 4, v. 7–8

Sacrifice

1. *Dhammapada*, XXV, v. 361, p. 81
2. *Kitáb-i-Íqán*, p. 232
3. *Bahá'í World Faith*, p. 368
4. Arabic *Hidden Words*, no. 46
5. *Promulgation of Universal Peace*, p. 148
6. *Divine Art of Living*, no. 13, p. 73
7. *An Early Pilgrimage*, p. 42
8. *Tablets of 'Abdu'l-Bahá*, p. 354
9. *Dawn-Breakers*, pp. 95–6
10. *Selections from the Writings of 'Abdu'l-Bahá*, p. 76

Self-Knowledge and Self-Respect

1. *Kitáb-i-Íqán*, p. 102
2. *Excellence in All Things*, p. 2
3. *Dhammapada*, I, v. 11, p. 17
4. *Dhammapada*, VI, v. 81, p. 31
5. *Gleanings*, CXXXVI, p. 294
6. *Gleanings*, I, pp. 4–5
7. *Tablets of Bahá'u'lláh*, p. 35
8. *Dhammapada*, II, v. 27, p. 20
9. *Gleanings*, CXXV, p. 266

Service

1. *Tablets of Bahá'u'lláh*, p. 167
2. *Paris Talks*, p. 177
3. Rev. 2:19
4. *Will and Testament of 'Abdu'l-Bahá*, p. 10
5. *Divine Art of Living*, p. 61
6. *Vignettes from the Life of 'Abdu'l-Bahá*, no. 29, pp. 55–6
7. *'Abdu'l-Bahá*, p. 3
8. *Vignettes from the Life of 'Abdu'l-Bahá*, no. 80, p. 91

Sharing

1. *Dhammapada*, XIII, v. 177, p. 51
2. Persian *Hidden Words*, no. 54
3. Matt. 5:42
4. *Tablets of Bahá'u'lláh*, p. 71
5. *Abbas Effendi, His Life and Teachings*, pp. 5–6
6. *Vignettes from the Life of 'Abdu'l-Bahá*, no. 27, p. 21
7. *Vignettes from the Life of 'Abdu'l-Bahá*, no. 31, p. 24
8. *Vignettes from the Life of 'Abdu'l-Bahá*, no. 27, p. 55

Silence

1. *Gleanings*, CXXV, p. 265
2. *Dhammapada*, XVII, v. 233, p. 61
3. *Upanishads* (Mundaka Upanishad, part III, i), p. 80
4. *Upanishads* (Chandogya Upanishad 7.6), p. 119
5. Quoted in *Dawn over Mount Hira*, p. 14
6. *Kitáb-i-Íqán*, p. 193
7. *Paris Talks*, p. 176

Sincerity

1. *Kitáb-i-Íqán*, p. 194
2. *Qur'án*, VI, v. 153, p. 168
3. *Dhammapada*, I, v. 100, p. 37
4. *Upanishads* (Chandogya Upanishad 7.16), p. 119
5. *Gleanings*, LXVII, p. 132
6. *Secret of Divine Civilization*, p. 96
7. *Vignettes from the Life of 'Abdu'l-Bahá*, no. 44, p. 31
8. *Gleanings*, CXIV, p. 233

Sorrow

1. *Tablets of Bahá'u'lláh*, p. 27
2. *Gleanings*, CXXX, p. 285
3. *Dhammapada*, I, v. 17–18, pp. 17–18
4. Proverbs 15:13
5. *Bahá'í World Faith*, pp. 395–6
6. *Gleanings*, CLIII, p. 329
7. *Bahá'í Revelation*, p. 91

Thoughts

1. *Dhammapada*, I, v. 2, p. 15
2. *Upanishads* (Chandogya Upanishad 7.16–25), p. 119
3. *Gleanings*, LXXXV, p. 168
4. *Yaçna*, XXXV, v. 4–6, p. 95
5. *Upanishads* (Chandogya Upanishad 7.16–25), p. 119
6. *Dhammapada*, I, v. 5–6, 11, 16, pp. 15–17
7. *Paris Talks*, p. 29
8. *Some Answered Questions*, pp. 245–6

Time

1. *Gleanings*, XCII, p. 184
2. *Tablets of Bahá'u'lláh*, p. 26
3. *Dhammapada*, VIII, v. 106, p. 37

4. *Upanishads* (Chandogya Upanishad 8.4.1), p. 121
5. *Some Answered Questions*, p. 179

Tranquillity

1. *Bahá'í Prayers*, p. 142
2. *Gleanings*, CXXXI, p. 286
3. *Bahá'í World Faith*, p. 232
4. *Bhagavad Gita*, 2, v. 71
5. *Dhammapada*, VI, v. 82, p. 31
6. *Dhammapada*, VII, v. 96, p. 35
7. *Gleanings*, LVI, p. 111
8. *Star of the West*, vol. 16, p. 401
9. *Gleanings*, XLIII, pp. 97–8
10. *Gleanings*, CXII, p. 218
11. *Gleanings*, CXXXI, p. 286
12. *Gleanings*, CXXII, p. 260

Troubles and Tests

1. Persian *Hidden Words*, no. 51
2. *Bhagavad Gita*, 2, v. 56
3. *Upanishads* (Katha Upanishad, Part II), p. 59
4. *Dhammapada*, VI, v. 83, p. 31
5. *Bahá'í World Faith*, pp. 363–4
6. *Selections from the Writings of 'Abdu'l-Bahá*, pp. 181–2

Trust in God

1. Tablet of Aḥmad, *Bahá'í Prayers*, p. 211
2. *Dawn-Breakers*, pp. 461–2
3. *Tablets of Bahá'u'lláh*, p. 155
4. *Gleanings*, CXXV, p. 264
5. Psalms 118:8
6. *Gleanings*, CXVI, p. 248
7. *Dawn-Breakers*, pp. 461–2

Trustworthiness

1. *Gleanings*, CXXX, p. 285
2. *Dhammapada*, XV, v. 204, p. 57
3. *Epistle to the Son of the Wolf*, pp. 54–5
4. I Tim. 6:20
5. *Gleanings*, CXIV, pp. 232–3
6. *Tablets of Bahá'u'lláh*, p. 37

Truthfulness

1. *Dhammapada*, XVII, v. 224, p. 60
2. *Rig Veda*, 10.85, v. 1, p. 267
3. *Bahá'í World Faith*, p. 384
4. John 8:31–2
5. *Dhammapada*, XXIV, v. 354, p. 79
6. *Dhammapada*, XIII, v. 176, p. 51
7. *Upanishads* (Chandogya Upanishad 7.16–25), p. 119
8. *Bahá'í World Faith*, p. 384

Unity

1. *Atharva-Veda*, III, 30, v. 1
2. *Gleanings*, CXXXII, p. 288
3. *Gleanings*, LXXII, p. 140
4. *Dhammapada*, XVIII, pp. 63–4
5. *Bahá'í World Faith*, pp. 257–8

Wisdom

1. *Yaçna*, XXXI, v. 12, p. 88
2. *Dhammapada*, I, v. 1, p. 15
3. James 1:5
4. *Epistle to the Son of the Wolf*, p. 55
5. *Dhammapada*, VI, v. 82, p. 31
6. *Dhammapada*, VI, v. 81, p. 31
7. *Tablets of Bahá'u'lláh*, p. 66

Work is Worship

1. *Bhagavad Gita*, 18, v. 46
2. *Bhagavad Gita*, 3, v. 19
3. Psalms 62:12
4. Proverbs 16:3
5. *Tablets of Bahá'u'lláh*, p. 26
6. *Yaçna*, XXIX, v. 6, p. 84
7. Persian *Hidden Words*, no. 80
8. *Paris Talks*, pp. 176–7